FRENCH POLITICS

AND ALGERIA

Current Political Problems

TAYLOR COLE, *Editor*

WILLIAM G. ANDREWS, *French Politics and Algeria*

WALLACE MENDELSON, *Capitalism, Democracy, and the Supreme Court*

NEAL RIEMER, *The Revival of Democratic Theory*

GEORGE W. SPICER, *The Supreme Court and Fundamental Freedoms*

In preparation

ROBERT S. RANKIN, *Civil Liberties and Martial Law*

WILLIAM G. ANDREWS

Tufts University

French Politics and Algeria

**THE PROCESS OF POLICY FORMATION
1954–1962**

New York

APPLETON-CENTURY-CROFTS

Division of Meredith Publishing Company

Library of Congress Card Number: 62-15310

682-1

FOR MY DAUGHTER

DONNA

May her troubles never be as big
As she thinks they are now.

Preface

SOMEONE has said that the French should be excellent constitution makers; they have had so much experience. It has also been remarked that the politics of the French are interesting because their problems are so perplexing. In the pages that follow, I try to turn to the advantage of scholarly inquiry both of these unfortunate French ailments: constitutional instability and chronic political indigestion.

In just three and one-half years the Algerian nationalist insurrection drove the parliamentary Fourth French Republic to an early grave. It plagued the presidential Fifth Republic for a similar length of time. The persistence, across two regimes so outwardly different, of a problem of such magnitude seemed to present an excellent opportunity for a comparative case study on the manner in which regimes deal with major problems confronting them. It is the purpose of this study to exploit (not cynically, I hope) this opportunity.

I believe that comparative government may profit from the careful examination of situations in which the variables influencing the effectiveness of different forms of government are reduced to a minimum. In this case, the society, the administrative substructure, the political elite, the general international situation, and, above all, the problem were substantially the same from one system to the other. The constitution and some of the top political leaders changed. This book attempts to describe and illustrate the differences and similarities in their operation and effectiveness.

In a general way, I deal with the attempts of the French to resolve the Algerian problem from November 1, 1954, to June 1, 1961. Particular attention is given to efforts to find a "political" solution, that is, to reform the Algerian political-governmental structure. Revisions and additions have been made to include developments through early August 1962.

After setting the stage with a chapter on the background of the nationalist insurrection and the policy making machinery of the two republics, I begin my inquiry into the policy formation process by examining the evolution of public and press opinion. The process of communicating popular opinion through political parties, interest groups, and elections to the constitutional organs of government is covered in Chapters 3 and 4. Finally, within the government, I have examined the manner in which the ball has been batted back and forth between the executive and the legislature. Because of the reconstruction of those institutions in 1958, the two republics are treated separately.

Wherever suitable, I have included illustrative material to supplement the narrative, description, and analysis. In many cases, with the benefit of the perspective of a few years, it would have been possible, even easier, to present the course of events more concisely without including verbatim excerpts from parliamentary debates, public speeches, newspaper accounts, etc. But I feel that the use of the two types of material best permits both the facts and the "feel" of the systems to be conveyed. Illustrative material gives events an immediacy that the detachment of scholarly re-creation lacks.

Of course, this approach has the defects of its strength. It captures the image of the big, well-publicized event, but is blind to the myriad, microscopic actions that have so greatly influenced, perhaps created, that big event. For instance, there is no chapter on the civil service (though it appears prominently in the chapters on the political executive) because it enters the public picture only through its open dealings with the political executive.

My judgments and conclusions are necessarily very tentative, limited by the valuable but incomplete sources available now in the United States. Much remains to be done. Memoirs will be published, interviews must be conducted, archives will someday be ransacked. All will produce material that will permit the picture drawn here to be deepened, corrected, and rendered in much greater detail.

I wish to express again in print my gratitude to Professor Mario Einaudi for his patient solicitude and inspirational guidance during the three years he directed my graduate studies and for his generous and kindly attention since then. All who have felt the impact of his intellect and personality are heavily in his debt, however inadequate may be our capacities to respond or however imperfect our attempts. Professor Alan Westin's *Anatomy of a Constitutional Law Case* provided the germ of idea out of which this book grew. I am grateful for the encouragement given me on this project by Professors Taylor Cole of Duke University, James F. Tierney of the Ford Foundation, Stanley Hoffmann of Harvard University, Henry W. Ehrmann of Dartmouth College, and Robert R. Robbins of Tufts University, and to Professor Betty B. Burch of Tufts University for the title and other suggestions. Professor Daniel Lerner of Massachusetts Institute of Technology gave generously of his time to read the manuscript and make helpful suggestions.

Mr. Robert Dohrenwend, a Dartmouth student, helped me with translations, especially a portion of the Assembly debates. Mr. James Jonas Clark, a Tufts student, conducted research for the section on the French press. He also assisted in the compilation of a chronology and a bibliography that was squeezed out by the publishing budget.

The reference staffs of Eaton Library at Tufts University, Widener and Littauer Libraries at Harvard University, and Baker Library at Dartmouth College patiently answered questions and obtained material in the ways that only expert librarians know. Mrs. Edna Nelson labored hard through a long summer and Mrs. Katharine Dempster gave up precious vacation time to type the manuscript cheerfully, carefully, and accurately. For help in paying for this assistance I am indebted to the Faculty Research Committees of Dartmouth College and Tufts University.

Finally, to my wife, who patiently bore the grinding strain of these scholarly endeavors which so often impinged on time that was rightfully hers, and who lent an eager hand in the endless task of retyping pages that were rendered illegible by my editing pencil, I owe the greatest debt of all.

They have contributed to whatever merit this book may have, but should not be held guilty by association for its defects.

W. A.

Contents

1

The Context of the Problem

THE GROWTH OF THE PROBLEM

Conquest and Colonization

On April 30, 1827 Hussein Dey of Algiers struck the French consul with a flyswatter. Seldom has a blow with that ancient weapon been so fraught with consequences. There ensued a three-year blockade of the port of Algiers, military occupation and active pacification of the North African country for some thirty years, relative peace and colonization for the next ninety-odd years, and finally the longest and bloodiest war for independence in the Afro-Asian nationalist surge.

The short-tempered swat by the Dey was the climactic act in a thirty-year dispute over payment for grain purchased in Algeria for the French Army at inflated prices. It served Charles X as a convenient pretext to invade Algiers in hope that imperial success might restore some of the luster to his tarnished crown. His hope was vain. The Revolution of 1830 drove him from the throne in the same month (July 1830) that his troops routed the Dey from his. The deposition of the Dey did not end Algerian resistance and the French soon realized that their hold on Algiers would be tenuous if the rest of the territory were not subdued. A series of military campaigns was undertaken to bring all of Algeria under French control.

After the military conquest, army leaders convinced the government that extensive settlement of the country by Frenchmen would help them maintain control. In recognition of this "mission of national interest," successive French governments adopted

1

measures to encourage the "implantation" of French settlers in the North African colony.[1] By 1905, this policy had resulted in the settlement of 17,200 colonial proprietors on 6,733,220 acres of land that had been granted by the State or purchased from natives under procedures that often were quite irregular.[2]

These immigrants were not all French. In 1847, for instance, the European population of 109,400 persons included 47,274 Frenchmen, 31,528 Spaniards, 8,788 Maltese, 8,624 Germans or Swiss, and 8,175 Italians.[3] At least until 1886 the French and the non-French Europeans were approximately equal in numbers and in some areas the French were in a substantial minority. Since 1889, official comparative figures have not been available because legislation that year automatically naturalized all non-French Europeans born in Algeria. Also, one of the Crémieux decrees of 1870 made French citizens of all Algerian Jews, though the Algerian Jewish community was not of French origin, or even European. Even so, as late as 1931 the official census disclosed that 148,342 of the 777,122 Europeans in Algeria were non-naturalized foreigners, another 70,050 were naturalized foreigners, and there were 97,046 Algerian Jews in the three coastal departments.[4] However, many of the settlers who are not of French stock are the most fervent French nationalists, and the claim by France that it speaks for all of them has not been wholly unjustified.

Present estimates of the population vary greatly. A French encyclopedia using pre-insurrection sources estimates the European population (apparently including Algerian Jews) at one million, of whom 700,000 are said to be French. It sets the native population at 7.5 million.[5] Another French source says that

[1] Alain Savary, *Nationalisme algérien et grandeur française*, Paris, Plon, 1960, p. 27.

[2] Calvelli, *Etat de la propriété rurale en Algérie* (Thèse de Droit), Algiers, 1905; cited in *ibid.*, p. 31.

[3] Colette and Francis Jeanson, *L'Algérie hors la loi*, 2nd ed., Paris, Editions du Seuil, 1955, p. 54. The Jeansons' political commitment to the Communist position on Algeria requires that their interpretations be used with caution.

[4] René Lespès, *Pour comprendre l'Algérie*, Algiers (?), Gouvernement Général de l'Algérie, 1937, p. 31, 33n.

[5] *Nouveau petit Larousse illustré*, Paris, Librairie Larousse, 1955, p. 1168.

"scarcely 11 per cent" of the Europeans are of French origin.[6] *Le Monde* has given the figure of one-third.[7]

Political Arrangements

As colonization increased, the settlers became an important political force. Undoubtedly, this had the effect, intended by the army, of strengthening the French grasp on Algeria; it also had the unintended result of diluting the army's influence in Algeria. Periodic efforts by the Paris government, often with the backing of the army, to assimilate the entire Algerian population—including the Moslems—to the French nation politically were systematically thwarted by the European settlers who feared the loss of their privileged status. Such measures also failed to conform to the reality that Algeria had never been and could not be genuinely and integrally French. Nor were realistic Frenchmen unaware that, given the usual fragmentation of French public opinion, equitable representation of Algerian Moslems in the French parliament would have given them the balance of political power if they voted as a bloc. France could have become the colony of her colony.

Instead, the European settlers strove for, and usually got, a high degree of internal Algerian political autonomy. This meant, in practice, domination by the settlers under the benevolent protection of French troops. After 1900, the Algerian government was endowed with a separate budget, levied its own taxes, and was responsible for all expenditures of public revenue, except military expenditures to which it contributed "only a very small part."[8] After World War II the Algerian Assembly was established. This body contained two "colleges" of sixty members each. The first college was composed of representatives of the Europeans and the very small number of "assimilated" natives. The second represented the other 90 per cent of the population. Through manipulated elections and the appointment of "official" representatives, the colonial authorities controlled enough

[6] Jeanson, *op. cit.*, p. 156.
[7] September 13, 1956.
[8] Lespès, *op. cit.*, p. 204.

votes in the second college combined with the European college to maintain European dominance.

Colon Influence in Paris

The Europeans in Algeria also made their political strength felt in Paris through elected representatives to parliament, interest groups, and political parties. The "North African lobby" was for many years one of the most powerful in France. Its power was manifested most spectacularly when *colon* interests were directly threatened, such as in the reform attempts of Clemenceau after World War I, Blum in 1936, and Mendès-France in 1954-1955. It was always active in a less conspicuous way, however, to dissuade successive Paris governments from meddling in the "private" affairs of Algeria.

The autonomous political supremacy of the Europeans in Algeria was used to perpetuate their economic and cultural domination. A customs union with France opened the homeland market to Algerian agricultural products while permitting established French manufacturers to prevent the emergence of Algerian industry. Furthermore, external tariff barriers enabled both parties to levy substantial surcharges over world market prices.[9]

Economic and Social Conditions

In domestic policy, the Europeans in Algeria were no less reluctant to profit from their political power. Although undoubtedly Algerian agriculture developed greatly under French rule, it was largely for the benefit of the European settlers. The 2 million Algerians of 1830 cultivated only about 1,235,000 acres compared to 11.7 million acres cultivated by the 8.3 million Moslems of 1954. But those 1.2 million acres were the best lands and many of the 11.7 million are marginal. One French writer has noted that in 1938, for instance, only 7 per cent of the cultivated land in one of the richest agricultural areas was held by Moslems and only 17, 13, 15, and 23 per cent in four other highly fertile regions, though in 1954 Moslems owned 68 per cent of all cultivable land in the country.[10] Furthermore, Moslem-

[9] Savary, *op. cit.*, pp. 31-32.
[10] *Ibid.*, pp. 33-34.

owned grazing land was much more extensive in 1830 than now. As a result, the standard of living of the rural Moslems had dropped sharply. In 1870 each Algerian had 21.5 bushels of cereal grains annually but by 1950 he had less than 7.2 bushels. The 2 sheep per capita of 1911 had become 1.8 by 1954.[11]

The holdings of Moslem landowners average 33.1 acres of which 21.4 are cultivated, but European holdings average 305.5 acres of which 243.0 are cultivated. Nor does the size of the farms tell the whole story. The land suitable for the most valuable crops is held almost exclusively by Europeans. They also own 95 per cent of the tractors and similar equipment and furnished in 1953 all of the 137 Algerian students at the leading agricultural school and 70 per cent of the students at the five lower agricultural schools.[12]

Besides the expropriation of choice land by the Europeans, it is not hard to find reasons for the superior development of European agriculture. A basic, underlying factor has probably been the greater dynamism of the European community and the support it has received from 40 million mainlanders and a powerful army. The design of the agricultural educational system favored the Europeans. Other governmental programs, such as awarding enormous tracts of valuable land to European joint-stock corporations and preferential treatment for Europeans in granting farm loans, enabled the European farmer to operate more efficiently than his Moslem counterpart.[13] Once the European economic ascendancy was established and the settlers gained control of an autonomous Algerian budget, a regressive tax structure was adopted which placed on the lower-income, predominantly-Moslem categories an excessively heavy burden.[14]

Not only did the Algerian tax structure fail to redress the balance, but social legislation in Algeria provided the neediest (that is, the Moslem) sector of the population with little benefit. In 1954 a French family of a given economic status was eligible

[11] Charles-Henri Favrod, La Révolution algérienne, Paris, Plon, pp. 112-123.
[12] Ibid., pp. 122-123; Savary, op. cit., p. 42; and Ivo Rens, L'Assemblée Algérienne, Paris, Editions A. Pendone, 1957, p. 279.
[13] Savary, op. cit., p. 14. See also Favrod, op. cit., p. 138.
[14] See Savary, op. cit., pp. 22, 40 for impressive statistics supporting these statements.

for family subsidies almost three times as large as a comparable Algerian family. Furthermore, the ineligibility of all but an infinitesimal number of rural families excluded the great bulk of the Moslems (74 per cent of whom are engaged in agriculture) but scarcely affected the Europeans (only 10.7 per cent of whom are engaged in agriculture). Unemployment and old age insurance legislation in Algeria operated in the same discriminatory manner.[15]

This use of public funds for the principal benefit of the European sector of the population was also evident in the educational system. In 1954 all European children but only 15.4 per cent of the Moslem children of school age [16] attended schools. Plans for the expansion of the educational system did not envision that the number of new schools would keep pace with the population growth. By 1956 the rebellion had caused the situation to deteriorate even further by forcing the closing of numerous schools in areas of combat, especially in the rural Moslem areas.[17]

Moslems were at an even greater disadvantage in the secondary and advanced levels in the educational system. Only one Moslem child of 175 attended *lycées* in 1954 compared to one European child of three. Ninety per cent of the population supplied only 18 per cent of the secondary school children and 10.9 per cent of the students at the university.[18]

As a result of these reduced educational opportunities, only 5.9 per cent of the Moslem male population and 1.6 per cent of the Moslem female population are literate. This educational discrimination put Moslems at a great disadvantage in the competitive examinations for civil service posts which, in the French system, are based on educational background. As late as 1958 not one of the 1,247 members of the highest category in the Algerian financial civil service was Moslem and there were only 271 Moslems among the 4,984 civil servants in the next three categories.[19] Only 183 of the 2,500 functionaries of the Govern-

---

[15] Jeanson, *op. cit.*, pp. 161-163.
[16] Favrod, p. 126, says one Moslem school-age child in six.
[17] *Ibid.*, pp. 167-168; Rens, *op. cit.*, p. 280; Savary, *op. cit.*, p. 19.
[18] Favrod, *op. cit.*, p. 126.
[19] Savary, *op. cit.*, p. 20.

ment General were Moslems and most of them had menial jobs.[20]

Significant differences in other nonagricultural professional activities between the two Algerian communities are apparent in the following table, which gives the percentage distribution of Europeans and Moslems in each category in 1954: [21]

Professional category	Europeans	Moslems
Business proprietors	36.2%	63.8%
Managers, intellectuals	92.7%	7.3%
Technicians	82.4%	17.6%
Office and commercial employees	78.7%	21.3%
Professional workers	50.9%	49.1%
Specialized workers	32.1%	67.9%
Manual laborers	4.8%	95.2%
Apprentices	54.1%	45.9%
Domestics	41.6%	58.4%
Unemployed	9.6%	90.4%

Particularly revealing are figures of 95.2 per cent of the manual laborers and 90.4 per cent of the unemployed being Moslem. The same situation prevailed in agriculture where 99.5 per cent of the members of the three lowest categories of agricultural workers were Moslem and unemployment was so widespread that the average Moslem farm worker was employed fewer than ninety days a year.[22] The very small number of Moslems who have entered the professions is also very striking. In 1954 there were only 99 Moslem physicians, 161 lawyers, 17 dentists, 44 pharmacists, 5 surgeons, 5 architects, 7 civil engineers, 21 engineers of other types, and 185 teachers in secondary and higher education.[23]

The Rise of Nationalism

Very early in the occupation of Algeria, the French adopted an official policy of treating natives and Europeans equally. In fact, this policy never satisfied the more aspiring and dynamic Algerians, for the French insisted that the equality be on their terms. French, not Arabic, was the official language; the French,

[20] Favrod, op. cit., p. 126.
[21] Translated from ibid., p. 17.
[22] Ibid., pp. 11, 15.
[23] Favrod, op. cit., p. 126.

not the Arabic, culture set the standards; acceptance of the jurisdiction of the French legal code was a prerequisite of full citizenship, in spite of Moslem attachment to Islamic law. The French
promised equality to the native Algerian, but the price was
abandonment of his Arabic-Islamic personality and competition
on European terms. Even so, many Algerians who accepted
assimilation were disillusioned because the French still did not
regard them as genuine Frenchmen à part entière. It was largely
among such Algerians that the seeds of dissidence took root
earliest and most firmly.[24]

The founder of modern Algerian nationalism was Messali
Ahmed Ben Hadj, the poorly educated son of a Tlemcen shoe-
maker. Messali served with the French Army in World War I
and later returned to France to find work. He soon became
associated with the French Communist party and, under its
aegis, organized the North African Star (Etoile nord-africaine,
ENA) in 1925. Later he broke with the Communists. Messali's
group was repeatedly dissolved by the French only to reappear
under another label, and he was in and out of French jails.
Other Algerian Moslem political groups such as the conservative
Society of Reformist Ulema (Koranic law scholars) and the
assimilationist reform groups of Dr. Bendjelloul and Ferhat Abbas were organized before World War II, but Messali remained
the dominant patriarch of Algerian nationalism.

The defeat of the French in World War II stimulated the
nationalist movement. Assimilationists such as Abbas had been
disillusioned by the defeat of the liberal Blum-Violette reforms
of 1937 and the racist policies of the wartime Vichy regime.
In 1943 a group of them presented de Gaulle with demands
for "the recognition of the political autonomy of Algeria as a
sovereign nation," although they favored special ties with France.
The demands were summarily rejected. Shortly after, Messali
brought his followers into the Abbas group and soon controlled it.

So far, the nationalist struggle had been nonviolent. On VE

[24] There are several good accounts of the development of the movement:
Richard and Joan Brace, Ordeal in Algeria, Princeton, Van Nostrand, 1960;
Joan Gillespie, Algeria: Rebellion and Revolution, New York, Praeger, 1961;
and Michael Clark, Algeria in Turmoil, New York, Praeger, 1959.

Day in 1945, however, Algerians parading with nationalist banners in the Allied victory celebration became involved in an altercation with police. The disorders spread, resulting in about 100 European deaths and a number of atrocities. The French riposted with bombers, tanks, strafing planes, and even naval bombardment, leveling many villages. Estimates of the number of Algerians killed vary from 17,000 to 45,000.[25] Many Algerians were imprisoned and the recently united nationalist organization was dissolved.

Messali and Abbas reconstituted separate groups in late 1946, both of which continued to work within the French governmental mechanisms for independence. Opportunities for political influence by Algerians apparently increased with the adoption of the Algerian Statute of 1947 but many of its key provisions were never implemented and others were sabotaged. When the sterility of the 1947 statute became apparent, a clandestine military unit (O.S.) was formed within the Messali group (M.T.L.D.), though the leaders continually deferred armed action.

Early in 1954 nine members of the military unit formed a secret revolutionary committee (C.R.U.A.) which decided on October 10 to take up arms against the French on November 1. The larger organization refused to support the action and never did join forces against the French. Abbas remained apart from the insurrection for many months after its beginning, though he subsequently became its chief statesman. He was ousted in favor of the more radical Benyoussef Ben Khedda in late August 1961.

By late 1954 Algeria was ripe for rebellion. A rising native elite felt it had been relegated to economic and political inferiority. It was convinced that French professions of generosity and assimilation were either insincere or impotent in the face of *colon* resistance. Population growth without corresponding economic development had increased the misery of the native population. Finally, the nationalists had sufficient organizational experience to launch a major enterprise.

[25] See Manfred Halpern, "The Algerian Uprising of 1945," *The Middle East Journal*, 1948, pp. 191-202.

THE POLICY-FORMING MACHINERY

The Constitution of the Fourth Republic

The constitutional frameworks of the Fourth and Fifth Republics are integral parts of the context within which the French searched for an Algerian solution. Relevant aspects of those systems will be discussed in detail at appropriate points in later chapters, but perhaps it will be useful to present here in a few pages their main outline as well as a summary account of the transition between them.

The Fourth Republic was founded in 1946 in a spirit compounded in roughly equal parts of hope, resignation, and disillusionment; idealism, realism, and opportunism; vengeance and generosity; marxism, democracy, liberalism, and Christianity; hindsight, foresight, and blindness; legalism, dogmatism, and pragmatism. The framers of the 1946 constitution emerged from the unifying forge of the wartime Resistance movements glowing with an idealistic fervor that was hardened by the conviction that their opponents were egoistic and short-sighted if not downright traitorous. Thus, their solidarity and militancy superimposed another fissure on the French body politic. They were determined to avoid what they believed had been defects in the prewar regime, but it was not wholly coincidental that the changes they proposed tended to their advantage over that of the political groups that had dominated the Third Republic. They were imbued with a zeal to install a regime of social and economic justice, but their labors produced competitive protestations of virtue more often than concrete achievements. The rival ideologies—communist, socialist, and Christian democratic—of the three dominant parties largely canceled each other out, producing a sterile pragmatism—a pragmatism of resignation rather than determination.

In concrete terms, the 1946 constitution was an ill-assorted mixture of compromises. No one was pleased, few were satisfied, many accepted it only with the intention of transforming it later. The strong-executive partisans among de Gaulle's followers compromised with the Communists, who advocated "assembly government," to found a regime that was little different from the impotent parliamentarianism of the Third Republic. The anti-colonialists at the constituent assemblies forced acceptance of an imperial disengagement policy but could not force its implementation. Abolition of an upper chamber was thwarted by referendal defeat of the first draft constitution, but the Council of the Republic created in the second draft was designed as a mere shadow of the powerful Senate of the Third Republic.

This criss-cross of countervailing ambitions, ideological imperatives, historical impediments, rhetorical flourishes, and practical exigencies produced a regime which concentrated authority in the lower parliamentary chamber. This assembly was restrained by: 1, the "reflective" upper chamber; 2, a ceremonial chief of state with the influence of an elder statesman; 3, a cabinet that had, in theory, the right to dissolve the assembly and appeal for the arbitration of the electorate in certain circumstances; and 4, most importantly, the imperfect realization among its members that irresponsible exercise of their prerogatives would lead to anarchy and paralysis that would benefit only their worst adversaries.

Politics in the Fourth Republic

Politically speaking, the divisions in French society were reflected and perhaps magnified by a multiparty system. There were six principal families of approximately equal strength: 1, the Communists; 2, the Socialists; 3, the Radical Socialists; 4, the Christian democrats (M.R.P.); 5, the traditional conservatives; 6, the antiparliamentary Right. The Communists, Socialists, and M.R.P. shared a disdain for the capitalist economic system, though it varied in intensity. The Radicals were good capitalists, but joined the Communists and the Socialists in their anticlericalism. The Communists agreed with the Gaullists and Poujadists of the antiparliamentary Right on the need for a new regime, but were poles apart in proposing a replacement. Most Socialists could work with the M.R.P. in developing a program of European integration that could win the support of large factions of Radicals and conservatives, but many other

Radicals, conservatives, and even Socialists joined the extremes in opposing it. In short, stable party coalitions were difficult because the major issues evoked contradictory responses. These centrifugal tendencies were not discouraged by the proportional representation electoral system.

In operation this political and governmental system produced a succession of cabinets surviving about six months on the average. The political groups providing most of the personnel for the ministerial merry-go-round (Socialist, Radical, M.R.P., and conservative) were usually the same, but faces and portfolios changed often. Besides creating a somewhat deceptive air of uncertainty about the continuity and stability of public policy, this situation made it very difficult for the average Frenchman to affix responsibility. In consequence, the accumulated dissatisfactions of the French were heaped on *le système* as a whole.

Beneath this swirling superstructure was a powerful, entrenched bureaucracy that could swallow up its political overlords, immobilize them in bureaucratic quicksand, and spew them forth with little damage to its own empire. Nevertheless, the French administration produced some of the truly notable achievements of the Fourth Republic, such as the Monnet Plan. The oversized administration, despite its flashes of brilliance, had little sensitivity to governmental will or popular sentiment, but it did give stability to the machinery of State and its enthronement was a consequence of the failures of the politicians as well as a product of its own ambitions.

The Fourth Republic was characterized, then, by the sterility of a domineering legislature, the multiplicity of dogmatic political parties, instability of cabinets, stability of coalitions, and stagnation of policy. Surprisingly, it also presided over the sudden rejuvenation, especially in the economic sphere, of a society that had languished long.

To that explosive mixture as it reached the boiling point were added two volatile ingredients: the Algerian dilemma and the Gaullist conspiracy. The result was the coup of May 13, 1958, the collapse of the Fourth Republic, and the establishment of the Fifth Republic.

The Fall of the Fourth Republic

No effort will be made here to unravel the many strands that wove the mesh of the thirteenth of May. Only a summary account will be attempted. The Algerian war was well into its fourth year with no end in sight. By accepting the principle of political equality for Algerian Moslems the Paris regime had angered the *colons*. Gaullist Defense Minister Jacques Chaban-Delmas had arranged several conspiratorial trips to Algeria for a Gaullist aide, Léon Delbecque. The army was exasperated by its impotence and *le système* was an easy scapegoat, while de Gaulle was a symbol of military pride and honor. Public opinion surveys disclosed massive indifference to the fate of the regime. Paris police demonstrations in March had indicated that they might also fail the regime in a crisis.

The confluence of these developments unleashed a variety of forces: determination by the *colons* to impose on Paris both a policy that would permit them to retain their privileged status and a regime with sufficient authority to carry it through; determination by the Gaullists to bring their chief back to power; determination by the army to recover its pride and honor. The will was there and so was the organization. On the other hand, as events proved, few would defend the regime.

A cabinet crisis lit the fire under the witch's cauldron. The government of Félix Gaillard had fallen on April 15 in the aftermath of the unauthorized bombing by French aircraft of a Tunisian border village alleged to have been harboring Algerian rebels. On May 13 the deputies invested M. Pierre Pflimlin who had dropped hints that he might negotiate a cease-fire.

A mob of European settlers seized possession of the main government building in Algiers. Gaullists like Delbecque gave the mob leadership and a concrete objective: *de Gaulle au pouvoir!* This covered the riots with enough respectability that, after some hesitation, the army lent its support. Meanwhile, de Gaulle was uttering ominous and enigmatic pronouncements on his readiness to assume power and his embarkment on the process of forming a government.

The government found it could rally no significant military units to bring into action against the dissidents and concluded that its only choice lay between abdication to de Gaulle and a military dictatorship. Its dying service was to arrange for de Gaulle's investiture as premier in the regular constitutional manner.

The Founding of the Fifth Republic

Immediately after his investiture by a vote of 329 to 224 in the Assembly, de Gaulle obtained authorization by parliament to draft a new constitution. Parliament required that the constitution incorporate the principles of universal suffrage, separation of powers, ministerial responsibility to parliament, judicial independence and protection of civil liberties, and "permit relations to be organized by the Republic with the peoples associated with it."

A drafting committee composed chiefly of civil servants and directed by Minister of Justice Michel Debré, longtime collaborator of de Gaulle, prepared a draft text during the summer. Late in August this was reviewed by a consultative committee containing some parliamentarians, by the cabinet, and by the Council of State. Minor changes were made in light of their recommendations. The completed text was made public on September 4, 1958, approved by popular referendum on September 28, and promulgated on October 4. Installation of the new institutions began with the election of the National Assembly in November, continued through the election of General de Gaulle to the Presidency of the Republic in December, and was completed with the designation of the members of the Constitutional Council, Economic Council, Senate, and the organs of the Community in the spring of 1959.

The New Regime

The new constitution was, in effect, an instrument for personal dictatorship. It was designed to give de Gaulle the means he believed necessary to accomplish the work he wished to do. The principal changes effected by the new constitution in the governmental structure of metropolitan France fall under six main headings:

1. The authority and independence of the President of the Republic were increased.
2. The prime minister and cabinet were made less dependent on parliament and more subject to the President of the Republic.
3. The power of parliament was reduced.
4. The upper chamber was brought more nearly onto a plane of equality with the National Assembly.
5. A quasi-judicial council was established to pass on the constitutionality of certain actions under certain conditions.
6. Invocation by the State, and especially the President of the Republic, of emergency powers was facilitated.

In addition, an organic law replaced the proportional representation electoral system for National Assembly elections by a single-member majority system with runoff elections.

The stage is set. The following pages present illustrative, descriptive, and analytical material designed to illuminate the functioning of the two regimes in the effort to solve the Algerian problem and, especially, to give that problem a political and governmental system that would so satisfy the average Algerian that the nationalist vision of the F.L.N. would no longer attract him.

The sequence of chapters follows the public flow of policy. Popular will is measured by public opinion surveys. The press reflects, informs, and persuades it. It is crystallized and diverted into constitutional channels by the parties and interest groups and determines through elections the personnel of the legislature and the executive, either directly or indirectly. Finally, the political executive supervises the formation of policy, seeks its legitimation by parliament, and is responsible for its implementation.

2

Public Opinion and the Press

PUBLIC OPINION

Both the Fourth and Fifth Republics are democratic in form. Democratic theory assumes that governments are ultimately responsive and responsible to the people. This responsibility is maintained primarily through elections and, more rarely, referenda. Such formal consultations are held infrequently, but presumably popular will is continuous. Furthermore, neither referenda nor elections provide a thoroughly accurate determination of popular will on policy questions. Inevitably, it is deformed because policy questions are only one of the determinants of a person's vote (and not necessarily the most important). Besides, there is always more than one policy issue in every election. No matter how completely one issue dominates an election it never has a complete monopoly. In order to determine popular attitudes on specific questions, sociologists have devised public opinion surveys. By interviewing a scientifically designed representative sample of the population, they claim to be able to tell with a high degree of accuracy the views of the population as a whole. Attempts to use opinion surveys in forecasting election results have not always been successful, but there is no reason to doubt that they provide a reasonably accurate reflection of general trends in opinion. In this chapter an effort will be made to analyze the evolution of French public opinion regarding the Algerian problem from the time of the outbreak of the rebellion until March 1960, the last month for which data is available at this writing.[1]

The Importance of the Problem

When the Algerian rebellion broke out in 1954, there had already been nationalist agitation in the North African French protectorates of Tunisia and Morocco for some time. Therefore, the first surveys by the French Institute of Public Opinion (I.F.O.P.) treated the insurrection as part of the general North African difficulties. Its last survey (September 1954) before the Algerian revolt, indicated that the public saw North African problems as the second most important task of the government with 24 per cent of the respondents listing either Tunisia (6 per cent), Morocco (7 per cent), or North Africa (11 per cent), behind E.D.C. (26 per cent) and on a par with wages (24 per cent).[2] The people became conscious of the gravity of the new development slowly. In mid-January 1955, more than two months after the insurrection, 27 per cent of the respondents ranked "halt the troubles in North Africa" among the most important tasks facing the government, but "economic and financial problems" (43 per cent) had replaced "international problems" (26 per cent) at the top of the list and "social questions" (35 per cent) also outranked North Africa. Further evidence that the insurrection was not taken seriously is shown by the fact that in the same survey 75 per cent of the respondents ranked "Indochina" and 22 per cent ranked the Paris Accords among the most important events of 1954, but only 17 per cent so ranked the "North African events," including the Tunisian and Moroccan troubles as well as the Algerian insurrection. Even as late as December 1955 only 25 per cent of the respondents saw North Africa as "the most important problem for France" at that moment, compared with 15 per cent for the next most

[1] All the statistics included in this analysis have been drawn from various issues of *Sondages: Revue française de l'opinion publique,* the quarterly journal of the French Institute of Public Opinion. In particular, the following issues contained the results of surveys relevant to public opinion regarding Algeria: 1954, 4; 1955, 1, 3, and 4; 1956, 3; 1957, 2 and 3; 1958, 3 and 4; 1959, 2 and 3; 1960, 3.

[2] There was a total of 142 per cent because of multiple answers.

numerous answer. After that the picture changed radically, as
the percentages in following table show:

	Apr. 1956	July 1956	Sept. 1957	Jan. 1958	Aug. 1958	Sept. 1959	Feb. 1960
North Africa or Algeria	63	60	51	37	40	68	78
Next most numerous response	20	10	27	36	19	14	5

The dip in late 1957 and 1958 resulted from concern over
inflation and constitutional reform. As these problems subsided,
Algeria recovered its dominance over the French consciousness.

Confidence in Nation and Governments

The I.F.O.P. has also asked five times since July 1956 whether
its respondents believed the situation was improving, worsening,
or remaining stationary. The deep pessimism of July 1956 became markedly more optimistic by January 1958 and then le-
veled off:

Situation in Algeria has:	July 1956	Sept. 1957	Jan. 1958	Feb. 1959	May 1959
Improved	16	12	29	21	21
Worsened	45	40	11	10	18
Not changed	15	40	48	62	46
No answer	24	8	12	7	15

This increased optimism was also reflected in the answers to
a question on the likelihood that Algeria will remain French.
The first three times, the respondents were asked if they believed it would still be French in five years. The last three times
the period was extended to ten years. The fifth time (January
1958) an additional choice of "perhaps" was added. If the
changes in the wording of the question are taken into account,
it appears that confidence that Algeria will remain French
increased fairly steadily from at least July 1956 until June 1958:

In your opinion will Algeria still be French in five (ten) years?

	Apr. 1956	July 1956	Mar. 1957	Sept. 1957	Jan. 1958	June 1958
Yes	31	19	32	28	27	42
No	25	28	24	37	22	18
No answer	44	53	44	35	12	40
Perhaps	—	—	—	—	40	—

Since then the question has been posed differently with these results:

Which [of the three options proposed by de Gaulle in his speech of September 16, 1959] *has the best chance to succeed?*

	Sept. 1959 (Paris only)	Oct. 1959	Feb. 1960
Association	38	35	48
Frenchification	24	23	27
Secession	17	12	6
No answer	21	30	19

Either there was a radical shift of opinion between June 1958 and September 1959 or de Gaulle convinced many of the 42 per cent in the June 1958 poll that "association" is a "French" solution. If it is assumed that as many as half do so regard it and if they are assimilated to the "frenchification" category, it appears that the optimistic trend has continued.

The steadily rising confidence was not uniformly transferred to the incumbent governments. In September 1954 and late January 1955, the survey asked if the respondents had confidence in the incumbent government to solve the "difficulties in Tunisia and Morocco." In late October 1955 the question was directed toward the "problems of North Africa." In nine later surveys, it was narrowed to "the difficulties in Algeria." In April and December 1959, the question was posed differently. The respondents were asked if their "opinion of the manner in which the government is handling the Algerian" problem was "very good, good, average, bad, or very bad." If the "average" answers are distributed equally between confidence and no confidence, a chart for the fourteen surveys looks like the ones on pages 20 and 21.

This indicates considerable vacillation in public confidence in the governments' Algerian policy. Confidence was highest under Mendès-France and Premier de Gaulle. It hit its low points under Faure, Bourgès-Maunoury, and de Gaulle-Debré.

The steadily rising confidence in France, but erratic attitude toward the governments may indicate why the Fourth Republic was so easily toppled. Frenchmen accepted mediocre government while they felt this reflected the status of their nation, but when they regained confidence in the nation they asked for a regime that would measure up to that image.

	Mendès-France		Faure		Mollet		Bourgès-Maunoury
	Sept. 1954	Jan. 1955	Oct. 1955	Apr. 1956	July 1956	Mar. 1957	Sept. 1957
Yes	60	55	29	37	38	39	26
No	13	20	38	27	30	30	43
No answer	27	25	33	36	32	31	31

Views on Negotiations

The I.F.O.P. has asked a number of questions concerning the substance of Algerian policy. Three surveys asked the respondents whether they would favor negotiations with the rebels to grant independence or all-out war if these were the only two alternatives:

	Apr. 1956	July 1956	July 1957
Negotiate	39	45	38
All-out war	39	23	36
Other answers	—	12	—
No answer	22	20	26

The survey has also asked if the respondents believed that the government should seek negotiations with the rebels for a cease-fire:

	July 1957	Sept. 1957	Jan. 1958	Feb. 1959	May 1959	Dec. [3] 1959
Yes	53	45	56	52	71	57
No	29	34	25	27	16	18
No answer	18	21	19	21	13	25

[3] In December 1959 the question concerned negotiations on the arrangements for the proposed referendum.

At least since July 1956 a decisive majority of those expressing an opinion have favored negotiations.

	de Gaulle			Debré			
	June 1958	Aug. 1958	Sept. 1958	Feb. 1959	Apr. 1959	Sept. 1959	Dec. 1959
Yes	68	68	51	51	34	60	41
No	11	15	24	24	49	20	37
No answer	21	17	25	25	17	20	23

Algeria's Future Political Status

Between October 1955 and September 1957 five surveys asked whether Algeria should retain her status as departments or be permitted "a less close connection." Through April 1956 neither the respondents nor the government were prepared to accept the latter alternative. But by March 1957, two months before Premier-designate Bourgès-Maunoury announced his intention to draft a new statute for Algeria, opinion was equally divided and in September 1957, shortly before the defeat of the loi cadre, it had become the more favored choice:

	Oct. 1955	Feb. 1956	Apr. 1956	Mar. 1957	Sept. 1957
Departments	47	49	40	34	36
Less close connection	26	25	33	35	40
No answer	27	26	27	31	24

After de Gaulle's declaration of September 16, 1959 a question asked which of the alternatives he proposed would best serve the interests of the metropole. In the three surveys since then, opinion has consistently supported "association," which obviously was de Gaulle's choice, too:

	Sept. 1959 (Paris only)	Oct. 1959	Feb. 1960
Association	38	35	48
Frenchification	24	23	27
Secession	17	12	6
No answer	21	30	19

Opinion conformed more closely to de Gaulle's position as his views became clearer. In fact, it has corresponded closely to official policy throughout the period. While the government said "integral part of France," opinion said "departmental status"; while the government said "special status," opinion said "less close connection"; while de Gaulle said "association," opinion agreed.

French public opinion seems to have accepted since early 1956 the view that Algeria was the most important French problem, but steadily since then has believed that the situation was improving. This confidence was not transferred uniformly to the governments that were apparently responsible for the improvement. On the substance of policy, opinion has generally been quite closely in step with the government.

THE FRENCH PRESS

Character and Circulation

The French have a lively press, though in many cases the newspapers are not as strong financially as their British and American counterparts because the institution of advertising is not so highly developed. The total average daily press run for daily newspapers in France in June 1960, a typical month, was 11,863,266 copies. Of these, probably at least 20 per cent went unsold, so the total actual circulation did not average more than 10 million. This compares with about 17.5 million in Great Britain and 58 million (English-language only) in the United States. The provincial press run averaged 7,170,105 and the Paris dailies averaged 4,693,121.[4]

There are in Paris nine *journaux d'information* (that is, newspapers ostensibly, at least, designed primarily to inform rather than persuade), two party dailies, and three "special" dailies. *France-Soir*, a popular evening paper with a printing of 1,381,000

[4] The data in this section has been drawn from *N. W. Ayer and Son's Directory; Ulrich's Periodicals Directory; L'Année politique* (hereafter cited as *A. P.*) for 1958, 1959, and 1960; Alexander Werth, *France, 1940-1955*, New York, Holt, 1956, pp. 735-742; Jean Chatelain, *La Nouvelle Constitution*, Paris, Berger-Levrault, 1959; and my own observations.

in June 1958, has the largest circulation. It has flashy headlines and is easily diverted from vital political news by gory tales of crime and sex. But it also maintains a large staff of writers and correspondents, publishes frequent, excellent *reportages*, and generally rises above the level of the usual tabloid. It is a *journal d'information*, but in common with most French newspapers is not averse to giving its news stories the proper slant—in this case, toward the right of center. *Le Monde* (230,000 in June 1958) is the French counterpart of *The New York Times*, a newspaper of record and the French "prestige" paper. *Le Monde* is much more serious, dull, and less sensational than *France-Soir*. It is "neutral," slightly left of center, and has a decided opposition bent, no matter who is in office.

Among the other *journaux d'information*, *Figaro* (501,000) is the most important, although the tabloid-type *Parisien Libéré* (875,000) has a larger circulation. *Figaro* publishes more material than *Le Monde* and is better written, but its coverage is not as complete. It is read primarily by the more prosperous Parisians and is moderately right-of-center politically. *Combat* (61,000) is similar to *Le Monde* in format, style, and political orientation (though it is not neutral). *Paris-presse l'intransigeante* (181,000) is virtually the same as, though perhaps a bit more sophisticated than, *France-Soir* and is owned by the same interests. *Libération* (125,000) is read by those who think communistically but are bored by *L'Humanité*'s sterile redundancy. *Paris-Jour* (148,000), which was first called *Paris-Journal*, is the heir to *Franc-Tireur*, a leftist paper that turned rightward. *Paris-Jour* is primarily commercial. *Aurore* (485,000) is right of *Figaro* and slightly superior in quality to *Parisien Libéré*.

The only two-party national dailies that have survived are the Communist *L'Humanité* (226,000) and the Socialist (S.F.I.O.) *Populaire* (15,000). *L'Humanité* peddles the rawest, most emetic party line tripe. It verges on caricature. Yet, blithely, it attempts to hold its dwindling circulation by following the comings and goings of Hollywood's most raffish adornments and of Europe's (non-French) royalty with unbecoming bourgeois avidity. *Populaire* is the smile that remains from Léon Blum's thriving prewar Cheshire cat. Its circulation is derisory and it rarely appears more than two or three times a week. Paris also has a Catholic daily (*La Croix*), two financial dailies, and a sports daily.

In 1960 there were 100 provincial dailies, some with considerable regional importance. As in Paris, the *journaux d'information* have the larger circulations though a number of party papers survive (especially Communist and Socialist). *Ouest-France* (550,000) in Rennes is militantly Catholic-conservative and has by far the largest provincial circulation. Other papers topping a quarter of a million press run are to be found in Lyon, Grenoble, Lille, Bordeaux, Toulouse, and Nancy.

The political coloration of the 200-odd weeklies runs the gamut from bright red to royal blue. All major political groups except the Radicals are represented and some political splinters that have not been taken seriously since the nineteenth century—if ever—still brandish fiery editorialists.

The press run of French dailies declined precipitously from a postwar high of more than 16 million for 203 newspapers in 1946 to a low of less than 10 million in 1952. The steady rise since then has been slowed down somewhat by price increases in 1958 and 1959. Four newspapers (*France-Soir, Parisien-Libéré, Aurore,* and *Figaro*) account for virtually all the circulation rise since 1952. In fact, their circulations have generally risen throughout the postwar period, even when most Paris newspapers were losing readers. Their common trait is that they are four of the five least political newspapers (*Paris-presse* being the other). On the other hand, *L'Humanité* has lost half its 1946 circulation, *Populaire* has kept only one reader in twenty, and all the other political papers of 1946 have become more informational or expired.

It is really not possible, except in one or two special cases, to correlate the changes in circulation since 1954 with events in Algeria. The upturn had begun two years before the rebellion and has been quite steady since then. It is notable, perhaps, that the sharpest rise since 1946 occurred during 1956, the year that public opinion surveys indicated the deepest public pessimism and the F.L.N. launched its first big spring offensive. Also, there was a great upsurge of press runs during the May 13 crisis. For instance, *Le Monde* increased by 18 per cent from the first full week to the second full week of May, *France-Soir* rose 22 per cent, and *L'Humanité* rose 40 per cent. Whether all these extra copies were actually sold is, of course, another question.

Front-page Algerian News

Front-page news content is another index of public attention to the Algerian problem. This is primarily and most accurately an indication of the extent to which the problem was impressed on the public consciousness by its news prominence. Also, it is a rough index of public opinion concerning the importance of the problem, because editors tend to anticipate and respond to the news judgments of their readers in using and placing news items.

To draw a profile of the front-page treatment of the Algerian problem during the insurrection, I have obtained by actual measurement the percentages of front-page Algerian news in *Le Monde*, *France-Soir*, and *L'Humanité*. In the case of *Le Monde*, the page one news on Algeria in every issue from November 1, 1954 to May 31, 1961 was measured. For the other two papers, issues of every fourth day were used.[5] All material (news articles, editorials, headlines, photographs, and cartoons) directly relevant to the Algerian problem was included. When an article treated more than one subject, including Algeria, and the Algerian portion was clearly identifiable, that portion and a proportionate amount of the headline were included. During the May 1958, January 1960, and April 1961 crises, the news of events in Algeria was included, but only their direct repercussions on the mainland.

Le Monde was given greater attention than the other two papers because it is the French "prestige" newspaper and because it has the most politically sophisticated readership in France. *France-Soir* was used because it is the most widely read French newspaper. Also, the I.F.O.P. has shown that it

[5] Because French dailies do not publish on Sunday, this is slightly more frequent than every fourth issue. Every fourth day is 91 issues; every fourth issue is 78 issues per year. Issues for May 1961 of *L'Humanité* were not available. I am grateful to Mr. James Jonas Clark, a worthy son of Tufts, for his patient assistance in the tedious job of measurement and calculation to obtain this data.

has the most representative readership.[6] *L'Humanité* was used because it is the only political party national organ that continues to appear as a regular daily. Because it is partisan, *L'Humanité* is a less dependable barometer of its readers' interest in a particular event. Prominence given Algerian news is determined more by the current party line than by the intrinsic importance of the news or reader interest.

The most striking fact that emerges from this analysis is that public attention to the Algerian problem was greatest from February through May 1956. At least 15.4 per cent of the front-page news in all three newspapers in all four months concerned Algeria. The only other months that all three papers topped 15 per cent were December 1960 and April 1961.[7] The average for the February-May 1956 period was 23.01 per cent, compared to 21.15 per cent for November 1960–February 1961, the next highest four-month average.

The 1956 period is significant for three reasons. It coincided with the first big F.L.N. spring offensive, it immediately preceded the low point in French public opinion optimism, and it was in the period of sharpest newspaper circulation rise since 1946.[8] On the other hand, the 1960-1961 period was one of good news generally. This was the period of the referendum and lively speculation that peace talks would soon begin.[9] The last three months of the period studied, March-May 1961, were also months of generally good news (the Evian talks got under way). They averaged 22.58 per cent Algerian front-page news.[10]

Tracing the evolution over the entire seventy-nine-month period, several observations deserve mention. The French newspaper public was slow in becoming aware of the gravity of the problem.[11] For the first fifteen months of the rebellion, Algerian news filled only 5.13 per cent of the front-page space. During that time in only three months did any newspaper top 10 per cent (*France-Soir*, November 1954, 12.3 per cent; *L'Humanité*,

---

[6] *Sondages*, no. 3, 1955, pp. 57-79.

[7] *Le Monde* and *France-Soir* exceeded 15 per cent in May 1961 but figures for *L'Humanité* for that month are not available.

[8] See pp. 18 and 24 above.

[9] It was also a time of bloody race riots in Algiers.

[10] The May *L'Humanité* not included.

[11] This supports public opinion survey findings. See p. 17 above.

June 1955, 12.7 per cent; and *Le Monde,* October 1955, 12.8 per cent). During the next six months only once did a paper (*France-Soir*, July, 8.5 per cent) fall below 10 per cent. From then until the beginning of 1960, there were no clear trends: Most commonly (51 of the 123 newspaper-months), from 5 to 10 per cent of the space was devoted to Algeria and the remainder of the newspaper-months were evenly divided between less than 5 per cent (35) and more than 10 per cent (37). Interest picked up during the settlers' revolt (January-February 1960), but languished again until preparations were begun for the referendum (November 1960). After that, fifteen of the twenty newspaper-months averaged more than 15 per cent and all but three averaged more than 10 per cent.

Significant differences among the three papers are discernible. *Le Monde* usually devoted more of its front page to Algerian news (13.8 per cent for the entire period) than did *L'Humanité* (8.8 per cent) or *France-Soir* (7.6 per cent). Only in 1954 did it lag behind both others and in 1955 it was slightly below *L'Humanité.* During only nineteen of the seventy-nine months did *L'Humanité's* coverage exceed *Le Monde's. France-Soir* topped *Le Monde* only ten times.

L'Humanité tended to react to important developments somewhat more slowly than *Le Monde. France-Soir* reacted as quickly as *Le Monde* but lost interest sooner. Perhaps *L'Humanité* marked time after a big event to permit the party to set the line, and *France-Soir's* audience lost interest more quickly because it is less sophisticated politically.

Finally, it should be noted that throughout the period the French press performed well its function of informing the people concerning Algerian developments. There has been a tendency by some right-wing papers to play down reports of army and police excesses and some of the more liberal papers have hesitated to publish material on that subject because issues containing such news have been seized regularly by the government at considerable inconvenience and financial loss to the papers. But, otherwise, the press has given the war good coverage. Even a popular sheet like *France-Soir* has kept regular staff writers in Algeria.

The quantity of material has, in general, been adequate. Even when Algeria was driven from the front pages by cabinet crises, international conferences, etc.—or, in the case of *France-Soir,* by a sensational kidnapping or, in the case of *L'Humanité,* by some big party event—there was often a page or more of Algerian news inside the paper. The disadvantage of each paper impressing its particular political bias on the news from Algeria was largely offset by the presence on every newsstand of a wide variety of slants.

PERCENTAGE OF FRONT PAGE DEVOTED TO ALGERIAN NEWS

	1954 (2 mos.)	1955	1956	1957	1958	1959	1960	1961
Le Monde	3.45	4.1	15.5	12.5	15.5	11.0	21.3	25.1 (5 mos.)
France-Soir	7.5	2.0	11.4	6.1	7.1	4.5	9.5	11.0 (5 mos.)
L'Humanité	5.0	4.3	14.1	8.2	8.0	4.0	6.7	25.0 (4 mos.)

This analysis of public opinion surveys, newspaper circulation, and front-page news coverage does not seem to bear out the contention of some observers that there has been a dramatic increase in political apathy since de Gaulle's return to power. In any case, there does not seem to have been the sharp decline in public interest in the Algerian problem that one might expect from an apathetic nation. Public opinion surveys show no tendency to thrust the problem aside. Newspaper circulation has continued to rise. As much front-page space is given over to Algeria as during the Fourth Republic.

Editorial Opinion on Algeria

Besides the modern newspaper's informational function, it has a job of contributing to the crystallization of political opinion through news interpretation and editorial persuasion. Because of the great diversity of political coloration represented in its press, especially among the weeklies, France is well served in this regard. The following excerpts from interpretive articles and editorials on Algeria illustrate this.

Already in 1955 and 1956 the lines of cleavage were drawn between the left-wing "reformist" press and the "blood and iron" of the right:

The already-designated interlocutor for M. Bourgès-Maunoury [minister of the interior], which he cannot challenge, is the Algerian

Assembly, on the condition that this Assembly truly constitute a democratic representation of the Algerian people and not, as is the case at present, a caricature of the Assembly, dominated by a handful of *gros colons.—Libération,* quoted by *Le Monde,* 5/18/55.[12]

It is agreed that Algeria cannot be considered a State, it would be enough to recognize both the existence of a national consciousness—thus a "national fact"—and the interests of an implanted European population in order to move toward a solution.—*Franc-Tireur,* quoted by *LM,* 3/17/56.

As far as the *fellaghas* and their instigators are concerned, illusions are not permissible. It is the duty of France . . . to show . . . that it will not recoil before any sacrifice to meet the first and most elementary of its responsibilities, which is to assure in North Africa the protection of its nationals and that of the Moslems who have placed confidence in it.—*Le Figaro,* quoted by *LM,* 3/17/56.

Left and Right clashed directly over Mollet's 1957 declaration of intentions:

The declaration of intentions does not respond to any of the essential questions posed today. It only arouses unfavorable reactions.

In France, no one finds anything new in it. . . . In Algeria, the French will remain uneasy. The Moslems will not find in it what they are waiting for: the recognition of an Algerian State. In the U. N., no new element will incline any delegation to modify its point of view.—*Combat,* quoted by *LM,* 1/11/57.

Our first reactions after the . . . declaration are very divided. On the one hand, justifiable apprehension about elections in a single electoral college. . . . But, on the other hand, unanimous approval of the firmness with which are dismissed any ideas of abandoning Algeria and any foreign intrusion, including that of the U. N.—*Le Figaro,* quoted by *LM,* 1/11/57.

It is Guy Mollet who is opposed to a "ceasefire," to any negotiations. It is he who formulates a policy of prerequisites that ruins in advance any possibility of a peaceful settlement.—*L'Humanité,* quoted by *LM,* 1/11/57.

The attitude of the press toward de Gaulle and his policies changed sharply between his 1959 announcement of the self-determination policy and his first steps to implement it with the 1961 referendum. Most of the left-wing press shifted from scorn to skepticism while the Right switched from warmth to wrath:

The "ambitious liars" of the FLN are revolting, from now on, only against universal suffrage. If international morality in this world of 1959 were not made up of vain words . . . tomorrow, everywhere,

12 *Le Monde* will be abbreviated *LM* in citations hereafter.

. . . support for the FLN would cease.—*L'Aurore,* quoted in *LM,* 9/19/59.

Does de Gaulle believe that he will do away with the Algerian underground and its influence by haughtiness, scorn, and insult? . . . Does he believe it possible to treat the Algerians as he treats his ministers? Not everyone is inclined to be a door-mat.—*Libération,* quoted in *LM,* 9/19/59.

We know that the 8th of January we are being invited to vote for self-determination, for a provisional statute preparing for association, and for an appeal for peace. The principles are good. They remain to be applied.—*Populaire,* quoted by *LM,* 12/22/60.

The Gaullist formula of Algerian Algeria will put an end to the terrorism and the conflict, neither now nor later.

It is obvious to all—except for one—that the Algerian Republic defined in the speech by Saint Charles could cease being utopian only on condition that a state of continuous warfare is installed in Algeria. —*Aspects de la France,* quoted by *LM,* 12/25/60.

The experts agree that . . . the referendum question is the equivalent of a blank check to the Chief of State. . . .

We will answer on the 8th of January a single question: *Yes or no, do you have confidence in de Gaulle?*

It is up to each person to examine his conscience and weigh his responsibilities.—*France Catholique,* quoted by *LM,* 12/25/60.

It is not enough to baptise a plebiscite with the name referendum for it not to be a plebiscitary endeavor. Referendum or plebiscite, it all depends on the way the questions are posed. . . .

It is not yet posed, but it is not possible . . . to doubt . . . that it will tend to cause a gradual and disguised abandonment of all the departments of Algeria and the Sahara.—*Journal du Parlement,* quoted in *LM,* 11/26/60.

De Gaulle solicits from the French . . . a massive "yes." What does it mean? This:

After all, I do not have the right to commit France and I know it. . . . But I ask you to cover me, and by your "yes" to commit yourselves in advance, you, Frenchmen, . . . to accept . . . secession with the misery and the shame it means. Thus . . . I will be covered. No one can blame me, nor bother me; the responsibility will have been yours.—*Rivarol,* quoted in *LM,* 12/25/60.

Thirty months ago it was emotion that made the tears flow. Today it is tear gas.

Why so much torment after so much exaltation? Is it not because it is forbidden today to shout both "*Vive de Gaulle*" and "*Vive l'Algérie française*"?—*Le Parisien Libéré,* quoted by *LM,* 12/11/60.

The examples above illustrate the general editorial attitude of the French press toward the Algerian question. Its editorial tone in the Fifth Republic has been at least equal in vigor to that under the Fourth. If anything, de Gaulle's press opponents have been more strident and his supporters less docile than those of his predecessors. In any case, there is no apparent reluctance to take clear-cut, polemical editorial stands—another indication that de Gaulle has not ended French political controversy.

3

Parties and Interest Groups

PUBLIC OPINION can be profiled in a rough way by public opinion
surveys. Its intensity can be measured to a certain extent by
newspaper coverage. Editorial opinion reflects it and perhaps
molds it somewhat. But it is diverted into and expressed in constitutional channels largely through the instrumentalities of
parties and interest groups. These organizations take raw public
sentiment, give it form through their own structures (perhaps
changing it a bit in the process) and bring it to bear on the constitutional organs of government. In de Gaulle's Republic he
registers, reflects, reacts to, and influences public opinion in
much the same manner as parties and interest groups. However,
he attempts to communicate with the opinion of the entire
French population, whereas by their nature, parties and interest
groups carve out much narrower niches for themselves. The
Gaullist manner of popular communication is treated in Chapter
6. Here, our concern is to illuminate the role of parties and interest groups.

PARTIES

Volume of Activity

There is a great deal more popular party activity in France
than in the United States or even in Great Britain. Other than
the quadrennial national conventions of the two major American
parties there are no plenary party assemblages in the United
States. Even the national committees meet—in almost complete
obscurity—only to settle campaign debts and handle other purely
housekeeping chores. They have very little political significance.
In Great Britain the three national parties hold annual con-

ferences and the central machinery functions with somewhat greater frequency in the interim.

In the Fourth French Republic, on the other hand, as many as ten or twelve parties of national significance held congresses each year and many of them also held several executive committee, central committee, or national council meetings annually. The latter type of meeting often had 200 to 300 participants and the congresses normally drew 600 to 1,000 delegates. In addition, most of these parties had active local units from canton and *arrondissement* committees to regional federations, that held frequent meetings.

Besides this regular organizational activity, special organs, such as the Radical "Cadillac Committee," which included both parliamentarians and representatives of the extraparliamentary structure, were brought into being or extraordinary meetings of regular units (congresses, executive committees, etc.) were called on the occasion of cabinet crises, elections, and other events of similar political import. All this added up to a considerable amount of party activity by ordinary Frenchmen.

Contrary to first impressions, party activity has not declined significantly under the Fifth Republic. In fact, despite a general growth in popular political apathy, the number of parties has increased. The four parties of Radical orientation have become five, there are two socialist parties, two Christian democratic parties and two Gaullist parties instead of one each, etc. The new parties feel as bound as do the old ones to hold annual congresses.

Ideological Character

The persistence and even increase in partisan activity is more understandable if the ideological orientation of French political attitudes is taken into account. Major new issues may produce schisms in existing parties, because the French electorate expects each party to take an ideological position on all questions and the parties respond accordingly. Minority factions in the parties are equally ideological in orientation and thus, on crucial issues become dissident, dissolving in many cases into new parties. The Algerian problem has been such a crucial issue.

Before 1958 when the Fifth Republic was set up, relatively few Frenchmen accepted Algerian independence as a patriotic alternative. Negotiation with the rebels was regarded with almost as much disfavor. As French public opinion and de Gaulle's official policy moved closer and closer toward implicit recognition of independence, the party factions left behind have, in most cases, split off. This interpretation of the impact of the Algerian quarrel on the parties gains support from the observation that only the Communists (who already had accepted independence) and the Independents (who have not done so yet) have escaped schism.

Thus the Algerian problem made another slice through the French public opinion that was already badly fragmented. Many voters who shared attitudes on the major questions that traditionally agitated the political scene disagreed on Algeria. They expected the parties to adjust to and reflect these changes, which the parties did in the only way possible—by splitting.

Therefore, the reflection of political opinion in the parties is no less accurate today than it was in 1958. On the other hand, the opportunity for this opinion to be brought to bear on policy through the parties is much reduced. De Gaulle has assumed this function himself by effectively removing policy formation from the purview of parliament. Opinion is still represented in the parties and the party lineup is extended into parliament, but it does not rise from there to the level of policy formation. Parliament has important authority neither legislatively nor electorally, though it may exercise legislative functions where de Gaulle permits. In all matters where de Gaulle chooses, it neither decides policy nor puts in office those who do decide it. The parties continue to represent particular interests, but de Gaulle, purporting to represent the general interest, has assumed the governmental and legislative functions they formerly exercised.

It might even be suggested that political controversy has been accelerated by its detachment from the responsibility of government, much as an engine accelerates when its fuel supply continues after its clutch has been disengaged. Politically active Frenchmen may be seized by a sense of helplessness, but this

has not yet been manifested by disinterest or decline in party
activity.

INTEREST GROUPS

The French bent for ideology is evident in their interest groups
as well as their parties. With some notable exceptions, most
American and British interest groups concern themselves entirely with promoting directly the welfare of the economic or
cultural segments of the population which form their membership. Most groups avoid a clearly partisan commitment and
also avoid taking stands on issues peripheral to their immediate
interests. They do this mainly because they fear that divisive
squabbles would result from attempts to give an official interpretation to the impact of these peripheral matters on the group.

In France, the people expect their interest groups to reflect
an ideological orientation as well. Thus there are communist,
socialist, Christian democratic, and even Gaullist labor unions.
There are veterans associations, peasant groups, student groups,
etc., to reflect each of the political lines.

Even where a social or professional category has sufficient
political cohesion to retain organizational unity, it often feels
called upon to announce a stand on a question that does not
affect its interests directly and peculiarly. In short, French interest groups are "politicized."

Whereas the parties exist primarily to put personnel into office
(parliament and the cabinet), the interest groups exist primarily
to influence policy formulation. When de Gaulle separated parliament from Algerian policy formulation, he sent the parties
down a side track. The interest groups kept their eyes fixed
firmly on policy, abandoned parliament where they had exercised such great influence during the Fourth Republic, and
latched on to the bureaucracy whose influence had increased
as parliament's had declined.

POLICY STATEMENTS

The positions of the major parties on Algerian policy are il-
lustrated by the following excerpts from official policy declara-

tions. As far as possible, they have been extracted from motions
passed at the plenary meetings, usually congresses, of the
parties. Thus, they express the views of the party members
rather than of the candidates, which are expressed in the campaign statements, or of the deputies, which are expressed in
Assembly debates. Schematically, French policy regarding a
political solution passed through four phases: 1, implementation
of the 1947 statute (November 1, 1954 to January 29, 1956);
2, Mollet's *triptyque* (cease-fire, elections, negotiations) and the
loi cadre (January 29, 1956 to June 1, 1958); 3, de Gaulle I:
"personality" but "solidarity" (June 1, 1958 to September 16,
1959); 4, de Gaulle II: Self-determination (after September 16,
1959). Declarations in each of those periods by most of the important parties are included below to show the relative positions of the various groups in each period and their evolution
since 1954. Some selected examples of interest group statements
on Algerian policy are also included. Their significance is reviewed at the end of the section.

Implementation of the 1947 Statute

1. *P.C.F.* The Central Committee calls for the reinforcement of
solidarity with the people of Algeria, by demanding the abrogation
of the state of urgency in Algeria . . . , the immediate cessation of
the repression in Algeria, the return to France of the troops and police
forces recently sent to Algeria, the opening of discussions with the
qualified representatives of the Algerian people with a view to the
establishment of normal relationships founded on the legitimate national aspirations of Algeria and conforming by that fact, to the
interests of the people of France.—Resolution of the Central Committee, July 8, 1955 (*Cahiers du communisme*, September 1955).
No congress was held between November 1954 and January 1956.

2. *S.F.I.O.* The present Algerian Assembly must be dissolved and
replaced, as a first step, by a parliamentary assembly composed half
of European Frenchmen and half of Moslem Frenchmen elected according to proportional representation by a single electoral college.—
Motion adopted by the national congress, July 3, 1955 (*LM*, 7/5/55).

3. *Radical Socialists*. The greatest urgency is commanded in
Algeria. . . . The protection of persons and goods . . . must certainly be assured in the shortest delay. But it cannot be exclusively
the work of force. . . . It is necessary to act at once for appeasement and the return of lost confidence. . . . Let us apply now,
without further delay, the measures decided upon eight years

ago: . . . communal liberties, . . . administration . . . broadly open to the [Moslem] elite, . . . increase of public and private investment, . . . social achievements.—Party declaration, 51st national congress, November 6, 1955 (*L'Information Radicale-Socialiste,* 11/26/55).

4. *M.R.P.* The congress . . . demands that the true instigators of the agitation and especially the Algerian Communist Party be rendered harmless. . . .

Believes, nevertheless, that the re-establishment of order will not be sufficient to resolve the Algerian crisis if a courageous reform policy is not put into effect without delay. . . . The Congress urges, in particular, that the integration of the Algerian populations in French life, with the exception of the religious status, be realized. —Excerpt from motion, national congress, May 23, 1955 (*LM,* 5/24/55).

5. *Social Republicans.* The Social Republicans call for a courageous and loyal policy of political, economic, and social reforms; the close association of the French Moslems of Algeria in the administration and in political life without discrimination and they oppose both the extremist sabotage of some and the retrograde spirit of others.—Motion voted by the 600 party workers and parliamentarians at the "Day of Study," June 5, 1955 (*LM,* 6/7/55).

6. *Independents and Peasants.* In all domains France has made its mark in North Africa. It will not leave. Any act of rebellion against French power and the traditional authorities is no more admissible on North African territory than it would be on the territory of the mainland. Therefore, it must be pitilessly repressed.

The congress demands that the representatives oppose the present policy of the government in North Africa, because, under the cover of reforms, which derive from equivocation their apparent audacity, this policy will finally leave behind it only despair and abandonment. —Motion voted by acclamation at the national congress, December 8, 1955 (*LM,* 12/9/55).

Triptyque and *Loi Cadre*

1. *P.C.F.* By orienting itself, not toward cease-fire and negotiations, but in fact toward a war of extermination of long duration, by sending to Algeria tens of thousands of young soldiers, recruits and conscripts, by maintaining the interdiction of the Algerian Communist Party and other Algerian national groups and by organizing an inhuman repression, the government is not serving the national interest. . . .

Only the rapid recognition of the national Algerian fact and the repudiation of the colonialist relationships imposed by force can lead to a solution conforming to the interest of the immense majority of Algerians of all origins and to that of France. There is no other means to restore peace and to permit Algeria to decide freely its future.—Motion, 16th national congress, July 21, 1956 (*Cahiers du communisme,* July 1956, p. 370).

2. *U.G.S.* After the failure of all attempts at halfway measures, the political decision which can unblock the situation can be no other than the recognition by the French Parliament of the right of independence and the affirmation of our will to negotiate with all the qualified representatives of the Algerian insurrection. In order to achieve this, the French government must neglect nothing. . . .

The congress urges an end to the Algerian war by the recognition of the right of the Algerian people to define its political status themselves.—Motion voted at its unification congress, December 8, 1957 (*LM,* 12/10/57).

3. *S.F.I.O.* The national congress urges the government to take new and courageous initiatives, including simultaneously, renewal of the "cease-fire" offer and the submission to . . . the National Assembly of a bill for a political regime, at least provisional. . . .

Pacification remains . . . indispensable to any political settlement. . . .

The party affirms its determination to rule out any notion of Algerian independence. On the other hand, it affirms its determination to give it broad autonomy of direction. . . .

The internal institutions of Algeria . . . must include:

(a) Local collectivities with assemblies elected by universal suffrage and by a single electoral college, and disposing of the maximum powers to insure the management of the vital interests of the populations;

(b) Territorial collectivities with executives and legislatures issued from assemblies elected by universal suffrage and by a single electoral college and including representation from professional, economic, and workers' organisms. These territorial authorities will possess extended powers. . . .

(c) An executive and a legislature possessing the powers indispensable to the exercise of their competence and charged with guaranteeing the Algerian personality above the level of the territories.

The bonds between Algeria and France will be assured:

(a) By the continuous arbitral power of the French Republic whose representatives will take care to see that the rights recognized to all Algerians, without distinction of origin, are rigorously respected and that no community is oppressed by another;

(b) By attributions retained by the political branches of the French government, limited to those which concern national sovereignty and the vital interests of the French Republic as a whole;

(c) By the participation in the political branches of the French government of representatives of Algeria. . . .

(d) By the institution of a fund for economic and social expansion in Algeria . . . supplied by an important and continuous contribution from the mainland and . . . managed as a common institution.

—Motion voted by 2,547 to 779 and 498 respectively for motions with more liberal wording. Seventy-eight votes were not cast. National congress, July 1, 1957 (*LM*, 7/2/57).

4. *Radical-Socialists.* A clear, realistic, and resolute [Algerian] policy must be affirmed at the same time as defensive military measures are taken, in order that no one may suspect our action of tending to re-establish a colonial regime that is definitely out-dated. . . .

We advocate . . . immediate achievement [of] . . . political and social reforms, purge of the administrative cadres responsible for past errors, liberation of political prisoners against whom no charges can be brought, etc. . . .

When this effort has been made, conciliation of the points of view can be and must be sought. A truce can be obtained. Then, it will be possible to define, in full agreement with all the Algerian populations, the definitive solution, avoiding the crushing of one ethnic group by another and assuring the emancipation of the Moslem masses that the mainland has been wrong to maintain until now in a situation of unjust inferiority.—Motion passed at the 52nd national congress by a large majority of the 3,000-odd votes (*l'Information Radicale-Socialiste*, October 1956). It was primarily as a result of this vote that the right-wing faction withdrew to form the dissident Radical party.

5. *Dissident Radical Socialists.* The committee denounces those who make of themselves advocates for our adversaries as well as "pretended conciliators." Purely military action cannot be sufficient, [therefore] the dissident Radicals urge that institutions permitting Moslems to participate broadly in the political life of Algeria be set up. —Summary of motion voted by show of hands by the 700 delegates, executive committee meeting, December 8, 1957 (*LM*, 12/10/57).

6. *M.R.P.* The Congress urges . . . that a *loi cadre* tending to assure to all Algerians full equality of rights and achieving the fundamental distinction of common interests of the Republic and interests peculiar to the Algerian departments be voted with a view toward permitting broad decentralization of Algeria in the framework of the Republic.—Motion, national congress, June 1, 1957 (*LM*, 6/2/57).

7. *Social Republicans.* The national council [reaffirms its] inflexible resolution to maintain French Algeria and . . . [bows] before the victims of the savage killings of the F.L.N. . . .

It warns public opinion against the risk of hasty elections and against conferring on the new representatives the double mandate of French parliamentarians and valid interlocutors.

It opposes the creation of State organisms, legislative and executive, at the Algerian level and . . . believes that no negotiated statute is possible at present and that it is necessary to affirm that the French legislative power is qualified to legislate for Algeria, a French land.

It proposes . . . the passage of an organic *loi cadre* which will permanently commit France, no matter what governmental fluctuations there may be. This statute must make of Algeria, integral part of the Republic, peopled by citizens equal in rights, a province formed of autonomous regions, each possessing extensive powers at the local level.—Motion voted June 2, 1957 (*LM*, 6/4/57).

8. *Independents and Peasants.* The Independents and Peasants affirm to all the Moslem populations that they will join them in defending the political, economic, and social reforms which will give them in absolute equality still more liberty, well-being, and justice. —Motion adopted unanimously by the third national congress, March 14, 1958 (*Combat*, 3/15/58).

9. *U.F.F.* Two formulas are proposed for the solution of the North African problems:

(a) A stroke of force: this solution, though it can be employed only at the last minute and in the last extremity, and on the sole condition that it be the emanation and the will of all the social classes and must not be envisaged as long as the possibility remains for the foreigner to intervene in a general and brutal repression.

(b) A national government. In these conditions the necessity of a government of national union in which ideological and partisan questions must bow before the imperative of public salvation.—Summary of motion voted by the 200 delegates, national congress, April 14, 1958 (*LM*, 4/15/58).

10. *The Catholic Church.* How can we not tell of our suffering and not call with all the fervor of our prayers and of our vows for the advent of peace, which alone conforms to the Christian ideal? . . .

To say that . . . is not to forget, assuredly, our duties to the fatherland nor the atrocities committed against our soldiers and against too many Frenchmen, and to which correspond sometimes, alas! . . . the painful excesses of certain of our own. It is to call . . . on the only light which may be capable . . . of making discernible in justice the legitimate aspirations of the peoples and of enlightening thereby all the souls with a view toward the establishment of a human and Christian peace, the light of the charity of Jesus Christ.—Speech by Cardinal Gerlier, Archbishop of Lyons (*LM*, 12/ /57).

De Gaulle I: Personality but Solidarity

1. *P.C.F.* The Gaullist government continues and aggravates the Algerian war. The monopolists wish to effect to their profit, in association with cosmopolitan financial groups (notably American and German), the exploitation of the Saharan oil. They intend, besides, to establish in Africa a base for atomic experiments. . . .

It is not the French government, but the Algerian people who can determine the future of Algeria. As long as the war lasts, a "plan" for the future of Algeria can, therefore, only be pure speculation. The duty of a French government is to make proposals capable of establishing between France and Algeria, new, peaceful relationships on an equal footing.—Excerpt from party declaration, XVth national congress, June 28, 1959 (*Cahiers du communisme,* July 1959, p. 524).

2. *P.S.A.* The national aspirations of the Algerians are as legitimate as those of any other colonial or dependent people. . . . An offer of a cease-fire [should] be made to the Algerian insurgents on the basis of this recognition of their national vocation, combined with guarantees for the economic, political, and cultural interests of the European minorities in Algeria and the Algerian workers in France. . . .

The negotiation of a cease-fire, without prerequisite or exclusion must include also an agreement on the military, administrative, and political conditions of the transitional period to permit the Algerian populations to express freely and in democratic forms their will concerning the organization of their national life as well as their relations with the other countries of the Maghreb and with France.—Motion voted by the 350 delegates, national congress, May 2-3, 1959 (*LM,* 5/4/59).

3. *S.F.I.O.* The congress affirms that . . . the extremist pseudo-solutions, integration or independence, appear equally illusory.

—The legislative elections of . . . 1958 did not produce in Algeria qualified representation of the populations permitting "the rest to be done." . . .

—In order to put an end to the combat, the offer of discussions with those who are fighting must be renewed in conditions which cannot be confused with a demand for capitulation. . . .

The negotiation on the cease-fire cannot exclude the search for an accord on the reciprocal guarantees permitting, in a later phase, and only then, discussion of the political solution with all the qualified representatives of the Algerian population without any exclusion.— Motion passed 3,358 to 269 with 92 abstentions over an "integrationist" motion after an "independence" motion was defeated 3,386 to 262 with 96 abstentions, national congress, July 12, 1959 (*LM,* 7/14/59).

4. *Radical-Socialists.* The party bows before the sacrifices of the French soldiers in Algeria but remains conscious of the impossibility of putting an end to the conflict solely by the weight of arms and of the necessity of bringing to it a political settlement. . . .

This long-term construction does not exclude—quite the contrary —the determined search for a rapid solution of the conflict. Parallel with this action all opportunities to achieve a cease-fire with the adversaries in combat must be seized. . . .

It must contain reciprocal guarantees for the two sides in order to exclude any suspicion of military or political treachery . . .

Algerian independence is more than ever stripped of all reality. But any solution which does not respect the originality of the Algerian personality would be equally doomed to failure. . . .

The future status of Algeria . . . must result from discussions undertaken among all the representatives freely designated by the

Algerian population. It will be applied only after ratification in democratic form.—Motion voted nearly unanimously, national congress, June 14, 1959 (*LM*, 6/16/59).

5. *M.R.P.* The congress declares itself in accord with the Algerian policy of General de Gaulle for the re-establishment of peace.— Motion voted by approximately 600 delegates, national congress, May 8-10, 1959 (*LM*, 5/12/59).

6. *C.G.T.* The Algerian war costs 900 billion francs a year from the budget of the State.

It is in order to assure its financing and its pursuance that ordinances striking the working class and the laboring masses have been issued. . . .

The C.G.T. will pursue, while intensifying it, its action for peace in Algeria, for a negotiation with the authentic representatives of the Algerian people. . . .—Motion adopted unanimously, national congress, June 18, 1959 (*LM*, 6/20/59).

7. *C.F.T.C.* The congress believes that, apart from the material burdens imposed by the conflict, the prolongation of the war encourages in Algeria and on the mainland the enemies of democratic institutions, provokes in the two camps a degradation of the conduct of individuals . . . , entails a moral disequilibrium in public opinion and in the mentality of the young. . . .

It affirms . . . the necessity of resolving the Algerian problem by a negotiated solution.—Motion approved, 9,918 to 2,129, over a motion making no reference to negotiations, national congress, June 21, 1959 (*LM*, 6/23/59).

8. *Association of Frenchmen of North Africa.* The congress affirms that any contact with the F.L.N., the M.N.A., or any personality representing them directly or indirectly will lead one day or another to the loss of French Algeria.—Motion voted by 200 delegates, annual congress in Paris, June 21, 1959 (*LM*, 6/23/59).

9. *National Federation of Republican Veterans.* The congress favors a courageous policy restoring confidence in Algeria to all the different communities and liquidating all the after-effects of the past. . . . Only a federal solution in the direction of the French Community will permit these first accomplishments to be attained, while awaiting the constitution of a confederal North Africa.—Motion, 31st national congress (*LM*, 6/30/59).

De Gaulle II: Self-Determination

1. *P.C.F.* For nearly seven years, the colonial Algerian war has been hanging over all French policies. The heroic struggle of the Algerian people, the international condemnation of the Algerian war, the struggle of the French people for peace have obliged de Gaulle to accept in words the principle of self-determination for the Algerian people. . . .

Since the first days of the Algerian war, the Communists have been
fighting for the recognition of the right to independence, . . . for
direct negotiation with the G.P.R.A. . . . Negotiations will open
when the people of France have imposed it on de Gaulle and on his
government. For that, the union of all the partisans of self-determination and of negotiation must be further strengthened and enlarged. . . .

The U.N. has called upon France to negotiate. . . . It is the only
means of assuring to the Algerian minority of European origin legitimate guarantees, to the exclusion of colonialist privileges.—Resolution
adopted by the 496 delegates, 16th national congress, May 14, 1961.
(*Cahiers du communisme,* June 1961, pp. 567-569).

2. *S.F.I.O.* The 52nd national congress recalls the constant objectives that the Socialist party has set for itself to lead to a durable
peace in Algeria.

(a) The solution of the Algerian policy must respond to the freely
expressed will of the Algerian populations and lead to the free
government of Algeria by the Algerians;

(b) It must guarantee respect for the rights of individuals and
those of ethnic minorities;

(c) It must not be imposed by force of arms and the search for a
cease-fire must be pursued continuously. . . .

The policy of self-determination can lead to a durable peace only:

(a) If negotiations are undertaken with those who are fighting,
negotiations bearing on the military and technical aspects of the cease-
fire;

(b) If the guarantees of self-determination are worked out in
consultation with the representatives of all those called upon to take
part in a decisive vote for the future of the new Algeria.—Motion
adopted by 1,876 votes to 1,299 for a more liberal motion, and 174
for a less liberal motion, national congress, July 3, 1960 (*LM,*
7/5/60).

3. *Radical-Socialists.* The Radical party, profoundly desirous of
seeing a worthy and durable peace established very soon in Algeria,

Renews *its adhesion to the self-determination policy,* which rec-
ognizes for all Algerians the right to decide freely their destiny.

Recalls, on the other hand, that national solidarity, equity, but also
concern for a durable peace and the future of relations between
France and Algeria require that . . . the rights of the Algerian
inhabitants of French stock be fully respected and guaranteed by
all means and all accords appropriate.

Urges that France take the initiative for an appeal for a reopening
of talks on a cease-fire and believes that, in the interest of this negotiation, the conditions of the exercise of self-determination must not be
excluded from the framework of the negotiation thus renewed.—
Unanimous motion, 57th national congress, October 8, 1960 (*LM,*
10/11/60).

4. *Republican Center.* The congress affirms that the Algerian problem has been aggravated by the irresolution of the authorities, by their evolutions, and their obvious impotence (while 400,000 of our children are fighting) to obtain the respect of the traitors and their accomplices for the elementary discipline without which there would be no more State. It affirms its indefectible fidelity to the defense of French Algeria and salutes with emotion the sacrifice of our army.— Unanimous motion, 2nd congress of the right-wing Radical party, October 9, 1960 (*LM*, 10/11/60).

5. *M.R.P.* The congress renews its adhesion to the self-determination policy and desires that the meeting at Evian will succeed in establishing in an Algeria associated with France and with the free world, a fair and durable peace founded on the cooperation of the communities and the guarantee of personal rights.—Motion, 18th national congress, May 14, 1961 (*LM*, 5/16/61).

6. *U.N.R.* In Algeria the presence of General de Gaulle at the head of the State and his authority, confirmed and increased by the referendum of January 8, 1961 have created the conditions for a settlement of the conflict for which the U.N.R. gives absolute confidence to the one who has the nation's mandate to achieve it.—Party declaration, national assize, March 19, 1961 (*LM*, 3/21/61).

7. *Independents and Peasants.* The national congress remains faithful to the constant position of the Independents and Peasants who have always demanded . . . that Algeria remain in the French Republic.

The national congress opposes all formulas which would lead to the Algerian Republic, because the Algerian Republic is independence, and independence for Algeria is anarchy first, communism later, and thus we would see the end of Algeria, but not the end of the war.—Motion adopted, 1,360 to 441 with 75 abstentions, national congress, December 1, 1960, over an alternative motion more favorable to de Gaulle (*LM*, 12/3/60).

8. *U.D.C.A.* The national congress with 700 members present authorized its leader, M. Pierre Poujade, to participate eventually in any government of national salvation of a nature to save Algeria (*LM*, 10/27/59).

9. *Club Jean Moulin.* It is not the role of France to dictate—not even to suggest—to its interlocutors the Constitution of independent Algeria. It is not for it, either, to negotiate the status of all the communities called upon to cohabit there. . . . Finally, it is no longer time to dream of a Franco-Arab co-sovereignty [in Algeria] that the numerical ratio of the populations does not justify.—Statement in the bulletin of this liberal, intellectual organization (*LM*, 2/5/61).

10. *C.G.T., C.G.T.-F.O., C.F.T.C., U.N.E.F.* The signatory organizations proclaim the imperative necessity to put an end to the [Algerian] war; they affirm that this objective can be attained only by direct negotiations between the French government and the pro-

visional government of the Algerian Republic [G.P.R.A.] on the conditions for implementing the self-determination and on the cease-fire.—Joint declaration of the four French labor and student organizations, the General Union of Algerian Workers, and the General Union of Moslem Students (*LM*, 2/27/61).

11. *League of the Rights of Man*. The will of the French people to see peace return to Algeria by way of negotiations was clearly expressed January 8.—Resolution voted unanimously, central committee of the League (*LM*, 1/18/61).

CONCLUSIONS

Consideration of these policy statements leads to several observations. In the first place, none of the parties has been able to maintain a consistent policy for Algeria. Even the Communists, despite their assertions to the contrary, did not assume a position favoring Algerian independence at the outset. The Independents, who have been more consistent than most of the parties, have become more intransigent in their conservatism as official policy has become more liberal and flexible. The Poujadists have really never been able to formulate a coherent stand on Algeria. The other major parties have evolved in much the way that official governmental policy has evolved, except that the Gaullists, who were very conservative during the Fourth Republic have since felt compelled to sacrifice their principles to their loyalty for "the Chief."

In the second place, most of the parties have reflected the dilemma of the nation: a wish that the rebellion could be suppressed by force but an awareness that this was not possible and that popular support for the insurgents could be weaned away only with "reforms," if at all.

Third, a comparison of the Algerian policies of the dissident parties with those of the parent parties indicates the extent of the role this issue played in disrupting those organizations.

Finally, the parties seem no less ready to take policy stands in the Gaullist period than they were in the Fourth Republic. This is further evidence that—at least with regard to Algeria—the impact of the regime has been less that of stifling politics than of raising policy formation above it. Political controversy rages as before but its rage is helpless, for de Gaulle has placed policy beyond its reach. He has de-politicized policy.

4

Elections and Referenda

FOUR CONSULTATIONS

THE ONLY FORMAL, regular constitutional means available to the French people to express their will on the Algerian problem have been elections and referenda. Algeria has not been a significant issue in elections at the local and departmental level. The upper parliamentary chambers in both the Fourth and Fifth Republics and the President of the Republic in the latter regime have been elected by electoral colleges composed predominantly of members of the local councils. Hence, public opinion concerning Algeria has had a direct channel through which it could operate only in the 1956 and 1958 National Assembly elections, the 1958, 1961, and 1962 referenda. In the 1958 referendum the voters adopted the new constitution. In 1961 they endorsed General de Gaulle's policy for the establishment of new political structures in Algeria pending an eventual referendum in Algeria on the relationship between France and Algeria. In 1962 they approved the agreement signed with the FLN and gave de Gaulle special powers to implement it.

The 1956 Elections

1. The Parties. Six principal party formations emerged from the 1951 elections: the Communists, the Socialists (S.F.I.O.), the middle-of-the-road Radical Socialists, the conservative Independent-Peasants and their allies, the Christian democratic M.R.P., and de Gaulle's R.P.F. During the course of the 1951 legislature, the R.P.F. was transformed as a result of a scission and of de Gaulle's withdrawal from politics into the much smaller Social Republican party. Immediately prior to the 1956 election, the Radical-Socialist party split. The majority under the leadership of M. Pierre Mendès-France expelled the Premier, M. Edgar Faure. Faure converted the R.G.R., a coordinating committee for the various Radical and allied groups, into a national electoral party to which a number of his primarily right-wing, Radical colleagues rallied. In addition, there was one significant new group on the scene, M. Pierre Poujade's U.F.F. The three electoral formations it sponsored were the electoral emanations of his tax reform organization, the U.D.C.A., which had attracted wide support among French shopkeepers.

Three parties (Radicals, Social Republicans, and Independents) had been associated in the Mendès-France government and the M.R.P. had joined them under Edgar Faure. The Socialists had supported Mendès but opposed Faure and the M.R.P. had opposed Mendès but supported Faure. The Communists were as constant in their opposition as were the Radicals in their support. The Social Republicans had been somewhat warmer toward Mendès than toward Faure while the reverse was true for the Independents.

2. *Campaign Statements.* Algeria was the most prominent issue in the campaign, although it vied for attention with a very wide range of other questions. It received less emphasis in the early part of the four-week campaign, but apparently the candidates responded to rising voter concern with the problem and gave it a dominant place in their appeals as the last blows were exchanged.

The Communists, as usual, took a wonderfully simple and irresponsible position:

The true crisis in North Africa lies in the exploitation by a handful of rich colonialists of peoples beaten down by servitude and misery. For not having wanted to resolve this problem in time, the governments of this legislature bear a crushing responsibility.

Before this situation we must be miserly with the blood of our young men of Creuse [1] who must not leave to defend those privileged persons.

—Immediate withdrawal from North Africa of all the forces of repression and of the conscripts.

—Opening of true negotiations with the qualified representatives of the peoples of Algeria. . . .

[1] The name of the *département* in which this platform was circulated.

—Setting in operation for all the overseas countries of a policy tending to the creation of a true French Union.

—No early call up of new groups of draftees.

—Immediate release of reservists and eligible conscripts.

(Secretary General of the National Assembly (ed.), *Recueil des textes authentiques des programmes et engagements électoraux des Deputés proclamés élus* . . . 2 janvier 1956, [hereafter cited as *Recueil 1956*]. Imprimérie de l'Assemblée nationale, Paris, 1956, vol. I., p. 355.)

The Socialists, with scarcely more precision, put their faith in reform of the Algerian Assembly and the embryo of Guy Mollet's famous "triptyque:" cease-fire, elections, negotiations.

Program. . . Algeria: Replacement of the Algerian Assembly by a parliamentary assembly elected by proportional representation by a single college (*Figaro*, 12/16/55).

The criminal Algerian war must be brought to an end and at the same time negotiations must be opened with valid spokesmen designated by free elections (*Combat*, 12/28/55).

We believe that peace necessitates energetic efforts by France in the following directions:

—Peaceful settlement of the present differences between France and the populations of North Africa;

—Construction of a true French Union. . . .

The Right has committed . . . criminal folly in Algeria by refusing for a long time to take into account modern realities and the aspirations of the populations (*Recueil 1956*, I:370-372).

The majority which has supported Edgar Faure . . . yielding to pressure from colonialists and feudalists, has not been able to avoid bloody troubles in North Africa and has preferred, instead of negotiation, the recall of several age groups of young Frenchmen in haste and disorder (*Recueil 1956*, I:473).

While not discounting the need to suppress the rebellion, the orthodox Radicals agreed on the need for institutional reforms and new elections. They also advocated other changes:

Free and indispensable elections must be organized in Algeria with the shortest possible delay . . . It is the administrative feudalism of the military that retards the solution of the Algerian problem (*LM*, 12/29/56).

Our aim is to save the French presence in Africa. We will not maintain it as long as we depend on force and repression. . . . Conciliation must be wanted and it can be found.

Grant of very broad powers to the government;

Solemn announcement of free, strictly controlled elections;

Dissolution of the municipal councils and elections in three months;

Dissolution of the Algerian Assembly, which no longer represents anything, and elections in six months;

Rapid promulgation of reforms, notably of an agrarian reform for the benefit of the fellahs (*LM*, 12/27/55).

Agreeing on the need for institutional changes while pursuing the military efforts, the Faure Radicals denied the feasibility of new elections, preferring, instead, contacts with the incumbents:

We must combat the terrorism with conviction while pursuing our economic and political task.

For Algeria the federal solution is no more satisfactory than integration. Though in no case should France separate herself from Algeria, we cannot, either, assimilate the Algerian population and territory to metropolitan France. I am convinced that Algeria must have a special institutional charter within the French community. . . .

Obviously, it is impossible to proceed immediately to elections. That is why we want a very broad consultation of all the elected representatives, of all the *notables* in order to elaborate a special charter assuring sufficient guarantees to the two populations (*LM*, 12/28/55).

Although also cognizant of the need for reforms, while continuing pacification, the M.R.P. left open the question of their character:

To transform the French Union there are not just two policies: the abandonment wanted by the Communists or the repression of blind colonialism. There is also association among united peoples (*Recueil 1956*, I:479).

We propose to seek together, right after the elections, the conditions for a policy of reforms and pacification in Algeria, in such a way as to assemble for constructive solutions the broadest union of representatives of the nation (*LM*, 12/29/55).

The search for peace and political solutions is not incompatible with the re-establishment of security (*LM*, 12/21/55).

Elements of both firmness and reform were present in the position of the Independents, but the former was stressed and given a clear nationalist tone:

The Independents have never separated their will for reforms from their care to defend the interests of France. . . . They have stood fast when it was necessary. The attitude of President Pinay at the U.N. when the majority voted to inscribe the Algerian question on

the agenda proves it. This attitude of national dignity was effective:
the inscription was withdrawn. . . .

We will not cease to denounce the demagogy of a policy which
consists of leading one to believe that French recovery can be assured by liquidating the French Union (*LM,* 12/20/55).

The loss of North Africa . . . would be not only the abandonment
of several million Frenchmen, but also, on the mainland, the closing
down of a fourth of our factories. In Algeria, the federalist solution
would lead to the Algerian Republic and this would lead to autonomy,
then to independence, thus to the eviction of France. It is for this
reason that we have chosen integration, but with a new statute taking
account of a legitimate evolution and respecting the particularism of
the country and of the populations (*Figaro,* 12/29/55).

The Gaullists (Social Republicans), since the withdrawal of
their chief, were given, even more than the other parties to the
Right of the Socialists, to speaking with a disconcerting range of
voices. M. Jacques Soustelle, the Algerian Governor General, had
already spoken out in favor of complete integration of the territory with mainland France and had become known as an
advocate of stern and unrelenting suppression of the revolt.
Another point of view in the party was expressed by M. Gaston
Palewski:

The increase in the terrorist activities, the tolerance, even ac-
quiescence that these activities encounter in a great majority of the
population, all this shows that . . . a constructive policy must be
elaborated to re-establish order in the minds and public peace and,
by means of courageous and spectacular measures, an end put to the
effusion of blood (*Combat,* 12/22/55).

The circle was completed by the Poujadists, whose quixotic
insouciance balanced the equally quixotic hyper-concern of the
Communists:

France is on the verge of collapse. Collapse of our Empire due to
the cowardice and the venality of governments under orders from
abroad and from financial interests without a fatherland (*Recueil
1956,* I:464).

In general, the Faure Radicals, the M.R.P., and the Independents defended the policies pursued under the incumbent
government, while the Communists, Socialists, and Mendès-
France Radicals argued that too much stress had been placed
on repression and too little on reforms that ranged from new
elections to the granting of independence. Some Independents

and some Gaullists, on the other hand, criticized the government for insufficient vigor against the rebels and for discussing reforms before order had been restored.

The Socialists and the orthodox Radicals combined with elements in the U.D.S.R. and Social Republicans to form the Republican Front electoral alliance. The members of this coalition, while not issuing any joint campaign statement on Algeria, were nevertheless in basic agreement in their hostility to the Algerian policy of the Faure government and on the need for greater emphasis on reforms.

3. *Election Results.* The most striking changes in the political alignment of the voters between 1951 and 1956 were the sharp decline of the Gaullists and the emergence of the Poujadists. The Socialists and the Communists registered virtually no change. The Independents increased slightly and the M.R.P. declined by a similar margin. The official national election returns lumped together both groups of Radicals. This showed an increase greater for the Radicals than for any other party that had competed in 1951.[2] A detailed analysis by a French scholar disclosed that the R.G.R. candidates polled the same percentages as in 1951, while the orthodox Radicals made the gains.[3]

4. *Views on Algeria and the Results.* It is difficult to discern in the results the reflection of any popular will concerning Algeria. A public opinion poll late in the campaign showed that 25 per cent of the respondents believed that "the problems of North Africa (Algeria and Morocco)" were "the most important problem of national interest which will have to be treated by the new government after the elections." "The problem of wages and purchasing power" came in second with 15 per cent.[4] This suggests that North Africa, and especially Algeria, was the most important single policy issue in the campaign. We cannot proceed from there to assume that the election was a sort of referendum on Algerian policy. Too many other factors inevitably influenced the voters. But no other measurement of electoral will on policy is available. Insofar as it was expressed in con-

[2] The official results were reproduced in *A.P. 1956,* p. 542.

[3] François Goguel, "Géographie des élections du 2 janvier," in Association française de science politique, *Les élections du 2 janvier 1956,* Paris, A. Colin, 1957, p. 488.

[4] *L'Express,* December 16, 1955.

| | Total Vote | | % of Registered Voters | | |
Parties	1951	1956	1951	1956	Difference
Communist and allies	4,910,547	5,454,589	20.02	20.37	+0.35
Other extreme left	146,058	78,042	0.60	0.29	−0.31
S.F.I.O.	2,744,842	3,180,656	11.19	11.88	+0.69
Miscellaneous left °	38,393	449,472	0.16	1.68	+1.52
Radical-Socialists °	2,110,992	2,876,398	8.60	10.74	+2.14
M.R.P.	2,369,778	2,374,221	9.66	8.87	−0.79
Independents and allies	2,433,586	3,086,414	9.92	11.53	+1.61
Miscellaneous extreme right		365,250		1.37	+1.37
Poujadists		2,451,555		9.16	+9.16
Others	87,346	47,990	0.36	0.18	−0.18
R.P.F., Social Republicans	4,125,492	948,854	16.81	3.54	−13.27

° Goguel, *loc. cit.*, p. 470, distributes these categories for 1956 as follows: Independent Left, Young Republic, and U.D.S.R. candidates allied with the Republican Front, 1.9 per cent; Republican Front Radicals, 7.4 per cent; R.G.R. and U.D.S.R. not allied with the Republican Front, 3.1 per cent. He assigns one Social Republican in three to the Republican Front.

stitutional forms in 1956 it was expressed in the parliamentary elections. Keeping in mind these reservations, being aware of the limitations of elections as expressions of popular will concerning policy questions, we can, nevertheless, for analytical purposes, reach these conclusions:

20.37 per cent of the registered electorate favored Algerian independence (Communists, though this stand was played down during the campaign itself).

22.4 per cent opposed the policies of the Faure government on the grounds that it placed too little emphasis on reform measures (Republican Front).

25.8 per cent defended, in general, the Algerian policies and performance of the Faure government (R.G.R., M.R.P., Independents, and those elements of the Social Republicans and U.D.S.R. not associated in the Republican Front), although many of the 11.53 per cent who voted for Independents desired greater emphasis on suppression of the rebellion and less on reforms.

9.16 per cent opposed the government from a strongly nationalist point of view (Poujadists).

17.2 per cent did not vote.

With such a distribution of votes no majority view could be deduced. It is true that the 52.55 per cent of the votes cast favored Communist and Republican Front candidates and may, therefore, be regarded as supporting a more liberal approach. But there was no majority for any particular liberal policy. Also, this makes no allowance for the abstainers. Can it not be assumed that in many cases they did not vote because they did not feel that there was a need to change? Or did they want change but did not vote because they felt that their votes would not effect such change anyway? After all, 47.45 per cent of the voters and 53.43 per cent of the total registered voters did not express themselves in favor of a more liberal policy.

About all that can be concluded from this is that the distribution of votes in the 1956 elections contained so many imponderables that it permitted a wide variety of interpretations concerning their meaning for Algerian policy.

5. *Popular Vote and Parliamentary Seats.* The Communists, Socialists, and orthodox Radicals—the three parties favoring Algerian policies more liberal than those of the Faure government —lacked one seat for a majority in the National Assembly after the 1956 elections. But, of course, as long as the Communists would not accept any policy that did not recognize Algerian independence and the other two parties refused to go that far, no common policy was possible.

On the other hand, the parties of the former majority were now sixty-five seats short of a majority and this did not take account of many unreliable deputies.

The absence of a majority on an Algerian policy in the electorate was reflected with little significant distortion in the National Assembly. The obstructionist and intransigent attitude of the Communists automatically excluded them from any majority. Consequently, a majority could be formed only by combining most of the "liberals" with most of the "stand-patters." This operation required a good deal of compromise, mostly effected at the level of the lowest common denominator. Almost by definition, this favored the "stand-patters." As a result, the voters, who had voted "liberal" over "stand-pat" by 52.55 per cent to 35.3 per cent were confronted by governments that were, in effect, prisoners of the stand-patters.

The 1958 Referendum

In form, the 1958 referendum enabled the French voters to decide if they wished to adopt the new constitution proposed to them. In fact, however, it was clear to all that ratification of the text was the price General de Gaulle required to remain in office. The form of the new regime was much less important to the French people than the identity of the man who was to govern them. Frenchmen lined up on the new constitution primarily on the basis of how they believed de Gaulle would handle the all-important Algerian problem. But de Gaulle had enunciated his Algerian policy in the very vaguest of terms. It was impossible to know what his policy was because he did not disclose it—if, in fact, he had one. Nevertheless, there was endless speculation on it, much more than on the nature of the Constitution. The following excerpts from statements made during the campaign indicate the variety of interpretations given his intentions both by his supporters and by his opponents:

CAMPAIGN POSITIONS

For "Oui" in the Referendum

For each person to respond *"oui"* in the present circumstances will mean that he wishes to act as a 100 per cent Frenchman and that he believes that the necessary evolution of Algeria should be accomplished within the French framework. (de Gaulle, 8/28/58.)

The members of the Algerian Committee of Public Safety of May 13 consider that by reason of the peculiar conditions in Algeria, the vote of the populations in the referendum is going to translate, essentially and above all, their will to see Algeria and the Sahara definitively and solemnly integrated into the Motherland. (*LM,* 9/7/58.)

The new Constitution will permit [the men who animate the national institutions] to struggle still more effectively for . . . the salvation of French Algeria. (Independents, *LM,* 9/7/58.)

The provinces Algeria and Sahara must be considered and put on the same plane as the mainland departments, so that its inhabitants, to whatever religion they may *subscribe, must be 100 per cent Frenchmen.* (Republican Convention, *LM,* 9/7/58.)

For [the solution of the Algerian problem] there is only one means:

to try to enter into negotiations with those whom we are fighting. (Marseilles S.F.I.O., *LM*, 9/9/58.)

The M.R.P. . . . approves a Constitution which institutes a strong republican State, capable of restoring peace in Algeria and of settling the question of its status in the French *ensemble*. (*LM*, 9/9/58.)

The Constitution must lead to elections in Algeria. From these elections will have to emerge the necessary interlocutors. This great question will finally have to be set on the way toward a settlement which will take into account the legitimate rights of both the Moslems and the Europeans. (M. Jean Monnet, *LM*, 9/11/58.)

Between the terms "independence" and "integration" the choice can only be for the measures which will integrate in the French nation the ten million Algerian Frenchmen. (Dissident Radicals, *LM*, 9/16/58.)

The Algerian problem . . . is neither settled nor on the way to being settled. On the contrary . . . the situation has become still more inextricable. (Radicals, *LM*, 9/16/58.)

Integration cannot be accepted. . . . The end to be attained [is] the harmonious coexistence of the two communities with recognition of an Algerian personality and of total equality of rights. (S.F.I.O., *LM*, 9/16/58.)

If we vote *"non"* . . . we are voting against France, against the army, against ourselves, against our happiness, against peace, . . . against Islam. (Moslem member of Algerian Committee of Public Safety, *LM*, 9/27/58.)

For "Non" in the Referendum

Search with Algeria for an agreement without ulterior motives, with the re-establishment of liberties, preparation of the discussion with true spokesmen and not puppets recruited by the army, cooperation of Morocco and Tunisia. (M. Pierre Mendès-France, Radical, *LM*, 9/7/58.)

We advocate the creation of an Algerian State, member of the French Federation. (Radical federation, *LM*, 9/9/58.)

The anguish of French Algeria is to be shared. . . . In the imprecision of the "evolution" of the future status within the "French framework" who does not see sprouting the redoubtable internal autonomy? (Independent deputy, *LM*, 9/2/58.)

For French Algeria. (Poujadist, *LM*, 9/17/58.)

The only solution for the Algerian conflict is negotiation on the basis of the recognition of the right of Algeria to independence. (U.G.S., *LM*, 9/23/58.)

Why is independence possible for all the African peoples and forbidden only to the Algerian people? (Communists, *LM*, 9/9/58.)

THE RESULTS AND THEIR MEANING

The new constitution was approved by 17.7 million votes to 4.6 million (79 per cent on the mainland and 3.6 million to 0.1 million in Algeria. What did this mean in terms of Algerian policy? Nothing, so far as its substance was concerned. The "*ouis*" ranged from "integration" to "independence" and so did the "*nons.*" It meant only that the French people believed that de Gaulle was more likely to be able to solve the problem than was any other visible alternative, and they gave him authority to do so.

The 1958 Elections

Barely two months after the referendum, the Frenchman returned to his voting booth for National Assembly elections. The voters in a parliamentary election would seem to have a better opportunity to express their will on an overriding policy issue such as Algeria than they had in the referendum on the Constitution. In the latter consultation they could only vote, in effect, for or against de Gaulle, whose Algerian policy was an enigma. Now, at least some of the candidates took policy stands.

In fact, there was little difference between the meaning of the two consultations. De Gaulle dominated the election as he had the referendum. He dominated both consultations because the Algerian problem dominated French political life and he had removed Algerian policy from the purview of parties and parliament. The constitution and the parliamentary candidates had meaning on this question only to the extent that they permitted the electorate to cast votes for or against de Gaulle. Candidates scrambled with undignified eagerness to attach themselves to his coat-tails, often by the flimsiest of threads. As his Algerian policy was no less ambiguous in November than it had been in September, any interpretation can be given to the significance of the results so far as popular views on Algeria are concerned. When not debating the relative strength of their attachment to de Gaulle, the candidates gave great attention to such local problems as the price of nuts, protection of the wine industry, or the need for housing in Bordeaux. Nevertheless, most parties did announce policy positions on Algeria.

CAMPAIGN STATEMENTS

Socialist Party (S.F.I.O.). This problem will not be resolved by "slogans." Thus integration cannot be accepted, not because we oppose equality of rights among human beings of different races—this would be contrary to Socialism—but because it is to be feared that it does not correspond to the sincere will of the population. . . .

The end to be attained being the harmonious coexistence of the two communities with the recognition of an Algerian personality and of equality of rights, the Socialist party cannot take a stand in favor of a solution which would lead to the elimination of the Algerian minority of European origin or the maintenance of an outdated regime of authority and privileges for the profit of one portion of the population to the detriment of the other.

The Socialist party . . . reaffirms that there cannot be any solution to the tragic Algerian problem other than a political one, that is, resulting from negotiations with the qualified representatives of the population, without any exclusions. . . . As long as this end is not attained, the military effort must be pursued. (*LM,* 10/21/56.)

French Communist Party. The prolongation and aggravation of the Algerian war casts light on the persistent impotence of the ruling classes to resolve this question. . . .

Six months ago the arrival in power of General de Gaulle gave rise to many illusions. . . . Now the facts speak. . . . All the world sees that the fiasco of the policy followed is complete. . . . The underlying cause of the failure is: no positive settlement of the problems raised is possible without the voluntary recognition of the right to independence of each colonial people. (*LM,* 11/16/58.)

The phony elections organized in Algeria will have as their only result the sending to the National Assembly of 71 enemies of peace, freedom, and the Republic. (*L'Humanité,* 11/22/58.)

M.R.P. We approve of the speeches [on Algeria] spoken by General de Gaulle . . . we find there what we have always advocated: the recognition of the Algerian personality and the affirmation of its close solidarity with the mainland and the establishment, with the elected representatives, of a new statute for Algeria within the French *ensemble.* (*LM,* 11/15/58.)

We intend to achieve broad agreement on the following objectives: . . .

To pursue in Algeria the policy defined by General de Gaulle. (*LM,* 10/14/58.)

Independent Party. Since 1955, the Independents . . . have led day after day an ardent fight to save French Algeria. The defeatists must be prevented from wrenching from our fighting soldiers and from our youth the African prospects and the energy resources of the Sahara that promise opportunity for the future of France. (*LM,* 11/18/58.)

Radical-Socialist Party. Our party has continuously urged that alongside the necessary pacification must be found a political solution within the French framework and that this solution must be such that the Algerian people can make their voices heard and deliberate on their fate. By their negative and destructive attitude, the extremists of Right and of Left defeated this liberal policy, which took concrete form in the *loi cadre.* . . . The Radical Party thus defends Algeria . . . , conscious that Algeria will be saved by the courage of our soldiers combined with the application of reforms that will truly raise the mass of the Moslems to the status of first-class citizens. (*LM,* 11/22/58.)

It seems indispensable . . . to pursue the installation of local collectivities freely elected. . . . Every occasion to move toward a cease fire must be sought and seized. (*LM,* 10/21/58.)

Center of Republican Reform (Left-wing Gaullists). Among the aims included in the contract which binds the members of the Republican Reform: . . .

In order to put an end to the war, to accelerate the evolution initiated in Algeria. On the economic and social plane, to apply without delay the measures announced at Constantine by General de Gaulle. On the political plane, to recognize solemnly the Algerian personality and its solidarity with France. (*LM,* 11/19/58.)

Republican Center (Right-wing Radicals). The safeguarding of French Algeria holds first place in our policy. (*LM,* 11/20/58.)

Our formation [i.e., party] was born of the battle for French Algeria. (*LM,* 11/4/58.)

Autonomous Socialist Party (Left-wing Socialists). Objectives to be attained in the shortest delay: the re-establishment of peace in Algeria by the recognition of the legitimate national aspirations of the Algerian people, by the establishment of new relationships between France and Algeria, including the protection of minorities, especially of the minority of European origin. (*LM,* 11/2/58.)

To sum up, the Communists still advocated independence; the Socialists and orthodox Radicals continued to stress reform measures with the Radicals regretting their 1957 *loi cadre;* the Independents, Bidault's dissident M.R.P., Morice's dissident Radicals, the Poujadists, and the extreme right, stood firmly for *Algérie française;* the M.R.P. and the various Gaullist groups consigned Algeria's fate to de Gaulle's providential hands.

THE RESULTS

The 1956 elections had used a system of list voting by departments with the seats distributed according to proportional representation. For the 1958 elections the government adopted the pre-World War II system of single-member constituencies with runoff elections wherever no candidate polled 50 per cent of the first round vote. The voters had a broader range of choices on the first round and, therefore, might be expected to have had a greater opportunity to find candidates expressing their will on Algerian policy, for inevitably some of the candidates did not remain on the ballot for the second round. Even if a minor candidate did remain, there was no assurance he would retain his voters, for they often feared they would help the candidate they liked least by voting for a favorite candidate who had no chance instead of a "second-best" candidate who was still in the race.

If we look, then, at the first ballot results, we see that the Gaullists made enormous gains over 1956 and that the Independents also increased their vote substantially. On the other hand, the extreme right and the Communists lost a large part of their vote. The Radicals declined less dramatically and the S.F.I.O. and M.R.P. vote was little changed.

Views on Algeria and the Results

Algeria loomed still larger in the minds of the French voter in 1958 than it had in 1956. At the earlier election the war was only fourteen months old and only 200,000 Frenchmen were fighting. By 1958, four years had passed and more than twice as many French soldiers were involved. All the reservations expressed above concerning the validity of interpretations of election results hold true for 1958 and, in addition, the personal involvement of de Gaulle made a clear expression of will on substantive policy still less possible. When discounted by those reservations, the remaining indications given by the results of the 1958 elections are that:

14.8 per cent of the electorate favored independence (Communists).

19.1 per cent favored liberal policies of one variety or another short of independence (miscellaneous left, Socialists, Radicals, and R.G.R.).

21.4 per cent voted to let de Gaulle do as he thought best (U.N.R., M.R.P.).

22.2 per cent voted for *Algérie française* (Independents, the right).

23.3 did not vote.

To put it another way, 33.9 per cent voted for liberalizing reforms, going as far as independence, 22.2 per cent favored integration, and 44.7 per cent committed themselves to go either way that de Gaulle chose to go, either by voting for his supporters or by abstaining.

Because of the ambiguity of de Gaulle's position and the continued division among the reformers, it was even less possible in 1958 than in 1956 to tell what the popular will was concerning Algeria.

Popular Vote and Parliamentary Seats

De Gaulle's ambiguity deprived the elections of any significance insofar as Algerian policy was concerned. The mode of election produced an Assembly in which the popular will was completely misrepresented, but, at the same time, in which there was a near-majority of mainland deputies committed to support de Gaulle's Algerian policy, whatever it might be. This near-majority vanished, however, when the seats filled by overseas constituencies and Algeria are included. (See chart p. 61.)

Thus, the 44.1 per cent of the mainland voters favoring reform candidates elected only 12.8 per cent of the deputies and *Algérie française* supporters with 28.9 per cent of the mainland vote won 43.0 per cent of the total Assembly seats. The Gaullists benefited almost as much. As in 1956, no Algerian majority emerged, but the situation was substantially altered by the existence of a bloc of nearly half the seats that, in theory at least, was at de Gaulle's disposal. They could be aligned with committed deputies on either flank to form a clear majority.

The 1961 Referendum

Of the four national popular consultations held during the first seven years of the Algerian war, only the 1961 referendum—

VOTES CAST AND DISTRIBUTION OF SEATS

	% 1st Ballot Vote	Total No. Deputies	% Mainland Deputies	% Total Deputies
Communist (independence)	18.9	10	2.1	1.8
Socialists	15.5	40	8.4	7.1
Left Radicals, etc.*	9.7	22	4.6	3.9
Total reformers	*44.1*	*72*	*15.1*	*12.8*
M.R.P.	9.1	44	9.3	7.8
U.N.R.	17.6	189	39.8	33.7
Total Gaullists	*26.7*	*233*	*49.1*	*41.5*
Right Radicals, etc.	3.2	20	4.2	3.6
Independents, other Right	25.7	150	31.6	26.7
Algerian deputies	—	71	—	12.7
Total Algérie française	*28.9*	*241*	*35.8*	*43.0*
Scattered and spoiled ballots	0.3	—	—	—
Overseas deputies	—	15	—	2.7
GRAND TOTALS	100.0	561	100.0	100.0

* R.G.R., Radical-Socialists.

Note. The chart above is, in part, schematic. For the bulk of the deputies to the right of the Socialist it is not feasible to locate their attitudes with exactness. For instance, although some Algerian deputies attached themselves to the U.N.R. group when it was organized, later events showed that their loyalty was very limited.

at least in form—enabled the electorate to express clearly its opinion on a question of Algerian policy. But though there were two questions posed, only one response could be given.[5] The voters were asked (1) if they approved the principle of self-determination and (2) if they approved the creation of new governmental institutions for Algeria. A voter could not answer the two questions differently. He had to say "yes" or "no" to both, even though he might approve of one and disapprove of the other.

The confusion of the two questions transformed the referendum into a plebiscite. De Gaulle and his supporters ensured this by warning that a "no" vote would send him back to Colombey. This tendency of officially convoked referenda to

[5] For the details of the proposal and the text of the question see pp. 125-127 below. The 1962 referendum later permitted similar expression.

become plebiscites is a common phenomenon. Also it is usually fairly easy for the government to evoke a favorable response, for the reasons stated before that there is no visible alternative.

CAMPAIGN POSITIONS

The six political parties that (1) had national organizations and (2) were represented in parliament were given the usual access to governmental facilities for propaganda (permission to display campaign posters and space on which to mount them, time on the State radio and television systems, etc.). Other groups, not qualified for official recognition, also declared their stands. Of the six privileged parties, only the Communists made a negative response at the national level. The U.N.R., M.R.P., and Socialists supported the "*oui*," and the Independents and Radicals left the question up to their local units.[6] Almost all the parties, whether right or left, that were not given official sanction opposed de Gaulle.

The Communists were not authorized to campaign in Algeria, but four Algerian organizations plus the remaining five major parties were. Of the four new groups, three supported de Gaulle. Soustelle's National Regroupment opposed him.[7]

The difficulty confronting the political organizations in taking positions on the referendum is apparent from the following statements:

In Favor

Algerians of French stock: listen to me, . . . follow General de Gaulle. He is the hope of France, of Algeria, he is your only protection. (The Count of Paris, pretender to the French throne, *LM*, 12/16/60.)

As royalists, . . . we cannot be deaf to this exhortation [by the Count of Paris]. . . . The confidence that he asks be given to the State and to its chief was not . . . shared by many among us. But we do not believe we know everything, and . . . a son of Saint Louis being what he is, knowing what we don't know, believes that . . . Algeria and the mainland can be led toward a common destiny by the present holder of power. (Royalist weekly, *LM*, 12/23/60.)

[6] *LM*, December 23-24, 1960.
[7] *LM*, December 24, 1960.

In case the French people reply massively "yes" to de Gaulle, as I am convinced they will, . . . the later instructions of the Chief of State [to the army] . . . will only be the obvious expression of the will of the country. (U.D.T., *LM*, 12/23/60.)

The Socialist party . . . will say *"oui"* . . . to the opening as soon as possible of negotiations for a cease fire and for the guarantees for self-determination. (*LM*, 12/24/60.)

A positive response to the referendum will take the character of an appeal to the end of fighting and to a peaceful confrontation. (U.N.R., *LM*, 12/22/60.)

Our *"oui"* confirms our adhesion to the principle of self-determination and . . . our will that . . . the coexistence and the rights of the communities, security, and personal liberty in Algeria be guaranteed. (M.R.P., *LM*, 12/20/60.)

Opposed

Both because of the plebiscitary character of the consultation and of the impossibility of speaking of self-determination after the idea of "Algerian Algeria" and even of "Algerian Republic" has been launched. (Republican Center, *LM*, 12/17/60.)

The policy practiced by de Gaulle cannot lead to peace. (Communist, *LM*, 12/17/60.)

The independence of Algeria would lead to racial hatred, to a still more savage war, and to the exodus to France of hundreds of thousands of men and women. (Independents, *LM*, 12/23/60.)

The Radical-Socialist Party . . . supports . . . the policy of self-determination . . . but [that] policy . . . is abandoned at the moment . . . the government declares one of the three options impracticable and proposes to establish a provisional regime . . . to prefigure the future status of Algeria. (*LM*, 12/23/60.)

The royalists of *Action française* refuse to follow M. de Gaulle to Algerian Algeria. (*LM*, 12/23/60.)

Only negotiations matter and the referendum poses no question concerning this negotiation. . . . [We] fear that the creation of provisional institutions by grant, far from hastening peace, will retard it. (P.S.U., *LM*, 12/22/60.)

A positive response is the surest means to orient the country still further toward submission to personal power without thereby resolving the Algerian problem. (R.G.R., *LM*, 12/24/60.)

"No" to the war, "no" to caesarism, "no" to the secession of Algeria, "no" to the sovietization of shores which are 800 kilometers from Marseilles, "no" to the racism of the F.L.N., "no" to the referendum. (Christian Democracy of France, *LM*, 12/24/60.)

"No" to the Algerian war, "no" to the blood spilled, . . . "no" to the refusal to apply self-determination. (P.S.U., *LM*, 12/20/60.)

The referendum is leading to a political Dien-Bien-Phu, it is leading us to the loss of Algeria. (M. Jacques Soustelle, *LM*, 12/22/60.)

Boycott the referendum . . . to protest against the setting up in Algeria of anticonstitutional institutions. (U.D.C.A., *LM*, 12/31/60.)

A preponderance of *"nons"* . . . would signify . . . the re-awakening of the citizen and it would not be difficult, then, to form a majority, even in the present Parliament. (A Radical-Socialist, *LM*, 1/4/61.)

To sum up, the Communists and several minor left-wing parties agreed with most of the more extreme groups on the right to oppose the government's bill, though for contradictory reasons. The Socialists, the M.R.P., and the various Gaullist formations supported it. The Radicals, Independents, and certain other groups were divided. In terms of policy, everyone to the left of a majority of the Independents favored self-determination in principle. A minority of the M.R.P. and S.F.I.O. and a majority of the Radicals and P.S.U. expressed fears that the reforms in the Algerian governmental structure would impair the chances for a negotiation. Opposition on the left focused primarily on de Gaulle's failure to commit himself to renewed negotiations, but there was also some opposition on the basis that a favorable vote would be a vote of confidence in de Gaulle's policies in general.

On paper, de Gaulle had little chance to get the massive support he needed. The only three major political groups to come firmly to his support (U.N.R., S.F.I.O., M.R.P.) had polled only 42.2 per cent of the vote in the 1958 first-round elections. In all the other groups a majority of the militants were hostile. In fact, of course, few doubted that he would carry the day easily, for, whatever reservations the political leaders had, they were in no position to offer a realistic alternative to the voters.

THE RESULTS AND THEIR MEANING

Of the 32.5 million registered voters, 24 million voted. Favorable ballots were cast by 53.65 per cent of the registered voters and 72.74 per cent of the voters.[8]

In terms of Algeria's future status, the "no" votes were cast for everything from *"Algérie française"* to independence. In view of the way de Gaulle had stacked the cards against "integration"

[8] *A.P., 1960*, pp. 134, 674. On the July 1, 1962 referendum in Algeria, see p. 196 fn. below.

no true friend of *Algérie française* could vote "yes." Almost anyone else could—and did. Even if the Communists and the hostile left accounted for only half the "no" votes (and they probably cast many more than that), there would remain—at most—only about 12 per cent of the voters on the side of "integration." All the remaining voters—about 90 per cent or more—must be assumed to have supported one or another of the liberal solutions—negotiations, "association," independence.

(*On the 1962 referendum see p. 66.*)

THE 1962 REFERENDUM

On April 8, 1962, a third referendum was held. De Gaulle asked the voters in France (but not Algeria) to approve a bill ratifying the agreement with the F.L.N. and granting him special powers to implement it, both as approval for the Algerian settlement and to confer "upon me the right to perform . . . the very trying task . . . of which the Algerian affair is one part among others."

The Communists, Socialists, M.R.P., and Radicals advised *oui* votes but denied that this reflected confidence in de Gaulle. The U.N.R. supported both the settlement and de Gaulle. The Independents could not agree on a stand. The P.S.U. called for invalidated ballots to support the settlement but oppose de Gaulle, and the "ultra" Unity for the Republic alone urged a negative vote, opposing both the settlement and de Gaulle.

The "*ouis*" carried, with 90.70 per cent of the valid ballots (17,505,473 to 1,794,553). 5 per cent of the ballots were invalid and 24.39 per cent of the electorate abstained.

CONCLUSIONS

Neither elections nor referenda provided adequate means for the electorate to express its will on the Algerian question. Either they permitted too many conflicting voices to sift through, or they acquired a plebiscitary character, or both. Nevertheless, they did produce certain indications. The advocates of stepped-up reform had attracted perhaps 46 per cent of the vote in 1956 and had grown to nearly 90 per cent in 1961 and 1962.

More important than their role as forums for the expression

of the popular will on policy questions, was the role of elections and referenda in producing a government. The 1956 elections did not afford the French people an opportunity to choose a government. The voters could only choose a parliament and parliament chose the government. The French voter did not feel psychologically responsible for the government in office when he had had no chance to express a preference. Parliament was blamed if the government failed.

In the first three consultations of the Fifth Republic, the voters spoke clearly on the question of the government. Regardless of the interposition of policy questions or parliamentary candidates, the import of the results on de Gaulle's tenure in the Elysée Palace was clear in all three cases. To vote for or against a policy proposed by de Gaulle or a candidate pledged to de Gaulle was to vote for or against de Gaulle. In every case, they supported him massively and thereby endorsed his policies, just as in presidential elections in the United States and parliamentary elections in Great Britain, the voters cast ballots for or against the incumbent government and its policies. The only difference, albeit a very important one, being that in France there has been no visible alternative to de Gaulle. In the third referendum the policy question obscured the personnel question. The massive majority that supported the Algerian accords had no means to express its general opposition to de Gaulle.

There is another difference between popular consultations in the two regimes. The Fourth Republic voter had little possibility to choose a government, but he had very real opportunities to express his preferences on policy. De Gaulle's dominance of the Fifth Republic deprives him of that choice. He must take de Gaulle and whatever policies de Gaulle may adopt or leap into the black unknown. This is Hobson's choice. The voter feels, rightly or wrongly, that the alternative to acceptance of the official position is de Gaulle's departure and inevitable chaos.

The failure of the de Gaulle regime to provide the voter with genuine opportunities to express his will in constitutional channels has created the breach between politics and policy. Elections are the clutch that links the engine of popular will to the wheels of public policy. De Gaulle has disengaged the clutch by depriving the popular consultations of meaning.

5

The Political Executive: The Fourth Republic

By MEANS of elections Fourth Republic voters designated the members of the National Assembly. The deputies, in turn, named the members of the government, or cabinet. Normally, the National Assembly assigned to the cabinet the task of formulating public policy, but it was not definitive in most areas unless approved by parliament. On occasion, the parliament by means of enabling acts gave blanket, prior endorsement to such policy as the cabinet might formulate within a specified time period for the attainment of specified objectives unless explicitly disavowed by parliament. Policy, whether approved by parliament or enacted in accordance with a previous delegation of authority by it, was executed under the direction of the cabinet.

This brief, schematic portrayal of the policy-formulating process suggests that the classic assumption that legislatures legislate and executives execute is oversimplified. In the Fourth Republic, the executive also played a role in legislating, a role that began prior in time to the role of the legislature. This observation is by no means original, but is perhaps necessary to justify my plan of treating the executive before dealing with the legislature. That was the way, in fact, that policy flowed in the Fourth Republic. The executive proposed and the legislature disposed. In the Fifth Republic this sequence is still more clearly followed, though, so far, the legislature has disposed pretty much as it has been told to regarding Algeria.

The National Assembly was called on to enact very little legislation concerning Algeria during the period following the 1954 insurrection. Through a succession of "special powers" acts

minister but a mere "delegate." Salan was replaced in December 1958 by a career civil servant, Paul Delouvrier, whose personality, background, and lack of a military command reduced the independence of the position still further. In November 1960, Delouvrier was replaced by another career civil servant, M. Louis Joxe, and the designation of the office was changed to "Minister of State for Algerian Affairs."

The Saharan ministry was retained until the formation of the Debré government, when its functions, along with those of overseas territories and overseas departments, were assigned to M. Jacques Soustelle as Minister delegated to the Prime Minister.

POSSESSION OF "SPECIAL POWERS"

The organic statute for Algeria at the outbreak of the insurrection was the Algerian Statute of 1947. This act was an aftermath of the bloody uprising of May 1945 and of the discontent manifested by certain Moslem spokesmen, including M. Ferhat Abbas, during the Constituent Assembly debates of 1946. It was designed to provide greater home rule and to increase Moslem participation in the territory's government.

By 1954 many of its key provisions still had not been put into effect because of the resistance of the European settlers. The Mendès-France government (June 1954–February 1955) had its full implementation as the cornerstone of its Algerian policy, but the Premier was so preoccupied with more pressing problems that he was not able to give adequate attention to Algeria until less than a month before his ministry fell. M. Edgar Faure, a leading member of the Mendès-France government, became premier in February 1955 and announced that he would continue most of his predecessor's policies, including implementation of the 1947 statute.

The Mendès-France government had considered requesting emergency powers in Algeria and probably would have done so had it survived longer. In any case, almost at once after being invested, Faure felt constrained by the increasing gravity of the Algerian situation to request from parliament a delegation of broad legislative powers to deal with the Algerian crisis.

In the latter years of the Third Republic, parliament had repeatedly delegated to cabinets authority to issue "decree-laws" having the character and effect of law. The founders of the Fourth Republic regarded this practice as one of the defects of the prewar regime and adopted a ban against delegated legislation virtually without opposition.[1] Nevertheless, by the time of the Mayer government in 1953, it had become obvious that in some areas, such as economic policy, parliament was incapable of taking positive action and that some delegation of "legislative" powers to the cabinet was imperative. At that time the Council of State expressed the opinion that it was no violation of the constitution for parliament to pass a law stating general policy principles and authorizing the government to enact decrees for their implementation. This device was used freely, especially in the area of economic policy, by later governments.

With the Faure request, this practice was extended into another area. Faure asked parliament for authorization to suspend certain civil and criminal procedural rights in Algeria by invoking a new device called *état d'urgence,* or state of emergency. This state was described by the government in the preamble of the bill as being intermediary between the normal state of common law and a state of siege in which broad powers would be transferred from civilian to military authorities.

The Interior Committee of the Assembly altered the government bill in a manner that reveals much about parliament's general attitude toward cabinets and toward legislation. The exceptional governmental powers provided by the bill were modified in only one minor respect: concentration camps were explicitly prohibited. But parliament's control over the cabinet in its exercise of those powers was tightened. Under the original bill, the state of emergency could be declared or extended only for a specific length of time and only by law, except between sessions of parliament when it could be declared by a full meeting of the cabinet provided parliament convened within forty-eight hours to consider the declaration. The committee eliminated this exception and stipulated that the powers would terminate

[1] Gordon Wright, *The Reshaping of French Democracy,* London, Methuen, 1950, p. 239; *Séances de la commission de la constitution, Comptes rendus analytiques.* Assemblée nationale constituante, Paris(?), 1946(?).

with the cabinet to which they were granted unless explicitly renewed by parliament within fifteen days of the investiture of a new cabinet.[2] In brief, the committee was willing to grant the exceptional police powers requested, if parliament's unlimited power to remove cabinets were not tampered with. The National Assembly passed the committee version without significant modification, 379 to 219, and the upper chamber concurred, 233 to 77.

The requirement that succeeding governments obtain explicit parliamentary renewal of the special powers was intended as a control on the cabinet, but the exigencies of the situation dictated otherwise. The first government (Mollet) on which this provision operated, used the opportunity to broaden its authority immensely. The Assembly was hoist with its own petard. It dared not deny the government's request for fear of providing it with an excuse for failure to solve the Algerian problem. Besides, with the exception of the Communists, most deputies agreed with the government's repression policy. This necessarily entailed permitting the government great flexibility in its choice of means and implied the abdication by parliament of most of its legislative authority in this domain. In effect, the sixteen articles of Faure's law with their provisions carefully designed to define, hedge, qualify, and control the special powers had been reduced to two sweeping sentences:

> The government shall have at its disposal in Algeria, the most extensive powers to take any exceptional measure required by the circumstances with a view toward the re-establishment of order, the protection of persons and goods and the security of the territory.
> When the measures taken by virtue of the preceding clause have the effect of modifying legislation, they will be promulgated by decree decided in a meeting of the full cabinet.[3]

This new formulation gave to the Minister Resident in Algeria "full powers" and to the cabinet the authority to invoke by simple decree either a state of emergency or a state of siege. Except that measures modifying existing legislation had to be decided by the full cabinet, "the power of the government" in

---

[2] For a summary of the original bill, including its preamble, and the full text of the law as passed see *A.P.*, *1955*, pp. 207-208, 662-663.

[3] For the text of the law see *A.P.*, *1956*, pp. 504-505; and *LM*, March 14, 1956.

Algeria was "without limit." [4] Nor was there a time limit under the new law, though it was not to survive the Mollet government without explicit renewal.

Parliament did not again seriously question the right of governments to have available extraordinary police powers in Algeria. But it was less cordial in 1957 when, with the spread of terrorism by the rebels to the French mainland, the government of M. Maurice Bourgès-Maunoury requested authority to wield some of the special powers on the mainland. The Assembly required amendment of the bill to reduce slightly the scope of powers, engaged in a very heated and lengthy debate, and compelled the government to pose a question of confidence before passing the bill.

In addition to removing virtually all restrictions on the government's police powers in Algeria, the Mollet law provided almost equally broad powers over economic, social, and administrative policy in Algeria. The cabinet was authorized "to take in Algeria all measures relative to" a wide range of policy areas including investments, public works, housing, agricultural equipment and land reform, industrial and farm subsidies, civil service recruitment, labor legislation, social welfare legislation, and the reorganization of the public administration and the local governmental organisms.

These powers were subject to four procedural limitations: 1, they had to be exercised by decrees decided upon in full cabinet session; 2, acting "on the report of the Minister Resident in Algeria and the interested ministers"; 3, and after having obtained the advice of the Council of State; 4, the decrees took effect immediately upon publication in the *Journal officiel*, but did not become permanent unless submitted to parliament within a year and ratified by it.

The law went still further in granting exceptional powers to the government in Article 4:

The government can, in any matter, by decree of the full cabinet, acting on a report by the Minister Resident in Algeria and the interested ministers and having heard the opinion of the Council of State, extend to Algeria, with such modifications as are necessary, the laws and decrees in effect in the motherland.

[4] Jacques Fauvet, *LM*, March 13, 1956.

The ambiguity and vagueness of the phrase "with such modifications as are necessary" obviously left the government wide freedom in implementing this provision.

Consideration of the sum of the powers delegated to the government by the law of March 16, 1956 and of the feasibility of implementing the meager controls it did contain makes clear the extent to which parliament had relinquished, insofar as the Algerian problem was concerned, effective legislative powers. At the time, it was argued that the only area in which the government did not hold full powers for Algeria was that concerning purely political matters such as electoral and legislative procedures [5] and even this reservation seemed too cautious when, a month later, the Algerian Assembly was dissolved by ministerial decree.[6]

POLICY CONCERNING ALGERIAN INSTITUTIONS

Implementation of the 1947 Statute

The policy of the Mendès-France and Faure governments concerning the political structure of Algeria was the gradual but accelerated application of the 1947 statute. After Mollet obtained his grant of broad powers for Algerian reforms, he made a number of structural modifications, though on the face of it the special powers bill seemed to authorize only administrative alterations.[7] These changes, however, were regarded as provisional and Mollet's famous *"triptyque"* of (1) cease-fire, (2) elections, (3) negotiations with those elected, was intended to lead to the eventual determination of Algeria's governmental structure. Several times during the Mollet government, official policy statements explicitly excluded the drafting of another *statut octroyée,*[8] although this possibility was being discussed increasingly in political circles as one necessary step on the road to a solution of the Algerian problem.

[5] Fauvet, *loc. cit.*

[6] *LM*, April 14, 1956. It was, in fact, already defunct as a result of a boycott by Moslem members.

[7] See p. 72 above.

[8] *A.P., 1956,* pp. 113, 220; *A.P., 1957,* p. 211. A *statut octroyée* is a charter granted unilaterally.

The *Loi Cadre*

1. The Bourgès-Maunoury Investiture. The promulgation of such a basic law, designated a *loi cadre*, became official policy after the investiture of the Bourgès-Maunoury government on June 12, 1957. It would be an oversimplification to say that the National Assembly explicitly approved this policy in principle by investing the new cabinet. Mollet had fallen less because of his Algerian policy than his social welfare policy, which was too costly for the conservative members of his majority, and Bourgès appeared before the Assembly at a ripe moment to obtain its approbation. The cabinet crisis had lasted three weeks and two previous aspirants had failed in attempts to solve it. Nevertheless, it must be presumed that, by investing Bourgès, the Assembly was approving this policy in principle, for in his investiture declaration he said:

> The tactic of the rebels is clear. They refuse a cease-fire. Thus they avoid free elections and, thereby, discussion of a statute. At the same time they turn toward international opinion to say that there has been no progress and that French commitments are not being kept. . . . We will not be outflanked by this maneuver. We will not allow ourselves to be hindered in the construction of a new Algeria.
>
> That is why . . . I have decided to submit as soon as possible a bill for a *loi cadre* which will serve as the basis for the progressive installation of new political structures. This installation will begin at the local level, it will pass next to the departmental level, then to that of the region. Each region will become a provisional political entity.
>
> Beginning with the provinces and their own political organs the structure of the "Algerian *ensemble*" will be elaborated.
>
> When elections become possible the elected representatives of the [Algerian] people will be called upon to examine this *loi cadre,* to adopt it, or to propose the modifications in it that they believe desirable. . . .[9]

By investing the Premier-designate after that pronouncement, the Assembly was, in effect, legitimizing the principle of a *loi cadre.* The government now had to work out a detailed statute incorporating the principle and submit it for legitimation by the National Assembly.

[9] *A.P.,* 1957, p. 522.

2. M. Lacoste Drafts a Proposal. Sometimes a minister becomes so identified with a policy that his presence in a cabinet
is a symbol of the cabinet's acceptance of the policy. His departure may be regarded as its repudiation. M. Robert Lacoste,
Mollet's Algerian minister, had become the symbol of a policy
of unrelenting firmness in suppressing the rebellion, but it was
made clear when he was retained in the Bourgès cabinet that
he also "conceded that a provisional statute must be put into
effect." [10] Yet, there was obviously a divergence in views between the new Prime Minister and the Resident Minister who
had borne primary responsibility for Algerian affairs and had
lived there for nearly a year and a half. This difference became
apparent as a result of a widely publicized speech by Lacoste
in early July. The Prime Minister had stressed his intention to
change the Algerian governmental structure, but his Minister
for Algeria emphasized the limits on the evolution. In particular,
he said that the *"loi cadre . . .* must not lead to independence"
and implied that the new governmental organization would not
be federal.[11]

It was Lacoste's responsibility to direct the preliminary work
on the *loi cadre,* but not until more than three weeks after the
formation of the new government did he meet with the three
secretaries of state for Algeria, the three Algerian prefects, General Salan and his collaborators, and several high civil servants
to begin work on the text.

After the meeting it was reported:

. . . the *loi cadre,* without treating all details, will not be limited
to fixing general principles.

It seems that the initial work reaffirmed the principle of the single
electoral college for all the assemblies envisioned. The protection of
the various communities in Algeria requires their equitable representation, to be provided for by the electoral law that will be drafted.

Communes and departments would be subject to the organic laws
in force on the mainland, but the new statute would confirm the
autonomy of the three regions which would have at their disposal an
executive and a legislature for their areas of competence.

The arbitral power of the representative of the French Republic
would be comparable to the system defined in the *loi cadre* for the
Overseas Territories.

[10] *LM,* June 12, 1957.
[11] *LM,* July 9, 1957.

The minister for Algeria would be assisted by a council including the representatives of the regional assemblies and the delegates of the economic and vocational organisms. (*LM*, 7/10/57.)

The double pressure—domestic and international politics—under which the government operated throughout the *loi cadre* crisis appeared at the very outset, as this dispatch shows:

The Council of Ministers this morning did not discuss the proposals of M. Lacoste. The studies have not been completed and the minister will first submit his plan to his Socialist colleagues. The government obviously wants to finish them before the U. N. session, thus the interest in a possible special session of Parliament. (*LM*, 7/12/57.)

The Premier made this desire explicit during a National Assembly debate.[12] Several days after his plea, the Assembly adjourned for the summer recess, but not before some of its more influential members gave Bourgès stern instructions on how to behave in their absence and made it clear that pressure from that quarter would continue:

The Independents and the Social Republicans who consider themselves part of the majority asked the Premier to consult them during the vacation on the major political questions and particularly on that of Algeria. M. Bourgès-Maunoury agreed. (*LM*, 7/26/57.)

And the Premier took the instructions seriously:

M. Bourgès-Maunoury . . . does not wish to confront the political parties with a *fait accompli*. As soon as the drafting of the *loi cadre* has advanced sufficiently, its text will be submitted to the representatives of the groups [in parliament] and the government will conclude [its work] only after having received their views. (*LM*, 7/28/57.)

No sooner had the Premier announced his good intentions than the cabinet plunged into an acrimonious and widely publicized free-for-all over the budget. It required his full attention for nine consecutive days to keep the squabbling ministers from each others' throats and to forestall—at least temporarily—the disintegration of the government. He then retreated for a week-long vacation that was, nevertheless, interrupted for conferences on the *loi cadre*. Commenting on a controversial press statement by Lacoste during this period, one writer said:

The fact that M. Lacoste felt bound to specify, in presenting his plan, that it was only his personal views . . . tends to confirm the

12 *LM*, July 19, 1957.

reports that divergences exist in this regard within the government. . . . The controversy bears, in particular, on the problem of the federative power. The Minister for Algeria favors an executive located in Algiers. . . . The Independents have serious reservations not only on the principle of elections by a single college, but also on the installation of an executive and a legislature in Algiers. The Social Republicans (Gaullists), equally hostile, hold out for the formula political, executive, and legislature in Paris and not in Algiers. (*LM,* 8/15/57.)

Finally, on August 20, work was begun in earnest:

It is three weeks later than the original schedule provided . . . that the government reopens the Algerian dossier. . . . The staff of the Premier's office has not remained inactive . . . but no element of information has so far been given which enables one to say the extent to which the investiture declaration has been outlined and filled in. . . .

It seems that the recent initiative of the Algerian Minister has not been wholly appreciated by the Premier. By saying, even with qualification, how he viewed the future of Algeria, M. Robert Lacoste opened the public debate even before the government took up the question. The choice of such a procedure caused some surprise in the entourage of M. Bourgés-Maunoury. (*LM,* 8/20/57.)

After another series of conferences among members of the staffs of the Premier and the Resident Minister, university professors of public law, and the secretary-general of the government-general in Algeria, the two principals (Bourgès-Maunoury and Lacoste) were able to agree on a report which contained these main points:

The new political statute must . . . guarantee the ties between Algeria and the mainland while permitting the peaceful coexistence of the two communities.

This result will be attained:

1. By the obligatory representation of minorities in the various assemblies, despite the institution of the single electoral college. There will be political equality as a result of an appropriate electoral arrangement not elaborated in the *loi cadre.*

2. By the "continuous arbitration of the Republic," carried out in Algeria by the Minister for Algeria and in Paris by an arbitral court whose decisions would not be subject to appeal. This court would be composed of persons having "civil status" [13] and persons having "Koranic status" in equal numbers and of members of the Council of State and of the Court of Appeals [*Cassation*]. Cases could be brought

---

[13] That is, subject to the French legal code.

before it by the representatives of the French Republic, the members of the assemblies, the presidents or members of municipal councils, etc.

The administrative organization . . . would include:

Territorial Organization. Division of Algeria into a certain number . . . of territories endowed with the broadest possible administrative autonomy. These territories would be administered by an assembly elected by a single electoral college, which would invest a council of government presided over by a representative of the Republic.

Federal Organization. In Algiers a "Federative Parliament," could be set up with coordinating competence particularly in economic . . . , social . . . , financial . . . , and irrigation matters.

Its members would be elected either by direct suffrage . . . or by the members of the territorial assemblies. It would also be possible to designate a certain number by direct suffrage and the rest by the territorial assemblies. After the expiration of a certain time, necessary for the territories to have time to acquire "an intense administrative life," and by this fact to avoid any risk of the creation at Algiers of a unifying and separatist power, the Federative Parliament could be delegated other functions by the territorial assemblies.

The "Federative Parliament" would invest for the duration of its mandate a "Federative Council" presided over by the representative of the Resident of the French Republic, he being the head of the executive.

The proposed bill . . . also sets, in a precise manner, the division of functions between the territorial authorities and the French Republic. The latter would keep, in particular, the army, the diplomatic services, general financial questions, civil and criminal justice, administrative litigation, secondary and higher education, mining, etc.

The Algerian people would continue to be represented in the French Parliament. (*LM*, 8/23/57.)

3. *The Cabinet Opens the Dossier.* Finally, on August 23—more than two months after its investiture—the cabinet, through its North Africa committee, began work on the *loi cadre:*

The meeting of the North Africa committee, enlarged to include most of the ministers, was devoted Wednesday morning to a general discussion of the *loi cadre* . . . on the basis of a written report submitted by MM. Bourgès-Maunoury and Lacoste. . . .

The text of the *loi cadre* is not yet ready and will not be studied at the Elysée until after several interministerial councils and after M. Bourgès-Maunoury has solicited the general agreement of the political groups. . . .

M. Bourgès-Maunoury has already encountered difficulty with his own staff in obtaining agreement.

Though it is quite easy to obtain a general "agreement" on rather vague principles (broad decentralization, division into regions, common institutions at Algiers), the problem becomes more prickly as soon as it concerns distributing authority between the central power and the territorial organisms envisaged or to define the tasks which would be entrusted to the institutions envisaged for Algeria.

The contradictions will be still more apparent when the Premier rounds the circle of political leaders to obtain their views.

M. Roger Duchet, since yesterday and before his Independent colleagues are officially received . . . has come to stand guard. In particular, he has reminded M. Bourgès-Maunoury that the Independents were categorically hostile to the creation of any executive "embryo" at Algiers. . . . However, [he] appears satisfied by the present proposal which would establish at Algiers only a simple "coordinating Assembly" for the regions, this Assembly being elected half indirectly (by the assemblies of the six or seven regions) and half by direct suffrage.

Does that which reassures M. Duchet appear sufficient for M. Pflimlin [M.R.P. leader] who must be consulted incessantly, and his friends?

M. Bourgès-Maunoury, in any case, must anticipate objections from those who fear that, by timidity, "another card will be burned" without decisive effect on Moslem opinion. (LM, 8/22/57.)

4. *Consultations with Party Leaders.* Using the Lacoste proposal and the cabinet discussions as guides, "experts" began preparation of a preliminary draft while the Premier embarked on the stormy seas of formal consultations with leaders of

political groups not represented in the government but whose support is necessary. This flexible procedure assuredly conforms to the character of the head of the government, who dislikes enclosing himself in rigid formulas.

It presents, on the other hand, a double advantage. By not proposing at this time a precise and tangible text to the political groups, M. Bourgès-Maunoury is declaring his readiness to take into account the views of the political groups with the aim of assembling the largest possible majority and he will still accept changes at the time of the discussion in Parliament. . . .

The desire of the chief of the government not to go too far yesterday in specifics presented, in his eyes, another advantage: that of deferring until later the most difficult decisions, especially those which concern the limits of the decentralization and the question of "federalism." (LM, 8/23/57.)

It didn't take the Premier long to discover the difficulties he faced in selling his proposal to the party leaders. He held sixteen meetings with representatives of nine different political groups over the next two weeks. Meanwhile, M. Lacoste was conferring with other political leaders in Algiers and Paris. Some of the divergences encountered can be seen from the following statements:

M. Mitterrand, U.D.S.R., very clearly posed the problem [of the extent of the legislative and executive powers to be transferred to Algiers] by declaring that an Algerian Assembly that was simply "coordinative" would be a "deception." For him internal federalism in Algeria assumes an Assembly effectively binding the States or territories by wielding "substantial, real powers of legislative import." Also, . . . a federal executive whose authority would be exercised "under the authority of a minister from the mainland" would be a "dupery." (*LM*, 8/28/57.)

M. Réoyo, U.F.F.: I recognize only one *loi cadre*, the French Constitution and its Article 88: "The Republic is one and indivisible. . . ." It is on this structure that we must re-establish order and peace in the Algerian departments. (*LM*, 9/1/57.)

M. Soustelle indicated that the Social Republicans are not hostile to regional decentralization. On the other hand, they believe that they must not present Algeria with the "poisoned gift" of a centralizing structure. The Algerian executive . . . could only be a coordinating executive, "capping" the different territories and presided over by the representative of France. (*LM*, 9/5/57.)

From *M. Edgar Faure* (R. G. R.), M. Bourgès-Maunoury encountered a prudent reserve. The former head of the government is waiting to have possession of a clear text before taking a position. . . . He only wondered . . . if the construction now under scaffolding . . . corresponds to present realities. (*LM*, 8/24/57.)

M. Rogier (Ind.) declared that he was fiercely hostile to any Algerian executive and . . . the single electoral college system. (*LM*, 8/24/57.)

MM. Queuille and Morice: The dissident Radical Socialist Party . . . believes that the future organization of Algeria must be based on a broad autonomy of the various regions that compose it, the affairs of the regions being managed, under the arbitration of a representative of the Republic, by an executive council elected by this assembly for a fixed term.

The Radical Socialist Party agrees to the creation above the level of the regions of an Assembly of coordination for economic and social organisms. . . .

On the other hand, it opposes the creation at Algiers of any Assembly of a political character as well as any autonomous executive. (*LM*, 9/7/57.)

5. *Reports to the People.* The Premier also made a report by radio directly to the people but—perhaps because of the traditional fear among Fourth Republic politicians that direct communication with the people smacked of caesarism—he said much less than had already been reported in the press.[14] After finishing his round of consultations, he reported on his negotiations to a special press conference, but again said nothing of substance that was not already known.[15]

6. *A Second Round of Consultations.* With the party consultations in mind, the Premier prepared a draft bill, requested a special session of Parliament, called a meeting of the Council of Ministers, communicated the text of his draft bill to the Council of State, and returned to the parties to hear their views on the concrete project:

> The *loi cadre* has undergone noticeable modification since it was "brought into the shop." Its authors have been led to follow through the consequences of the basic principle that they have chosen: that of internal federalism. They have accentuated the decentralization by distinguishing clearly between the President and the effective head of the executive councils of the territories, and in the same spirit they have reinforced the federative power which will be located in Algiers. (*LM*, 9/10/57.)

The new text was considered by the executive organs of some of the parties before the meeting of the Council of Ministers with these results:

> *Social Republicans.* The Political Committee of the Social Republicans . . . met for more than three hours and a half Tuesday afternoon. . . .
> In the motion that was adopted . . . the committee declares . . .:
> "The committee criticized, in particular, as incompatible with the maintenance of French Algeria:
> "(a) The creation in Algiers of State institutions including a political assembly and an autonomous executive;
> "(b) The possibility for the Parliament to delegate essential attributes of sovereignty;
> "(c) The politicization of the local institutions which would come

14 *LM*, September 1, 1957.
15 *LM*, September 12, 1957.

about through making the territorial governments responsible to their assemblies.

"(d) The continuous incitement to revision." (*LM*, 9/12/57.)

M.R.P. The National Bureau of the M.R.P. examined the *loi cadre* for five hours. A delegation . . . was received at 10:30 P.M. by M. Bourgès-Maunoury. At the close of this meeting the following statement was published:

"The National Bureau of the M.R.P., . . . reaffirms its conviction that a *loi cadre* . . . to be effective must permit . . . the functioning of new communal, territorial, and federative institutions whose powers must be real and clearly defined." (*LM*, 9/12/57.)

Communist Party. The Political Bureau of the Communist Party, meeting Tuesday, decided to convene the National Committee on September 18 and 19 to "intensify the necessary struggle of the working class and of the people of France against the Algerian war." (*LM*, 9/12/57.)

7. *Trouble in the Cabinet.* Despite the Premier's agonizing efforts to elaborate a proposal that would attract wide support, basic disagreements remained, even within the cabinet, when the draft was submitted to it September 11. After three long cabinet meetings, the following report appeared:

Controversy remains on an essential point: that of the federative organisms to be installed in Algiers. . . .

The Cabinet Council worked out a provision for the Federative Executive Council to be composed of persons designated for four years by the territorial assemblies. This formula won the approval of the great majority of the members of the government, but encountered and continued to encounter from the opening moment of the Council of Ministers meeting the hostility of M. André Morice.

The Minister of National Defense certainly could not ignore the motion voted by his dissident Radical friends last September 5, a motion which formally rejected "the creation in Algiers of any Assembly with political character as well as any autonomous executive." The very fact that he did not quit Wednesday and that he engaged in the discussion on the appointment of an executive, . . . is evidence of his desire not to disrupt the solidarity of the government.

His intention not to burn his bridges as of yesterday, not to make a decision before seeing again his political friends who will meet Monday also seems to indicate that he has not been insensitive to M. Queuille's profuse counsels of patience and moderation.

M. André Morice having made this morning a certain number of counterproposals, the question remained to know if it was possible to arrive at a compromise worthy of the name. . . .

The Socialists had demanded at their last national congress the installation of an executive and a legislature possessing powers indispensable for the exercise of their competence and charged with guaranteeing above the level of the territories the Algerian "personality." . . . Any step taken in the direction of M. André Morice endangers, in these conditions, the agreement they made among themselves.

In that case, M. Bourgès-Maunoury would also have to reckon, outside the government, with the vigilance of the Popular Republicans. They affirmed recently that the new institutions must be endowed with real powers. . . .

MM. Bourgès-Maunoury and Lacoste raised Thursday with M. René Coty the possibility of a rupture of ministerial solidarity. The working out of a mediocre compromise would certainly permit the avoidance of such a possibility, but this would be to the detriment of a *loi cadre* of which one scarcely sees what would be the sense and the utility if it were not liberal and evolutionary. . . .

The Right is not disposed to relax its vigilance. The decision made by M. Duchet to advance the date of his return from the United States, the visits of the Algerian senators to M. Bourgès-Maunoury, the reactions of the *Echo d'Alger* . . .[16] are sufficient evidence of that. (*LM*, 9/14/57.)

Even the advisory Council of State bore little water to the government's mill:

That high assembly approved the bill. It made only modifications of form, but discussed it for a very long time in executive session. The substitution of words reflects juridical reservations. Its decision was difficult but constitutes, anyway, only an opinion. (*LM*, 9/17/57.)

The Premier made one last effort to bring into line his Minister of National Defense before throwing the bill to the lions in the Palais Bourbon:

M. Bourgès-Maunoury received M. André Morice again for a long time late in the morning. The Minister of National Defense submitted to him in the name of the dissident Radicals new "counterproposals" for the *loi cadre* bill . . .

M. Bourgès-Maunoury is endeavoring to regain the support of the Independents and dissident Radicals without thereby losing that of the S.F.I.O. and the M.R.P. . . . [and is proposing a] compromise that would consist of suppressing in Article 14 the sentence: "The Federative Council . . . *elects* each year its president." This council would remain presided over by the Minister for Algeria and its deliberations would be executory, but they would be applied *under the authority of one of its members*—and no longer *of a president*. . . .

[16] Right-wing Algerian newspaper.

The modifications in form seemed acceptable to the M.R.P. and to the S.F.I.O. But they did not appear sufficient to M. André Morice. The resignation of the Minister of National Defense thus remains pending. (*LM*, 9/18/57.)

8. *The "Round-Table" Conference.* The dissident Radicals persisted in their opposition, M. Morice tendered his resignation, which was not immediately accepted, and the *loi cadre* was submitted to National Assembly. After the fracas in the Assembly's Interior Committee (described on pp. 137-140 below), the Premier, with the approval of the Council of Ministers, called a meeting "of a certain number of political personalities to seek a *rapprochement* leading to the formation of a broad national majority on the *loi cadre*." [17] Thus a new procedure of French parliamentary government was born, marking another long step in the degradation and paralysis of the regime. The cabinet, whose composition had always depended on a proper *dosage* among the majority parties, was now compelled, in order to prevent its own disintegration, to summon fresh and more official party representatives to solve a policy question too difficult for the cabinet itself. These "round-table" conferences were later used by the Félix Gaillard government on several occasions to deal with questions other than the Algerian problem. The formation of the original round table was reported this way:

The "Round-Table" procedure may seem singular on first view. It is concerned with the settlement of a conflict which exists in the government itself. The solution of the problem has already suffered by being discussed in the public square. Conciliation becomes more difficult when considerations of pride and personal prestige enter in.

What, then, can be the utility, the object, and the effectiveness of the "last chance conference"?

(1) Its convocation . . . will at least have permitted:

—*avoidance of the break up of the Council of Ministers on Wednesday morning.* The resignation of M. André Morice would have been followed, not only by that of the three other representatives of his party in the government, but also by that of M. Robert Lacoste.

The Minister for Algeria does not agree with the critique and does not share the fears of the Minister of National Defense. He justifies and defends the draft bill as it was submitted to Parliament. But it is very certain that the resignation of his colleagues would place him in a delicate position in Algeria;

17 *LM*, September 19, 1957. For a summary of the bill submitted originally to the Assembly committee, see pp. 136-137 below.

—time to await the decisions of the National Council of the Social-ist Party. Neither M. Lacoste nor M. Gazier have favored the rupture in the Council of Ministers. M. Guy Mollet is, like them, eager to avoid the defeat of the *loi cadre.* . . . So is M. Pineau. . . .

(2) If the convocation of the Round Table has been opportune to the extent that it prevents, at least provisionally, the break-up of the cabinet and a defeat in Parliament, what is its object? . . .

—to rally to the present text those who are hesitant. The Premier has observed that many of those who criticize it discover in their turn the problem. They propose solutions which already have been presented to the government and not retained;

—to modify the draft bill to rally the opponents. The positions taken on one side and the other are so categorical that no compromise is possible . . . ;

—to empty the text of "details" and defer them to implementing decrees or later laws. The operation would be justified to the extent that the present proposal defines not only a framework but descends to the means; but if it does this it is precisely to satisfy those who wanted to include in it numerous safeguards for French sovereignty.

The idea of a "thinned-out" bill is attractive. It would not resolve the difficulty; it would defer it. It would not settle the conflict; it would prolong it. (*LM,* 9/20/57.)

The nine-and-one-half-hour first meeting of the round-table conference failed to reach agreement. This report shows why:

The conference turned rapidly into a dialogue—often tense—between M. Roger Duchet and M. Guy Mollet . . . [who speak for] the two large parties they head. On their agreement or their disagreement depends the fate of the *loi cadre,* the government, and the legislature.

There was on one side, then, M. Guy Mollet, supported by M. Joseph Perrin . . . M. P.-H. Teitgen, . . . and M. Edgar Faure. . . . On the other were M. Roger Duchet and M. Marcellin, supported on substance but not always on tactics by M. Soustelle and, outside the conference, by M. André Morice, with whom he conferred after the second session. . . .

There were also conciliators, some discreet like M. Queuille; others eager like M. Roclore . . . ; still others tireless and determined like M. Houphouet-Boigny. Finally, more than ever, M. Daladier was taciturn.

Although the entire draft bill was examined anew, it was on Article 12 that the conference stumbled again. [The Independents and Soustelle sought to designate the Minister for Algeria as the head of the "federative" executive, but] M. Guy Mollet . . . argued that to have the Minister for Algeria direct the federative council would be to prevent him from playing his role of arbiter and would involve him directly in all the conflicts among territories. . . .

His voice rising, the Socialist leader reproached the Moderate leader for having supported his government only because it assumed responsibility for the military action although that had a *raison d'être* only if it led to a political solution. . . .

To attempt to resolve the conflict the Premier proposed to defer until later the organization of the federative council. A special law would provide it. Taking up this idea, M. P.-H. Teitgen . . . proposed that this be accomplished, instead, by a decree. . . .

After having conferred during the night with M. André Morice, M. Roger Duchet rejected this compromise which had been accepted by M. Guy Mollet. The decree procedure seemed more perilous than that of the law. No one could know what use would be made of it by the government then in power. . . . (*LM,* 9/21,22/57.)

The following day these changes were made to win the support of the right-wing deputies:

The attributions conferred by the territorial assemblies on the Federative Assembly must be "with an aim toward coordination and may not impair the autonomy of the territory." . . .

The second paragraph of the same article was deleted. It stipulated that Parliament, by means of a law, could transfer to the federative and territorial organs certain attributes reserved to the Republic. . . .

The institutions provided can be modified "by concordant resolutions" and not simply "by agreement" of the territorial assemblies, the Federative Assembly, and Parliament.[18] (*LM,* 9/24/57.)

In addition, it was agreed that the Federative Council would not be set up for at least eighteen months. By that time, new Assembly elections would have been held in which the Right expected to make substantial gains.

The text thus agreed upon was submitted to the Assembly and rejected, bringing about the fall of the cabinet. These developments are presented in detail on pages 138-159 below. M. Félix Gaillard succeeded M. Bourgès-Maunoury to the premiership on November 5, becoming on his thirty-eighth birthday the youngest head of the French government since the time of Napoleon. His government obtained the participation of the M.R.P., the Independents, and the Social Republicans in addition

18 That is, all of these assemblies had to agree.

to the parties that had been in the previous coalition except the dissident Radicals.[19]

9. *The Gaillard Government Resumes the Task.* During his investiture address, M. Gaillard stated his intentions regarding the *loi cadre:*

> First of all, . . . Parliament must . . . resume the discussion of a draft *loi cadre,* defining the principles on which is based the Algerian policy of our country.
>
> This text must signify without equivocation that our country is not contented with only the necessary action of repressing terrorism, but that it seeks a political solution to the Algerian problem.
>
> Within the framework of indissoluble bonds between the mainland and this territory, the Algerian personality must find its full flowering. It will achieve that only by respecting the ethnic communities that compose it and by insuring their equitable representation in the administrative organs. . . .
>
> The concern to ensure the coexistence of the Algerian communities must be reconciled with the equal rights of the individual within a single electoral college. Toward this end, the government will define the procedures of the electoral law, taking into account the concern which was manifested on certain Assembly benches during the first discussion of this text. The two bills will be submitted to Parliament simultaneously.[20]

Elaboration of the new bill was easy in comparison to its unfortunate predecessor. Because the positions of the adversaries were well known, most avenues of compromise had already been explored. Also, the Premier was prepared to accept a weaker bill than had been M. Bourgès-Maunoury. The political atmosphere was also conducive to conciliation. The regime had just passed through two long ministerial crises. The country had been without governments for 58 of the 169 days after May 21. In the view of the supporters of the Republic it was no time to precipitate a new crisis. It is not surprising, then, that only one week after the new government was invested the following report appeared:

> M. Robert Lacoste and his collaborators have drafted a new *loi cadre.* . . . The new text retains most of the [previous] one . . . ; in particular it retains the federative organs in Algiers. But M. Lacoste has adopted an idea advanced by M. Soustelle and accepted by M. Guy Mollet: that of the representation of the "communities."

[19] There was, however, a dissident Radical secretary of state.
[20] *A.P., 1957,* p. 538.

[Soustelle] proposed the creation of an Assembly of Communities in Algiers and [Mollet] envisioned one in each territory. The new bill satisfies both. It has . . . :

(a) Alongside the territorial assemblies, consultative assemblies of communities, composed, on a basis of parity, of representatives of the Algerians with Koranic status, of Europeans, and of economic, cultural, and social groups;

(b) Alongside the federative council in Algiers, itself issued from the territorial assemblies, a federative council of communities with consultative power;

(c) An arbitration procedure between the territorial assemblies, whose function would be comparable to that of legislative assemblies, and the councils of communities, whose roles would be comparable to that of the Council of the Republic. . . . In case of disagreement, the Minister for Algeria could either implement the decision taken on second reading by the territorial assembly or refer the dispute to the mainland Parliament.

The mechanism . . . is thus heavier and more complicated. . . . But . . . it is one of the conditions necessary to win the support of a sufficient number of opponents and, in particular, of Independents, of whom 41 voted against the [first] bill.

The government also hopes to accomplish this by presenting, simultaneously, a bill for an electoral law. There again the same principles are being retained and especially the single electoral college. But . . . the present bill specifies the . . . the form of balloting. In order to ensure "equitable and authentic" representation of the communities, it institutes a system of proportional representation. . . . Each list would elect as many candidates as the number of times its vote contains a quotient resulting from the division of the total number of voters by the number of seats to be filled. The "remainders" would be distributed at the level of the territory among the groups having presented lists in more than eight constituencies throughout Algeria. (*LM*, 11/10/57.)

The institution of the "councils of communities" entails, in effect, the deletion from the proposal of the arbitral court. . . . The Council of State becomes the only means of recourse.

The councils of communities . . . will have . . . competence only in the financial domain and over problems concerning the coexistence of the communities. (*LM*, 11/13/57.)

With several minor changes, the bill received the endorsement of the Council of State, was approved by the Cabinet Council and the Council of Ministers, and was dumped into the hopper of the National Assembly. Having worked out again a bill incorporating the principles that had been legitimized by the Assembly in June, the cabinet now solicited legitimation for the details. It was granted by a vote of 269 to 200 on November 29. (See pp. 160-161 below.)

CONCLUSIONS

Viewed in retrospect, the contemporary newspaper accounts of the efforts to draft an Algerian *loi cadre* acceptable to parliament paint in shrieking colors the portrait of a regime in full disintegration. In a great modern state, confronted by all the ravishing problems of a global economy, electronic technology, nuclear weapons, ideological warfare, and colonial disengagement, the governmental organ best equipped to devise public policy realistically is the executive. Small, composed of specialists, with all the resources of the bureaucracy available, it can act with much greater assurance than can the unwieldy, ill-equipped, disparate legislature. Yet, in the Fourth Republic the executive descended deeper and deeper into a pit of weakness, indecision, and complacent despair. By the time of the Bourgès-Maunoury government, its dance of death had reached phrenetic tempo. Conferences multiplied, consultations were heaped on top of consultations, day-long council meetings fused into one another while clashes between weary and cynical politicians threw chips and sparks that were deflected across the land, arousing universal disgust and dismay. Newspapers could always be sure that someone on the cabinet would breach the integrity of the conference to embarrass a political adversary. Yet, through all the smoke and flame the whole world scoffed at the possibility that the object of so much passion and energy would ever be put into effect.

The ultimate mark of this disintegrative process was the invention of the round-table conference. Admitting its paralysis, its incapacity to perform its assigned functions, the cabinet issued a desperate cry for assistance from its chief adversaries. Public authority was diverted from constitutional channels. Whereas the Assembly and the Government bore the responsibility, an extraconstitutional round table was called on to make the decisions.

In the end, the bill that received the endorsement of a reluctant cabinet was ill-conceived. It was so diluted by safeguards for the European minority in Algeria that few believed it could win the confidence of the Moslems, that it could persuade them that France was sincerely trying to build a "new Algeria" in which they would enjoy full and equal political rights. Yet it was for that purpose it had been conceived, fought for, and now passed on with resignation and foreboding to an ill-tempered legislature.

6

The Political Executive:
The Fifth Republic

THE PRELIMINARY PHASE

Interment of the *Loi Cadre*

THE *loi cadre* was never put into effect, interred with the regime
that had produced it. Though the Fourth Republic expired,
though the *loi cadre* was forgotten, though the men who had
dominated the one and spawned the other were driven from
office or eclipsed by the Olympian figure of Charles de Gaulle,
the dilemma of political reform in Algeria remained.

Nothing in de Gaulle's investiture declaration nor in the statements he made during the crisis preceding it indicated the solution he desired nor the method he would use in finding it, except
that it could be found only within the framework of a new
French constitution.[1] On June 3, 1958 the National Assembly
renewed the special Algerian powers in the form first voted for
the Mollet government, but de Gaulle did not use them to introduce permanent constitutional reforms any more than had
his predecessors. The following day he made a speech in Algiers
in which he endorsed the single electoral college for the election
of Algerian deputies and presidential electors and added that
"with these elected representatives we will see how to do what
remains."[2] The obvious implications of this were: 1, the 1957
loi cadre was to be abandoned except the principle of the single
electoral college; and 2, the Mollet *triptyque* was to be dis-
mantled; the cease-fire need not precede elections and the

[1] *A.P., 1958*, pp. 538-541.
[2] *Ibid.*, p. 544.

eventuality of "negotiations" with those elected was framed in terms of typically Gaullist ambiguity. In later speeches he transposed the first two terms of the *triptyque* by indicating that the definitive form of the Algerian political structure could not be determined until after "calm" returned to the territory.[3]

In his June 4 speech he gave the first hints of the form of Algerian governmental system he favored by ruling out—at least implicitly—the communal basis that had acquired such prominence and such importance in the final version of the *loi cadre.* Later in June he discarded another feature of the *loi cadre* by saying that one of the problems facing France was "to act in such a way that [Algeria] may always be body and soul with France" while a federal bond was to be forged between France and "the associated peoples of Africa and Madagascar." This implied that Algeria was to retain a unitary, rather than federal, bond with France.[4]

Personality and Solidarity

After the 1958 referendum on the new constitution, de Gaulle broached the question of the future political status of Algeria more directly in his famous Constantine speech:

I believe that it is completely useless to determine in advance by words that which, no matter what, actions will sketch bit by bit. But in any case . . . [it is] certain [that] the future of Algeria . . . — because it is the nature of things—will be built on a double base: its personality and its close solidarity with the French mainland.[5]

This vague formula was repeated in various terms in numerous speeches by de Gaulle over the next few months. Always there was the refusal to attempt to predetermine the form of the future Algerian institutions, except to say that—by the nature of things— it would be both distinctively Algerian and bound to France.

De Gaulle as Head of State

When the institutions of the new republic were set in operation in January 1959, M. Michel Debré replaced de Gaulle as Premier and de Gaulle assumed the office that had been re-

[3] *Ibid.,* pp. 550-552.
[4] *Ibid.,* p. 545.
[5] *Ibid.,* pp. 561-562.

fashioned to his measure, the Presidency of the Republic. In fact, however, de Gaulle continued to play the dominant role in the formation of Algerian policy. Debré made occasional declarations on Algerian policy, but always stressed the identity of his views with those of de Gaulle. When observers detected divergence in their statements, they discounted Debré.

De Gaulle's activity as well as Debré's attitude reflected this fact. Not only did de Gaulle conduct himself in a radically different manner than had the heads of state of previous French Republics, but he also behaved differently from the heads of their governments, their premiers—and, indeed, differently from *his own* premier.

He made extended tours through the provinces in the grand monarchic manner with retinue and all, delivering speeches repetitiously, endlessly. He held regal, stage-directed press conferences. He spoke directly to his countrymen by television and radio when occasion demanded. His language reflected his incessant concern with establishing and maintaining his authority.[6] He identified governmental policy with himself, himself with the State and, more than the State, with France, her eternal self.

All of these activities did not, of course, bear directly on the Algerian question, but they all were aimed at creating for de Gaulle general authority and, therefore, *ipso facto*, authority to deal with Algeria.

PREPARATIONS FOR A "NEW INITIATIVE"

Parliamentary Contacts

A new phase in formulating and implementing policy for reform of the Algerian governmental structure opened in August 1959. After more than a year in office, during which de Gaulle refused to depart from the very vaguest pronouncements

[6] His writings, in more or less explicit terms, have also harped on this theme. See, especially, his essay written in 1932: *Le Fil de l'épee*, Paris, Berger-Levrault, 1944, which was published in English translation as *The Edge of the Sword* (trans. by Gerard Hopkins), New York, Criterion Books, 1960. For a ruthless and incisive exercise in dismantling Gaullist rhetoric see Jean-François Revel, *Le style du Général*, Paris, Julliard, 1959.

on Algeria, his statements and those of his subordinates began to acquire sharper definition.

At the end of July 1959, Debré met with a group of deputies from Algeria and reaffirmed his position that "under the terms of the Constitution, Algeria is sovereign French land," that "there could be no question of political negotiations or foreign mediation" but

> . . . no doubt it will be advisable to examine later the problem of the eventual special administrative organization for Algeria, unity not necessarily implying administrative uniformity. (*LM*, 7/31/59.)

Debré clarified this point further in a reply to a written parliamentary question. He said, with reference to Algeria, that "the rules of sovereignty set by the Constitution can be modified only by constitutional revision," but that new "territorial collectivities" could be created and adopted by legislative or administrative action, and he denied that the 1958 Constitution had abrogated the 1947 Algeria Statute.[7]

Those statements were applauded by the partisans of "French Algeria" and were generally interpreted as supporting the opponents of modification of Algeria's relationship with the mainland. They did not, however, exclude the possibility of changes through constitutional amendment, nor did Debré express opposition to such changes. Viewed in this light, they give a more ominous cast to the rather cryptic remark that de Gaulle was reported to have made the same day. De Gaulle told the steering committee of the Senate of the Community, "as long as a territory is engaged in civil war it is impossible for us to develop the prosperity that we wish to bring to it" and he referred specifically to Algeria. This was interpreted as suggesting new moves regarding Algerian political structures, an impression that was soon heightened by reports that the President would visit Algeria before the resumption of general political activity in the autumn and by Debré's trip there the second week in August.

In this atmosphere and after conferring with General Challe, Guy Mollet, and the prime minister, de Gaulle left for a three-week vacation at his country home.

[7] *J.O.*, August 14, 1959, p. 1544; *LM*, August 2-3, 1959.

The Cabinet

1. Theme Topic Assigned. After Debré's trip, the following report was published:

The agenda for the extraordinary Council of Ministers, convened Wednesday afternoon at the Elysée Palace, contains only two points: a report, presented by M. Debré on his recent trip to Algeria and a communication from M. Couve de Murville on the international situation.

General de Gaulle, who will interrupt his vacation in order to come to preside over the meeting, prepared with the Prime Minister these deliberations during their conference Monday at Colombey. Their conversation lasted two and a half hours. (*LM*, 8/12/59.)

After the Council of Ministers meeting, this account described the further evolution of the search for a policy:

Opened by M. Michel Debré's report on his recent information trip to the other side of the Mediterranean, the debate in the Council of Ministers expanded to an examination of all of the present factors in the Algerian problem, not only administrative and economic, but also military and political. It was, in effect, a question essentially of preparing for the forthcoming visit by General de Gaulle and, beyond that, of studying an eventual "initiative" which could later mark a new step in French Algerian policy. . . .

General de Gaulle . . . is concerned with the political problems of Algeria, which he has reserved to himself [rather than the budgetary, military recruitment, and administrative problems that are being dealt with under the direction of the Premier]. As is known, before making a statement he has the habit of obtaining the advice of the ministers, of hearing their suggestions. After which, he decides alone, generally without revealing the decision, or stating the reasons for it, until the day he makes it public.

In the present case, it is a complete examination of the Algerian portfolio, the chances and ways for a solution of the conflict and of the prospects for the future that he is undertaking. . . .

So far, General de Gaulle has not revealed his intentions, nor even said that he has formed them. . . . (*LM*, 8/13/59.)

During the meeting there was a "first exchange of views" on the question of the long-term political solution in Algeria:

In effect, the President of the Republic posed to the ministers several questions on the advisability and the nature of an eventual "initiative," and on the general orientation that should be given the governmental policy. These questions had less to do with the form and the content of a new offer of a "peace of the brave"—on this point General de Gaulle will decide alone—than on the evolution of Algeria toward a definitive political status. . . . (*LM*, 8/14/59.)

General de Gaulle asked the ministers to submit to him before the meeting planned for August 26, notes summarizing, on one hand, their personal suggestions for the development of the Algerian policy and, on the other hand, their reactions to the analysis of the bases of the policy that he sketched. This analysis [included the view that] . . . politically the Algeria of tomorrow will be what the Algerians want it to be. It can be formed only through universal suffrage—and especially through recourse again soon to this direct form of expression by the people (canton elections, etc.). . . . (*LM*, 8/19/59.)

Precise questions were posed to the ministers, who were asked to say how they foresee the future evolution of the territory, what formula for the future they prefer, what means they envision for its attainment, finally what immediate consequences might be entailed by the policy thus defined in all the other areas of governmental action and public life. (*LM*, 8/25/59.)

This theme for meditation . . . will also be proposed . . . for consideration by the officers of all ranks that General de Gaulle will see August 27-30 during his trip [to Algeria]. (*LM*, 8/19/59.)

2. Themes Submitted. Widely reported speeches by the Prime Minister during the weeks preceding August 26 returned to the vague generalities of previous months, apparently keeping the way clear for whatever policy was worked out by de Gaulle. Debré's assertion that "the destiny of France is coupled with the Algerian destiny" won applause from the proponents of *Algérie française,* but did not really exclude evolution toward an autonomous or even independent status.[8]

This did not mean that the Premier did not have personal views on the question or that he would not express them in cabinet meetings, as this report of a full cabinet meeting shows:

Several ministers have replied to the questions posed by the President of the Republic August 12 with written notes submitted to M. Michel Debré. He has taken into account their remarks and their conclusions in the presentation that . . . he read to the Cabinet Council [Tuesday]. No discussion followed this communication, no debate took place. Some found in the words of the Premier the expression of the reflections and the suggestions that they had made to him in writing or orally; some preferred to reserve their comments for the Council of Ministers; others, who have hardly spoken up so far on Algerian policy, continue to observe the same discretion. (*LM*, 8/27/59.)

[8] The text of one speech was published in *LM*, August 18, 1959. Another was reported in *LM*, August 25, 1959.

The silence of the ministers was not maintained during the Council of Ministers meeting the following day:

> The greatest part of the governmental deliberation . . . was devoted . . . to Algeria. . . . M. Michel Debré repeated the presentation he had made the previous day in the Cabinet Council. . . .
>
> Next, each member of the government was asked to make known his responses to the precise questions that had been posed by the President of the Republic at the previous Council or the remarks that had been suggested to him by M. Michel Debré's communication.
>
> The ministers showed themselves to be, by a large majority, favorable to a liberal evolution of the French policy in Algeria. . . . Above all, they proposed original formulas in which could be cast a special statute determining the relations of Algeria with the mainland and with the other member-States of the Community. . . .
>
> The word "integration" was pronounced with more or less insistence by several ministers, four or five, in fact, remaining attentive to, if not truly convinced by, this "doctrine." . . .
>
> The government . . . is leaving it up to de Gaulle to choose and explore the ways toward a political solution. . . . The President of the Republic concluded the debate with a brief speech. Without revealing his intentions, he is said, however, to have shown that he generally approved the evolutive theses presented by the majority.
>
> During their remarks, each of the ministers was obviously led to treat the effect of the solution he envisaged on the affairs of his department. . . .
>
> The Council having been heard, it is more than ever up to General de Gaulle to take the responsibility for the Algerian policy. (*LM*, 8/28/59.)

Courtesy to the Parliamentary Majority

After the Council meeting, Debré conferred with five ministers for an hour and then entertained at lunch eleven representatives of the four parties composing the government's majority in the National Assembly and the Senate. One of the deputies indicated later:

> . . . the Prime Minister did not directly report on the Council of Ministers of the previous day. The clarification of a general order that he furnished us has reassured us regarding the firmness of the government in defending French positions. (*LM*, 8/29/59.)

A Sedative for the Army

At the same time that Debré made his courteous but quite uninformative gesture toward parliamentarianism, de Gaulle, the

real source of authority, began a four-day tour of military estab-
lishments in Algeria, delivering several speeches and learning
the views of the army concerning Algeria. After his first stop
this report appeared:

General de Gaulle arrived at noon at the main square of Saïda, a
small town where Moslem delegations had been waiting for him under a leaden sky for a long time. . . .

He could be seen coming from afar, a tall, khaki-colored silhouette
[accompanied by the top French army and naval commanders in
Algeria and the Mediterranean]. As he does each time, the President
of the Republic moves through the crowd, shaking the hands of the
Moslems, in the midst of whom he becomes lost at times, while his
party waits for him.

General de Gaulle shakes still more hands under trees that young
boys have climbed and then he stops. A military parade begins . . .
[and] when it ends and the police have, after some difficulty, cleared
the way . . . General de Gaulle proceeds to the *Hôtel de Ville* [City
Hall] nearby. . . . He reappears on the balcony, thanks the population for its "very moving welcome" and [makes a brief speech in which
he says nothing of substance. He delivers another short talk to the
local dignitaries inside the Hôtel de Ville, but says little more.] . . .

The inhabitants of Saïda run again to see at close hand General de
Gaulle when he goes next to the headquarters of the operational
sector to hear Colonel Bigeard describe the military action assigned
to the professional corps and to mingle with the members of the Moslem commando unit. . . .

At a late hour General de Gaulle is the luncheon guest of the municipal council. Nine tables have been set and at each are found several young officers—about twenty—with whom the President of the
Republic intends to converse until Sunday. . . .

Another indication of his will to learn the opinion of the Algerian
army . . . is that a seat is reserved for a guest of his choice in the
helicopter which will fly him from place to place. (*LM,* 8/28/59.)

In the evening, at Cassaigne, . . . the dinner was again the occasion for an encounter with twenty officers around a separate table.
. . . Was the atmosphere less propitious for a fruitful exchange of
reflections? It must have been because one of the participants after
the meal said: "No one went to confessional." (*LM,* 8/29/59.)

And so went the tour. At each stop, he spoke to civilians on
the need for fraternal relations and to the military on the need
for energetic "pacification." He sought out the lower-ranking
officers and asked endless questions even of the most technical
sort, yet he gave very little indication of his own views on Algeria's status. On the whole, he led the colonialists to believe

that he was still on their side. He was not, however, completely able to dissimulate his views—if, indeed, he wanted to—as this comment shows:

> The word "self-determination" has become a key word since the last trip of General de Gaulle to Algeria. . . .
>
> However, in re-reading the public speeches of the President of the Republic . . . one does not discover the word, even though it is constantly implied by the declarations of the sort: "The Algerians will make their destiny themselves."
>
> It was before the officers, in the intimacy of military posts and mess halls that General de Gaulle used this word.
>
> The spokesman for the general staff indicated to reporters that General de Gaulle had "on several occasions spoken of self-determination." (LM, 9/3/59.)

A Promise to Ike

Upon de Gaulle's return from Algeria, he met with President Eisenhower and endeavored to win American support for French policy in Algeria with this result:

> Considerable progress has been made. Although no one reports publicly an agreement on Algeria, which anyway, is not . . . an "object of negotiation," M. Hagerty's confirmation that a declaration by General de Gaulle was forthcoming and announcement that it would be followed by a declaration from the White House is significant of the very new climate that reigns. (LM, 9/5/59.)

But a few days later Debré denied before a joint meeting of the Foreign Affairs and National Defense committees of the National Assembly that his confidence of American support at the next U.N. debate on Algeria resulted from concessions made by France in regard to its Algerian policy. He asserted that his position on Algeria had not changed.

Announcing the Decision

1. *To the Cabinet.* On September 10, de Gaulle began the process of informing his compatriots of the substance of the long-awaited "new initiative." At the first Council of Ministers meeting since his Algerian trip he announced that he would deliver on "September 16 a radio broadcast in which he will define his

Algerian policy." He thus made the ministers the first to be informed of his plans but:

No discussion followed . . . this announcement. . . . On the content of the declaration that the general will make the greatest discretion is being observed. If its "liberal" spirit is generally not doubted, uncertainty remains concerning the plan of action, which has no less importance. (*LM*, 9/11/59.)

2. *To the Community.* The next group to be taken into de Gaulle's widening circle of confidants was the Executive Council of the Community, which met the following day:

General de Gaulle, for diplomatic as well as national reasons, still holds the view, . . . that he defines the Algerian evolution in his capacity of President of the Community. . . . (*LM*, 9/13/59.)
General de Gaulle explained to the African and Madagascan Prime Ministers his forthcoming declaration on Algeria and received their unanimous approval. . . .
The President of the Community presented to the session only principles. . . . He . . . detailed . . . what he meant by the formula "self-determination" of the Algerian people. (*LM*, 9/12,13/59.)

3. *Drafting the Declaration.* De Gaulle then withdrew to his country home to prepare the speech. Upon his return to Paris Tuesday afternoon, September 15, he conferred with several political leaders and Debré appeared before the Senate Committee on Foreign Affairs, Defense, and Armed Forces. The extent of Debré's eclipse in Algerian policy formulation is highlighted by the fact that he would say on Algerian policy no more than:

The President of the Republic will show tomorrow that France has in Algeria a well-determined policy. (*LM*, 9/17/59.)

4. *The Cabinet Again.* Wednesday morning at a meeting of the Council of Ministers:

The President of the Republic made known the main lines of the declaration on Algeria to be broadcast at 8 P.M.
Forecasts [concerning its content] can be made with assurance, but some very important points remain uncertain. . . .
It may seem abnormal that in circumstance so grave, the government has been as little informed as consulted, that it is through its own head that General de Gaulle commits in this way, with all the risks that are entailed, the destiny of the country. This is so because he is certain that alone he can overcome the opposition, the dissent,

the hatred; that alone he possesses sufficient prestige as much on the mainland as in Algeria, to put an end to [the] conflict. (*LM*, 9/17/59.)

5. *To the People.* Having received the advice of "his" ministers, having heard the views of the army and having promised it that—whatever might happen—it would be permitted to continue its task of pacification until completed, having informed his ministers and his allies (the United States and the member states of the Community) of the main outline of his decision, General de Gaulle now appeared before his people and the world to announce, apparently for the first time to anyone (except perhaps Debré), the details of his decision. No members of parliament had been consulted nor had any civilian authorities in Algeria. Even the ministers had not been informed of the details of the decision before the broadcast nor had they been permitted to discuss the broad outline in its final form.

Through this declaration, as in his comportment concerning the Algerian affair during recent weeks, General de Gaulle has again shown himself to be the author and only originator of Algerian policy much more than an arbiter. (*LM*, 10/1/59.)

After reviewing the political, military, social, and economic achievements of his government in Algeria and discussing the prospects for the future, de Gaulle, in his broadcast of September 16, broached the question of Algeria's future political status:

All Algerians should have the means of expressing themselves through truly universal suffrage. Up to last year they have never had it. They have it now. . . .

As soon as violence has subsided, the path may be used even more broadly, and more freely. Next year, the General Councils will be elected, from which, later, will be drawn a number of Administrative, Economic and Social Councils, which will discuss with the Delegate General the development of Algeria. . . .

We can now look forward to the day when the men and women who live in Algeria will be in a position to decide their own destiny, once and for all, freely and in full knowledge of what is at stake. Taking into account all these factors—those of the Algerian situation, those inherent in the national and the international situation—I deem it necessary that recourse to self-determination be here and now proclaimed. In the name of France and of the Republic, by virtue of the power granted to me by the Constitution to consult its citizens—if only God lets me live and the people listen to me—I pledge myself to ask the Algerians, on the one hand, . . . what, when all is said and done, they wish to be; and, on the other hand, all Frenchmen, to endorse that choice.

The question, obviously, will be put to the Algerians as individuals. For since the beginning of the world there has never been any Algerian unity, far less any Algerian sovereignty. . . . As for the time of the elections, I will decide upon it in due course, at the latest, four years after the actual restoration of peace; that is to say, once a situation has been established whereby not more than 200 persons a year will lose their lives, either in ambushes or isolated attacks. The ensuing period of time will be devoted to resuming normal existence, to emptying the camps and prisons, to permitting the return of exiles, to restoring the free play of individual and public liberties and to enabling the population to become fully aware of what is at stake. I would like to invite, here and now, observers from all over the world, to attend, without hindrance, the final culmination of this process.

But what will this political destiny finally be. . . ? Since it is in the interest of all concerned—and especially of France—that the question be answered without ambiguity, the three conceivable solutions will be put to the vote:

Either—secession, where some believe independence would be found. France would then leave the Algerians. . . . They would organize, without her, the territory in which they live, the resources which they have at their disposal, the government which they desire. I am convinced personally that such an outcome would be incredible and disastrous. Algeria being what it is at the present time, and the world what we know it to be, secession would carry in its wake the most appalling poverty, frightful political chaos, widespread slaughter, and soon after, the warlike dictatorship of the Communists. But this demon must be exorcised, and this must be done by the Algerians themselves. If it should appear, through some inconceivable misfortune, that such is indeed their will, France would undoubtedly stop devoting so much of value and so many billions of francs to a cause shorn of any hope. It goes without saying that, on this assumption, those Algerians regardless of origin, who might wish to remain French would do so in any case, and that France would arrange, if need be, for their regrouping and resettlement. On the other hand, everything would be arranged so that the operation of oil wells, the handling and shipping of Saharan oil—which is the result of French efforts and which is of interest to the whole western world—would be ensured in any event.

Or—out-and-out identification with France, such as is implied in equality of rights: Algerians can accede to all political, administrative, and judicial functions of the state and have free access to the public service. They would benefit, as regards salaries, wages, social security, education and vocational training from all measures provided for in Metropolitan France; they would live and work wherever they saw fit throughout the territory of the Republic; in other words, they would be living, from every point of view, regardless of their religion or the community to which they belonged, by and large, on the same footing and at the same level as other citizens and would become part and parcel of the French people. . . .

Or—the government of Algerians by Algerians, backed up by French help and in close relationship with her, as regards the economy, education, defense and foreign relations. In that case, the internal regime of Algeria should be of the federal type, so that the various communities—French, Arab, Kabyle, Mozabite—who live together in the country would find guarantees for their own way of life and a framework for cooperation. (Press release, French Press and Information Service.)

Significance of the Decision

De Gaulle's decision was, in certain respects, similar in form to M. Bourgès-Maunoury's announcement in his investiture speech that his government would draft a new statute for Algeria. Neither decision was self-enacting. De Gaulle's announcement of a decision in principle did not, on the face of it, seem to require formal legitimation in the way Bourgès-Maunoury's investiture declaration was legitimized by the investiture vote. But, as the rest of this chapter will show, de Gaulle discovered that his decisions of principle also required legitimation. In addition, both de Gaulle's and Bourgès-Maunoury's decisions required the definition, legitimation, and implementation of detailed measures before the political status of Algeria would be altered. The 1947 statute remained—on paper—the formal basis of the Algerian political structure. Both decisions in principle were promises, but little more. De Gaulle's promise was even more hypothetical than Bourgès-Maunoury's for it did not need to be implemented before the restoration of "calm." This all-important escape clause was not inserted into the *loi cadre* until the "round table."

The de Gaulle plan did explicitly open the possibility for Algeria's separation from France whereas this was expressly excluded by the Bourgès proposal. Even this liberal gesture was somewhat modified by the manner in which de Gaulle stacked the cards in favor of the third alternative—association. "Association" sounded very much like the *loi cadre* sounded when first outlined by Bourgès-Maunoury: internal self-government; single electoral college; bound to France for economic, educational, defense, and foreign affairs; federalized internal governmental structure based on the ethnic communities. De Gaulle did not describe in detail the form of the bond with France nor was his list of "common" affairs as long as that in the *loi cadre*. Otherwise, it is difficult to see how his "association" differed materially from the Bourgès *loi cadre*. Had the mighty de Gaulle labored for nearly sixteen months and produced no more than Bourgès-Maunoury began with? In substance, perhaps; but the promise of self-determination rather than a unilaterally granted statute and the inclusion of secession as an alternative were bold strokes that Bourgès would not have dared. In fairness to Bourgès, however, and to the Fourth Republic it must be added that the passage of time probably aided de Gaulle; the French people undoubtedly were more receptive to such an initiative in 1959 than in 1957 because of their increasing war weariness.

Five steps were required to make an Algerian policy change effective: 1, decision on the principle; 2, legitimation of the principle; 3, elaboration of the details; 4, legitimation of the details; 5, implementation of the policy. Bourgès advanced as far as definition of the details, but failed to legitimize them through parliamentary enactment. Gaillard cleared that hurdle, but passed from the scene without implementing the law. For both Bourgès and Gaillard legitimation meant approval by parliament. De Gaulle had destroyed parliament as a genuine forum but had retained it in form. As a consequence he felt constrained to obtain parliamentary approval for his decision, even before defining it, but then decided that this was not sufficient. Eventually, he decided it was necessary to confirm this sanction by direct popular referendum, but it was a long time before he clearly perceived this need. He first tried informal ratification by popular enthusiasm.

LEGITIMATION OF PRINCIPLE, DEFINITION AND LEGITIMATION OF DETAIL

Appeals for Popular Support

No conferences on Algeria between de Gaulle and parliamentary or governmental leaders were reported in the days fol-

lowing the declaration. The next Council of Ministers meeting
on September 23 was wholly taken up with budgetary discussions.

The following day, however, de Gaulle began a four-day cir-
cuit of twenty-one northern French towns and cities plus all the
villages in between, defending his policy in countless public
speeches and explaining it to innumerable local notables. His
tour was not solely devoted to the Algerian problem, but he
constantly placed it uppermost. Receiving warm acclaim everywhere, he told his countrymen that he was confident the Algerian problem would be settled, that free choice by the Algerians was the best way to settle it, and that his decision had
the "profound agreement of all France." His visit to Douai was
typical:

The general arrives at 9:47 A.M. at the Douai station where he is
welcomed by the mayor. . . . He shakes the hands of the young
students of the mining school. A procession forms, but at the entrance
to the *Rue de Paris* the Chief of State descends from the auto and
walks along the street, which is lined with miners. Other miners in
mining attire form an escort for him. Throughout the city an immense crowd applauds the general, who is the object of an ovation
when he reaches the *Hôtel de ville.* . . . During this time the car-
illon in the belfry is picking out the sour notes of *Le P'tit Quinquin.*
After having been welcomed by the first deputy mayor and being
presented to the municipal council and the *notables,* General de
Gaulle delivers a speech. . . .
"There is one problem that is immediate, bloody, and complex. We
have chosen to resolve it in a way worthy of France. (*Applause.*) It
is by the free determination of those concerned, that is, above all, the
Algerians, that we will resolve one day or another, this problem."
(*Applause.*) . . .
The crowd gave the general a long ovation.
Between Douai and Cambrai, several stops, as usual, in the flag-
bedecked villages where the people gathered around the mayor.
(*LM,* 9/27/59.)

While de Gaulle strode the low road to the people, Debré
took the high road to parliament in preparation for the autumn
session. This manner of proceeding reflects some of the confusion at the very highest level concerning the nature of the
Gaullist regime. De Gaulle placed greatest dependence on the
people directly rather than as refracted through the parliamentary lens. Yet personal appearance tours through a few

provincial areas could not really provide him with unequivocal, formal endorsement of his policy. On the other hand, approval by parliament was sufficiently formal and the government was assured of a large majority, but it would have contradicted the principles of Gaullism to have rested entirely or even primarily on the support of a parliament whose long-term dependability could not be assumed. Having reached a decision in principle and having declared its intentions, the government floundered about for sixteen months in search of a satisfactory formula for obtaining its legitimation.

Parliamentary Endorsement

Debré met with M. René Pleven, a leader of his parliamentary majority, and later conferred with spokesmen from all the majority groups to discuss general policy, including that concerning Algeria.[9] The Cabinet Council decided to permit a debate following the declaration of general policy with which Debré was to open the new session of parliament and, after some reflection, the Council of Ministers authorized Debré to pose a vote of confidence following the debate. The declaration by Debré was made in the National Assembly on October 14 at the same time that M. Edmond Michelet, a former senator and Minister of Justice in Debré's cabinet, was addressing the Senate on the same matter. The Senate was not permitted to debate the declaration. Both speeches followed de Gaulle's declaration step-by-step in their treatment of Algerian policy. The forty-odd speakers who took part in the Assembly debate stressed the importance of the Algerian policy to the neglect of the other points in the government's declaration. Thus, the vote approving Debré's declaration of general policy by 441 to 23 with 28 abstentions and 56 other deputies not taking part, must be interpreted as a massive vote of confidence in the government's Algerian policy. If the government had regarded Assembly endorsement as sufficient for legitimation of the policy in principle, it could have moved ahead to the drafting of a concrete proposal and its legitimation and implementation without further endorsement of the principle.

[9] *LM,* September 30, 1959.

Back to the Army

Parliamentary endorsement was not enough. De Gaulle continued to conduct himself as though it were necessary to demonstrate directly the popularity of his Algerian policy. Repeating the sequence he had followed before his September 16 declaration, de Gaulle issued a statement to the army and the administration in Algeria on October 28 and held a press conference on November 10. Later in the month he undertook another grand provincial tour. The statement of October 28 was plainly designed to mollify the army before reaffirming a "liberal" policy on November 10.[10] He reassured the army concerning the three aspects of the question that concerned them most: 1, he played upon their loyalty to him personally and their military discipline by stressing the extent to which the Algerian policy was his personally; 2, he held out the promise of eventual military victory by implying that complete pacification remained his aim; 3, he consigned the day of reckoning to the indefinite future.

Directives transmitted separately by Debré to Delouvrier and Challe were still more reassuring:

> The Algerians will reply successively to two questions. The first: "Do you wish that Algeria achieve its destiny with France or without France?" The second: "Since you have chosen to be with France, do you wish to be administered like mainland *départements* or do you wish to be managed in accordance with such detailed statutes as will be drafted between now and then under the control of the government?" (*LM*, 11/5/59.)

This arrangement would require that at least 50 per cent of the voters favor secession rather than as few as one-third if all three options were on one ballot. The preference of the army is obvious. The directives also affirmed the government's determination to repress the rebellion, assure the choice of the "most French" solution, and denied that the declaration could be considered a "point of departure" or "basis for discussion" with the rebels. Rather, it is "a plan and a policy." Continuing the campaign to neutralize the army before the press conference of November 10, Minister of the Armies Pierre Guillaumat in yet another communication to Challe added two important qualifica-

10 *LM*, October 30, 1959.

tions to the previous explanations. No foreign or international participation in conducting the referenda could be permitted nor could its arrangements be objects for negotiation with the F.L.N. Furthermore, even if a cease-fire were negotiated, the army would still be needed to maintain order and, during the referenda, "the army will be present, with the necessary troops." [11]

It cannot be said that as much care was given the cultivation of parliamentary favor as of military approval. But, in addition to the debates in the chambers, Debré appeared before the central committee of the U.N.R. for the first time in his ten months as premier to support the successful move to expel nine U.N.R. deputies who had voted against his government after the general policy debate.[12] This was an obvious move to maintain intact the main bulwark of the governmental majority by imposing effective sanctions for indiscipline.

The November 10 Press Conference

1. The Form. The press conference of November 10 was a typical and illuminating manifestation of de Gaulle's philosophy of leadership: authority enshrouded by mystery and ceremony. In some respects, to de Gaulle's mind, the forms observed in leadership are more important than its content. Thus, it is useful for an understanding of the manner in which the executive power operates in the Fifth Republic to evoke the atmosphere at the press conference:

On the one side as on the other of the little platform, draped in red silk, which was set up opposite the stage in the Grand Festival Hall [of the Elysée Palace], seats had been reserved for the members of the government and the collaborators of the President of the Republic. All the ministers and secretaries of state . . . and two of the ministers-councilor were there in their places, in an order arranged according to both protocol and hierarchy, which was not without significance: M. Debré, alone in front, then MM. Soustelle, Lecourt and Malraux. . . .

At exactly 4 P.M., the center door-curtains between two large Gobelin tapestries . . . suddenly parted and General de Gaulle assumed his seat. At once, the traditional: "Ladies and gentlemen, I am very pleased to see you." Three minutes to permit the photographers

11 *LM,* November 8-9, 1959.
12 *LM,* October 18, 1959.

and movie cameramen, who form a dense mass at the base of the platform, to operate at leisure under the bare light of the projectors. The usual dismissal: *"Voilà, messieurs,* I thank you." And then the preliminary statement. The rites are scrupulously observed. . . .

The four anticipated questions receive in turn, in the guise of replies, the four declarations prepared on atomic, Algerian, Community, and veterans policies. The authors of two unexpected questions . . . drew brief replies stamped with irony, good-natured or icy, and sat down amid laughter. For an hour and five minutes—fifteen minutes of preliminary declaration and fifty of response to questions—the President of the Republic speaks in a firm voice, without ever consulting his notes, citing from memory impressive series of figures and giving, except for brief moments, the impression of improvising. . . . A good number of the listeners are visibly subdued by these meditations out loud which blend history and diplomacy, the past and the future, forming a continuous bond between thought and action. . . .

One more sentence, after the fourth and last "response," in order to echo, in the guise of conclusion, the customary invocations—France, solidity, firmness, conscience—and, while the tall silhouette disappears between the suddenly opened draperies, the noisy hall slowly empties. (*LM,* 11/12/59.)

2. *The Content.* Some notion of the manner in which de Gaulle handled the questions that obviously had been planted is given by this excerpt of about 20 per cent of his reply on Algeria:

I am going to give . . . some figures which will, perhaps, shed some light on what . . . will gradually happen if there is no cease-fire. . . . The rebellion has killed 1,800 civilians of French stock in five years, that is, one out of 600 in all and one out of 3,000 per year. It has killed 12,000 Moslem civilians in five years, that is one out of 700 in all, one out of 3,500 per year; that is, happily and substantially less than died during the same period in ordinary traffic and working accidents. During the same five years, 1,400,000 men served in the forces of order, of whom 13,000 died on the field of honor, that is, less than one per cent. In comparison . . . to these losses, how lamentable it is to count the 145,000 Algerians who have been killed on the side of the insurrection. . . .

But the general activity in Algeria proves, above all, that, though the insurrection is distressing to her, it does not prevent her development. . . . It is a fact that Algeria has never worked more and has never worked better than today. The 1959 harvest has just been completed: it has been completed . . . everywhere, and in better conditions than ever. The total foreign trade . . . for Algeria, which was 325 billion francs in 1954 before the insurrection, reached 700 billion francs this year. In Algeria in 1954 something like 700 million kilowatt hours were consumed. Nearly one billion 400 million will be consumed in 1959. In 1954 12,000 housing units were constructed in Algeria. This year 31,000 were constructed and next year 55,000 will be constructed. In 1954 something like 400 or 500 kilometers of roads and highways were built. This year 2,500 kilometers will have been built. There were 450,000 children in school in 1954. At the opening of school this fall, 860,000 were enrolled. (*LM*, 11/12/59.)

3. *The Significance*. Though one cannot put a finger on direct contradictions between de Gaulle's pronouncements and those of Debré and Guillaumat, the differences in emphasis, tone, and content are striking. In de Gaulle's second discourse, the word "army" never crossed his lips. Although he made several references to military matters, he did not say that the army would remain after the cease-fire. He did not say that it would "be present" during the referendum. He did not say that negotiations with the rebels could concern only military questions and, in fact, he opened the way for discussions concerning the conduct of the referendum. Nor did he specify a two-stage referendum nor insist on the imperative that Algeria remain French. As Debré curried the Right, de Gaulle solicited the Left. It was as if de Gaulle had sketched a scene in pencil with his September declaration, Debré daubed in some black, and de Gaulle added some red. Neither splashed over the other, but they had opposite effects on the total impression. When both were finished, moreover, much of the canvas remained blank and much else was obscure and fuzzy.

4. *A Pause*. De Gaulle's second tour of the autumn took him for five days through Alsace. As usual, he stopped in every little hamlet (making thirty-seven stops on a typical day), visiting factories, laying wreaths, shaking hands, expressing irrepressible optimism in dozens of short talks, and meeting warm receptions everywhere. But nowhere did he add any new element to his Algerian project and, in fact, most of his statements were limited to glittering generalities.

After that tour Algerian policy was returned to the icebox for nearly two months. Debré made a brief visit to Algeria on December 6 and 7 during which he continued to express himself in tones different from, though not directly contradictory to, those used by his chief. De Gaulle refrained from any comment on Algeria during a six-day trip to West Africa. He met with the presidents of the parliamentary groups of the National Assembly on December 15, but made no response when one of his visitors attempted to draw him out on Algeria. Only one paragraph in his New Year's message concerned Algeria and here he rose to new heights of ambiguity, although he did repeat his pledge that "all tendencies may take part in complete freedom and security in the debates which will prepare for" the referendum.[13]

The Settlers' Revolt

1. Resumption of Activity. The middle of January saw a resurgence of activity on the part of the government with respect to Algeria, reaching a bloody and unexpected climax in the settlers' revolt on January 24. On January 15 it was announced that de Gaulle was summoning the five appropriate ministers, Delouvrier and Moris, and the six top Algerian military commanders for a conference on Algerian policy January 22.[14]

In anticipation of that conference, he met with three Algerian parliamentarians hostile to his self-determination policy and indicated that it remained unmodified.[15] He also obtained from the Council of Ministers on January 20 renewal of "its will to pursue the [Algerian] policy defined by the Chief of State, decided upon by the government, and approved by parliament." [16] After the conference it was announced that de Gaulle would deliver a radio-television address on Algeria on January 29 and that he would visit that territory for several days beginning February 5. It was also reported that:

Before the end of 1960 new General Council elections will be held [in Algeria]. After them, the government will convoke in Paris commissions composed of representatives of the parliamentarians, general councilors and municipal councilors to study the principal political, economic, and social problems and to formulate proposals regarding them. . . . (*LM*, 1/23/60.)

13 *LM*, January 2, 1960.
14 *LM*, January 15-22, 1960.
15 *LM*, January 21, 1960.
16 *LM*, January 22, 1960.

2. The Insurrection and First Reactions. This timetable was somewhat altered by the settlers' revolt that began on January 24. A German newspaper, in an account of an interview, attributed to General Jacques Massu, military commander in the Algiers region, insubordinate remarks. Though he denied them, he was summoned to Paris by de Gaulle and relieved of his command. This news reached Algiers at the same time as the report of the Algerian conference and precipitated a demonstration. Massu had been regarded by the settlers as very sympathetic to their viewpoint. The army in Algiers took no part in the demonstrations, which soon became insurrectionary, but it did nothing to suppress them either. The manner in which the executive moved to remove this violent impediment to its Algerian policy is typical. Debré had begun a tour of Brittany and de Gaulle was at his country home when news of the violence was received at about 7:30 P.M. Sunday, January 24. At 9:50 P.M. Debré left Rennes by plane for Paris.

11:20 P.M.—The Prime Minister arrives at the Hôtel Matignon accompanied by MM. Chatenet, Minister of the Interior, and Michel Maurice-Bokanowski, Secretary of State. He confers with MM. Guillaumat; Chatenet; Moris; Brouillet, manager of General de Gaulle's office; and General Ely, chief of the general staff.

11:59 P.M.—General de Gaulle, who returned by car from Colombey-les-Deux-Eglises, arrives at Elysée Palace.

12:10 A.M.—M. Michel Debré goes to see the President of the Republic. . . .

2:45 A.M.— . . . The Prime Minister returns to Hôtel Matignon. He informs General Ely and M. Moris of the text of the message by General de Gaulle. . . .

3:15 A.M.—First broadcast by the French Broadcasting and Television system and Radio Algiers of the message from General de Gaulle [which was re-broadcast every hour thereafter]:

"The riot which has just broken out in Algiers is a foul blow struck against France. A foul blow struck against France in Algeria. A foul blow struck against France before the world. A foul blow struck against France within France.

"With the government, in agreement with parliament, called upon and supported by the nation, I became head of the State in order to revive our country, and especially to bring about the triumph in shattered Algeria, by uniting all its communities, of a solution that is French.

"I say with all lucidity and in all simplicity that, if I were to fail in my task, the unity, the prestige, the fate of France, would be compromised with the same stroke. And, first of all, it would no longer have any chance to pursue its great work in Algeria.

"I beseech those who have arisen against the fatherland, misled though they may be by lies and calumny, to return to national order. Nothing is lost for a Frenchman when he rallies to his mother, France.

"I express my profound confidence in Paul Delouvrier, delegate general; to General Challe, commander in chief; to the forces which are under their orders to serve France and the State; to the Algerian people who are so dear and who have suffered so much.

"As for me, I will do my duty.

"*Vive la France.*" (*LM*, 1/26/60.)

Although it was clear from the outset of this new test that de Gaulle had full charge of the government's moves to reduce the insurrection, he did not completely bypass the constitutional organs of prime minister and cabinet. The instructions to Delouvrier and Challe (the nonpolitical officials) were drafted in consultation with Debré and Guillaumat. These directives were ratified by a Council of Ministers meeting that convened at 3:30 P.M. January 25. That the cabinet meeting was not perfunctory is indicated by this report:

Unanimity . . . was easily reached on the absolute, vital necessity to put an end as rapidly as possible to the Algiers insurrection. Several voices were raised to regret that the riot leaders had not been taken into preventive custody. All agreed that the policy of self-determination be boldly reaffirmed and maintained integrally and that it be confirmed to the civil and military authorities in Algeria that the government will concede nothing to the riot.

Divergences . . . occurred on the question of whether, if all possibility for a peaceful resolution becomes exhausted, the "camps" of MM. Ortiz and Lagaillarde should be assaulted. Several ministers, in a clear minority, expressed very sharp emotions at the thought that blood might again flow. . . . The great majority . . . believed that the authority of the State must be demonstrated . . . after all the means of persuasion and conciliation have been exhausted. . . . (*LM*, 1/27/60.)

After the meeting, Debré conferred for half an hour with de Gaulle, then flew unannounced to Algiers accompanied by Guillaumat, Moris, and several aides. The trip had not been discussed by the Council of Ministers. He confirmed to Delouvrier and Challe their instructions and received a group of Algerian parliamentarians. Upon his return to Paris at 10:05 A.M. Tuesday, he met with three other ministers, reported to de Gaulle, and delivered a radio address in which he painted a bleak picture of the consequences if the insurgents succeeded, reaffirmed both the self-determination policy and his determination that France must stay in Algeria. Of particular interest in understanding the relationship between Debré and de Gaulle in the conduct of the government are these passages:

I have reported to General de Gaulle on the situation in Algeria. . . .

Addressing myself to all those in Algeria who wish to think and act as Frenchmen . . . in the name of the government, I say this to them, and what I am going to say has the agreement of General de Gaulle, who, moreover, as he has already announced, will address the nation Friday and then travel to Algeria:

"French policy has been clearly defined by the Chief of State; it has received the support of parliament. It has the support of the nation. . . ."

Debré also announced in a very brief passage, a new decision in regard to the elaboration of a detailed proposal for reorganization of the Algerian governmental institutions:

Without further delay, the government proposes to summon to Paris this year the elected Algerian representatives in order to work out with them the organization of a renovated Algeria. (*LM*, 1/27/60.)

Wednesday morning Debré and de Gaulle continued consultations with other officials, including a meeting between de Gaulle and the president of the Constitutional Council. Another meeting of the Council of Ministers was held in the afternoon. Discord within the cabinet was discussed more openly now:

The discussion . . . first concerned the maintenance of the policy of 16 September. The principle of self-determination is to be solemnly reaffirmed. . . . On this point the agreement of the ministers is complete.

The examination of the insurrectional situation which reigns in Algiers and of the means to put an end to it caused . . . divergences . . . to appear. If the official thesis remains that of firmness, the ministers who have opposed any solution by force believe that they obtained assurances and appeasement. Those who stress . . . the absolute necessity of putting an end to the insurrection as soon as possible . . . admit a certain uneasiness. General de Gaulle . . .

has unveiled nothing regarding his intentions and has asked the ministers to protect the secrecy of the deliberations. For the moment, it is in the public speech of the Chief of State that each places his hope for a solution. (*LM*, 1/29/60.)

According to reports, the divisions within the cabinet were reflected in the administration. Contradictory instructions were given. Measures were modified by subordinates, were delayed, or were not implemented.[17] The authority of the State was still being challenged by insurgents who showed no sign of weakening before "forces of order" with little resolution to bring them into submission and there were signs that the administration on the mainland was not completely dependable. Everything did indeed depend on the impact of de Gaulle's speech.

3. *The Speech of January 29.* Apparently de Gaulle drafted his speech without consultation with his ministers. At 4 P.M. he summoned Debré to his office to inform him of the contents of the speech. At 6 P.M. the Prime Minister presided over a short meeting of the full cabinet, advising it of the "main lines of the Presidential declaration." At 9 P.M. Debré conferred for two hours with several ministers, but the meeting was described by one of the participants as "purely social, where no decisions were made." At 5 P.M. de Gaulle, reciting as usual from memory, delivered the radio-television address, saying in part:

If I have put on my uniform to speak on television today it is to stress that I am speaking as General de Gaulle and as the Chief of State. . . .
[After repeating the conditions of his self-determination policy, he said:]
In short, self-determination is the only policy that is worthy of France. It is the one defined by the President of the Republic, decided by the government, approved by parliament, and adopted by the French nation . . .
Self-determination is the only means by which the Moslems can exorcise the demon of secession. As for the details of this or that French solution, I intend that these shall be worked out at leisure when peace has returned.
When that has been done, I reserve the right to commit myself, at the proper moment, to that which I hold to be right. . . .
Faced with the foul blow that has been struck at France, I first of all address myself to the community of French stock in Algeria. . . .

[17] *LM*, January 30, 1960.

Frenchmen of Algeria, how can you listen to the liars and the conspirators who tell you that in granting free choice to the Algerians, France and de Gaulle want to abandon you, to withdraw from Algeria, and to surrender it to the rebellion? . . .

How can you doubt that, if one day the Moslems decide . . . that the Algeria of tomorrow must be closely united with France, nothing would cause more joy to the country and to de Gaulle than to see them choose between this or that solution the one which would be the most French? . . .

I implore you to return to law and order.

I now turn to the army. . . . I say to all our soldiers, your mission does not permit any equivocation or interpretation.

You have to liquidate the rebel force that wants to chase France from Algeria. . . . When the moment has come to undertake the consultation, you will have to guarantee its complete and genuine freedom.

Now as you know, I am the supreme authority. It is I who bear the destiny of the country. I must therefore be obeyed by all French soldiers. . . .

Public order must be restored . . . your duty is to restore it. I have given, I give the order for that.

Finally, I address myself to France. *Eh bien!* My dear and old country, here we are, then, once again faced with a heavy trial. By virtue of the mandate that the people have given me and the national legitimacy that I have embodied for twenty years, I call on everyone to support me whatever happens. . . . (*LM*, 1/31/60.)

The response was immediate and unequivocal. The morale of the insurgents collapsed. They withdrew their call for a general strike. The soldiers in Algiers stopped fraternizing with them and drove off their crowd of sympathizers. The army leaders received favorably de Gaulle's command to restore order. Even a drenching downpour in Algiers lent aid. Forty-eight hours later negotiations for the surrender of the insurgents were opened and the revolt ended.

4. Aftermath of the Revolt: Immediate Repercussions. The government's moves to reassert its authority did not end with the collapse of the insurrection. After a series of conferences by de Gaulle and Debré with members of the cabinet, high-ranking civil and military officials, the presidents of the two parliamentary chambers, and the head of the Constitutional Council, parliament was called into extraordinary session. Despite reservations expressed by many parliamentarians concerning the need for additional "special powers," their sweeping character, or their im-

precision, the National Assembly by 441 votes to 75 and the
Senate by 225 to 39 approved the request by the government
for permission to issue for a period of fourteen months, in accordance with Article 38 of the Constitution, "ordinances" having
the effect of laws. The decision to request this authority apparently was made by de Gaulle and approved by the cabinet.
In the words of the preamble of the bill, its purpose was to
enable the government "to take by ordinance the measures necessary for the maintenance of order, the safety of the State and
the pacification and administration of Algeria," but not "to undertake . . . broad reforms." [18] Debré said specifically during the
Assembly debate that the ordinances "will not touch the political
institutions" of Algeria.

The government also initiated criminal action against the in-
surgent leaders and took extremist opponents of its Algerian
policy into custody. Other consequences of the insurrection, discussed below, bore more directly on the question of Algeria's
future political status and are of greater interest in this study.

5. *Induced Acceleration.* There is every indication that de
Gaulle was beginning a new series of moves to promote eventual
implementation of his referendum decision at the time of the
revolt. Indeed, this was one cause of the uprising. Therefore, it
seems unlikely that all the steps taken after January were reactions to those events. On the other hand, the revolt probably
stimulated implementation of action already planned and induced
new decisions.[19]

Action of long run import following upon the settlers' revolt
falls into two categories. In the first place, there was reorganization and development of mechanisms designed to obtain legitimation of the self-determination decision. There was also some
definition of governmental policy concerning the form of the
eventual political structure. Between the 1960 revolt and the
January 1961 referendum greater public attention was directed
to the former objective, but, incidentally to it, significant progress
was made toward the latter goal as well.

The process of legitimation proceeded at three levels. At the
top, the executive was reorganized to bring Algerian policy more

[18] *LM*, February 3-4, 1960.
[19] *LM*, February 11-12, 1960.

completely and directly under the authority of the President of the Republic. Secondly, while relations between the executive and the elected representatives of the mainlanders continued to be handled much as before, efforts were made to develop new contacts with other representatives emanating from Algeria, and especially from the Moslem population of Algeria. Finally, concerted and extensive activity was undertaken to broaden and deepen the direct contacts between the executive (and especially the President of the Republic himself) and the people on the mainland. This activity culminated in the January 1961 referendum which marked a new turning on this problem. It constituted formal popular legitimation of de Gaulle's decision both in principle and in detail and had other significant implications.

Reorganization of the Executive

A direct and immediate consequence of the January 1960 troubles was a dramatic reshuffle of the Council of Ministers. It was the sixth time that important changes had been made in the thirteen-month-old Debré cabinet and there were more to come.

The most important change was the elimination of Jacques Soustelle, *Algérie française* leader and the "principal adversary in the cabinet to de Gaulle's Algerian policy." He had been second-ranking member in the cabinet. H. Cornut-Gentille, the Minister of Posts and Telecommunications, whose views on Algerian policy generally conformed to Soustelle's, was also replaced.[20] These changes made the cabinet more homogeneous and more completely in accord with de Gaulle's Algerian views. It is generally believed that Debré wavered while de Gaulle stood firm during the January revolt, so it may also be said that the new cabinet was lined up more closely with the President than with the Premier on Algerian questions.

The next step in bringing Algerian policy more directly under the President was the creation on February 14 of a Committee of Algerian Affairs responsible directly to the President of the Republic and presided over by him. Besides the Premier, the Minister of Interior, and the Minister of the Armies, its regular

[20] *LM,* February 6, 1960.

members were the Delegate General in Algeria, the Secretary
of State for Algerian Affairs, the Armed Forces chief of staff and,
whenever possible, the commander-in-chief in Algeria. Other
high officials and cabinet ministers attended its deliberations
from time to time.[21] As *Le Monde* noted:

> The creation of this committee, a sort of "privy council," institutes
> a new echelon of decision within the government. . . . It deprives, in
> part, those of the ministers who are not members of their right of
> oversight of Algerian affairs and thus accentuates the Presidential
> character of the regime. (*LM*, 2/16/60.)

The committee seems to draft Algerian policy in accordance
with instructions from de Gaulle and submits it for cabinet approval. This committee directed the establishment and the work
of the Moslem *commissions d'élus,* made arrangements for the
referendum, and prepared the decrees to implement its decisions.[22]

The final institutional change tending to concentrate Algerian
authority in the President was the creation on November 22 of
the Ministry of State for Algerian Affairs, reporting directly to
the President of the Republic. M. Louis Joxe, a high civil servant
who had long been a close aide and troubleshooter for de Gaulle,
was named to the office and instructed to give special attention
to preparations for the planned referendum.[23]

The cabinet was not excluded from deliberation of Algerian
affairs by these last two developments. Its endorsement was constitutionally required for ordinances and decrees and, even
where cabinet advice or approval was not obligatory by law or
by the constitution, in practice it was usually sought. All major
policy moves received cabinet handling in the same manner as
before. Nevertheless, the creation of two higher echelons of
specialized agencies inevitably reduced the influence of the
cabinet in this area.

Representational Reforms

At the same time that de Gaulle was gathering into his hands
all the strings for control of Algerian policy at the executive

---

21 *LM*, February 18, 1960.
22 See below, pp. 122-132.
23 *A.P., 1960,* p. 317.

level, he sought to expand his means for developing popular support, both indirectly through elected representatives and directly.

On the representational level, he continued to deal with parliament as before—through the cabinet and through occasional courtesy meetings with small groups of deputies. Never did he communicate directly with parliament in its corporate capacity, although there was some consideration of constitutional revision to permit him to address parliament in person.[24] Never did he engage in negotiations or deliberations with the parliamentary delegations he received. Always he listened to their views and sometimes he informed them of his.

Alongside parliament he created or revived two additional elective bodies, which emanated from Algeria and specialized on Algerian questions. The first of these was the Algerian General (Departmental) Councils that were elected May 29. The other was Commissions of Elected Officials (*commission d'élus*) created on July 19 and set in operation two months later.

De Gaulle had announced the elections and subsequent creation of consultative committees as early as his September 16 speech, but the date for the elections was advanced from autumn 1961 after the January revolt.

General Council elections had not been held in Algeria since 1955. At that time the double electoral college system was still used, with each of the two main ethnic communities electing an equal number of members. The councils were replaced by appointed administrative commissions in February 1956 because of the intensification of the nationalist rebellion.

The single college system and multimember constituencies were adopted for the 1960 elections. Each party nominated candidates equal in number to the seats to be filled. In 97 of the 113 election districts all the candidates of the party which won the largest number of votes were elected. In the remaining 16 districts, largely urban, the seats were distributed by proportional representation. Each list in each constituency where Europeans numbered from 3 to 10 per cent of the population was required to contain one European candidate and, where they numbered 10 to 20 per cent of the population, at least one

24 *LM*, October 16-17, 1960.

and as many as one half of the candidates were European.

The elections returned 301 Moslem and 149 European members. Supporters of de Gaulle's policies won 298 seats and the *"Algérie française"* lists won 88. The remaining 64 seats were won by miscellaneous and unaffiliated candidates.[25]

With local councils again in place, de Gaulle constituted his *"commissions d'élus."* There were four categories of members: 1, sixteen deputies and eight senators representing Algerian constituencies were elected by the respective parliamentary chambers; 2, the chairmen of the thirteen Algerian General Councils served by right, and the Councils elected, in addition, fifty-one of their members; 3, twenty mayors or members of the municipal councils were appointed by the Delegate General in Algeria upon nomination by the prefects; 4, twelve members of Chambers of Commerce and of Agriculture in Algeria were appointed by the Premier.

De Gaulle took little risk in the composition of the commissions. More than 25 per cent of the members were governmental appointees and another 20 per cent were designated by the parliament he controlled. The remaining nearly 55 per cent emanated from the General Councils in which his supporters had very recently won 65 per cent of the seats.

The "commissioners" were grouped into four commissions treating (1) rural modernization, (2) local government, (3) administrative decentralization and regionalization, (4) relations between the communities.

In his speech at Algiers on June 4, 1958 de Gaulle had announced that "the ten million Frenchmen of Algeria . . . will elect . . . their representatives for the political branches of government. . . . With these elected representatives, we will see how to do what remains." [26] In his September 16 speech, he said, "Next year there will be election of General Councils, from which will be drawn later certain great administrative economic, and social councils, which will deliberate, alongside the Delegate General, on the development of Algeria." [27] When they were

[25] For information on the elections see *French Affairs*, nos. 102 and 105, May 17 and June 22, 1960, French Press and Information Service, New York (mimeo).

[26] *A.P., 1958*, p. 544.

[27] See above, pp. 102-104.

created, however, it was made clear that they were assigned purely consultative functions bearing on current Algerian problems. They had no formal authority and were not to deal with Algeria's future political status. It was announced that they were so restricted in order not to predetermine the decision to be made by the Algerian people concerning their governmental system. It was also reported that the government did not wish to prejudice the possibility of cease-fire negotiations with the rebels.[28]

The government intended that the commissions should be representative and informative, transmitting Algerian public opinion to de Gaulle and relaying the government's views to the people, rather than policy formulating bodies. This was underlined by M. Roger Moris, Secretary General for Algerian Affairs who was in general charge of the commissions, at the time the first commission was installed:

> We are led . . . to undertake immediate action in Algeria. But the reforms that we wish to introduce necessitate the support of the men. It would be vain to carry out agrarian reforms if those interested do not understand us, if those who must benefit from them do not agree. The role of these commissions will thus be strictly consultative. (*LM*, 9/18/60.)

The commissions had troubles from the outset. One member defected from the first commission even before it was installed.[29] Others followed suit.[30] Despite the fact that the sessions were held behind closed doors, well-substantiated reports soon circulated that bitter controversies had developed within the commissions and that the governmental representatives intervened firmly to keep opposition viewpoints in check.[31]

Nevertheless, the commissions were all installed, held several meetings each, submitted reports by the end of January 1961, and disbanded. They recommended that the local governmental bodies be given more power, that the all-Algerian authority be

[28] On the constitution of the commissions and the functions see *J.O. lois et decrets*, July 19, 1960; *Le Monde*, July 16, 21, 24-25, 30, 1960; *A.P.*, 1960, pp. 77, 78, 82, 92, 302-304; *French Affairs*, No. 112, January 1961, French Press and Information Service, New York (mimeo).

[29] *LM*, September 21, 1960.

[30] *LM*, September 29, 1960.

[31] *LM*, September 28, 1960.

weakened, that three "regions" with "consultative councils" be formed, and that representatives of communal (that is, ethnic) and economic groups be included in the councils at various levels.[32]

The limited competence of the commissions, their "rigged" composition, the extent of the government's control over their deliberations, the close conformity of their recommendations with the substance of the government bill submitted to the January referendum, and the alacrity with which the government accepted those recommendations and began to implement them [33] all suggest that the *commission d'élus* were designed to contribute toward the legitimation of policy rather than its formulation. Their reports endorsed emerging governmental policy.

In a sense, their activity did tend toward the legitimation of the principle of self-determination—at least to the extent that their members were authentic representatives of the Algerian people—for they worked on the assumption that there would be self-determination and, thereby, implicitly endorsed that principle.

On the other hand, their explicit recommendations concerned the details of governmental organization. To pretend that they pertained only to Algeria before the self-determination referendum is unrealistic. Voters in a referendum tend to opt for visible, concrete alternatives rather than plunge into the unknown. Thus, plebiscites generally elicit affirmative responses because the average man sees no clear alternative to the man in office. Decentralization, regionalization, communalization, all lend themselves well to the "association" alternative which de Gaulle obviously favored. If structures peculiarly suitable to this alternative were set in place and in operation before the referendum, the Algerians would have strong psychological reasons to endorse them.

Thus the commissions served two purposes besides contributing implicitly to the legitimation of the principle of self-determination. They also served as a screen through which the government defined the details of its decision and as a device for the partial legitimation of the detailed proposal.

[32] *LM,* December 29, 1960, February 21, 1961; *French Affairs,* No. 112.
[33] See below, pp. 130-132.

The 1961 Referendum

1. Preparations. The representativeness and competence of the commissions were too questionable to permit de Gaulle to rely exclusively on them for legitimation of his policy. Nor was it feasible to rely on parliament. Consequently, he renewed his campaign for direct endorsement of it by the French electorate.

During the suppression of the January revolt the possibility of a popular referendum for this purpose had been proposed, but was rejected for the time being.[34] Instead, de Gaulle sought to rally public support for his proposal through a new series of provincial tours. In February he spent four days in Languedoc; in July he was six days in Normandy; in September it was Brittany for six days; and the following month Savoy and the Dauphiné for another six days. In March, de Gaulle toured army posts in Algeria and in April Debré made a civilian tour of the territory.

The President appealed for support of the self-determination principle in his radio-television speeches of June 14 and November 4 and his press conference of September 5. During his October tour in the Southeast, de Gaulle had alluded to the possibility of a referendum on his self-determination principle and there had been speculation before the November speech that it would contain an announcement concerning that. In fact, he merely dropped this hint: "If the ordinary . . . powers are not enough, it is up to me to consult the country by means of a referendum." [35]

Immediately after the speech, steps were taken to transform the hint into reality. The Committee on Algerian Affairs met on November 5. On November 7 de Gaulle conferred with M. Chaban-Delmas and a Cabinet Council meeting was held preparatory to a Council of Ministers meeting two days later. After the latter meeting, the following account was rendered:

> At the . . . meeting . . . the Chief of State . . . indicated that he would see, one by one, the ministers who might wish to tell him of their disquiet or pose to him questions on his Algerian policy. This

[34] *LM,* January 29, 1960.
[35] *French Affairs,* No. 107, November 4, 1960, French Press and Information Service, New York (mimeo).

invitation which implied a reminder of the commitment to solidarity and fidelity of the members of the government, elicited no response.

General de Gaulle [then] . . . cast some light on his intentions and specified, in particular, the spirit with which he is broaching the new state of the Algerian affair.

From this presentation, long and detailed, the President's listeners drew the impression, above all, that he had decided to press very actively, against all and everything, for the implementation of the projects that he sketched last week. . . . (*LM*, 11/11/60.)

Departing from custom, de Gaulle remained in Paris over the week end, consulting his top aides on Algeria. After the next meeting of the Council of Ministers this statement was issued:

General de Gaulle made known his intention to submit, when the moment comes, to the country, by way of referendum, a government bill relative to the organization of the political branches of government in Algeria, while awaiting self-determination. (*LM*, 11/17/60.)

Apparently he did not ask for the cabinet's approval of his decision, but simply announced it. But he did confer individually over a period of several days with most of the members of the government.[36]

The next step to prepare for the referendum was de Gaulle's appointment of M. Louis Joxe as Minister of State charged with Algerian Affairs. After "a first examination of the conditions of organization of the forthcoming referendum," at the next cabinet meeting, it was announced that Joxe and M. Chatenet, Minister of the Interior, would present definitive proposals concerning it a week later.[37] The proposals were discussed at the next ministers' meeting, but no action was taken pending the National Assembly debate on Algeria, December 7-8, except to announce that the referendum would be held January 8.[38]

While the President's Committee on Algerian Affairs and a cabinet committee worked out the details of the popular consultation, de Gaulle met one by one with the leaders of the five major political parties (not the heads of the parliamentary parties) and the presidents of the parliamentary chambers.[39] The text of the referendum question was submitted to the Con-

[36] *LM*, November 19, 1960.
[37] *LM*, November 24, 1960.
[38] *LM*, December 1, 1960.
[39] *LM*, December 2, 1960.

stitutional Council on December 6, described in rather general terms to the National Assembly the following day,[40] and approved by the Council of Ministers on the eighth: [41]

Do you approve the government bill submitted to the French people by the President of the Republic concerning the self-determination of the Algerian populations and the organization of the public powers in Algeria before self-determination? [42]

The Government Bill contained two articles:

Article 1. As soon as security conditions in Algeria will permit the re-establishment of the full exercise of the public liberties there, the Algerian populations shall make known, through a consultation of the electorate by direct universal suffrage, the political destiny they choose in relation to the French Republic.

The conditions of this consultation shall be determined by a decree taken in the Council of Minister.

The legal documents which would eventually be drawn up as a result of self-determination shall be submitted to the French people in accordance with constitutional procedures.

Article 2. Until self-determination has been effected as provided for in Article 1, decrees taken in the Council of Ministers shall arrange for the organization of public powers in Algeria in accordance with the provisions of Article 72 of the Constitution and on the following bases:

(a) Conferring on the Algerian populations and their representatives the responsibilities relative to Algerian affairs by instituting both an executive organ and deliberative assemblies having jurisdiction over all the Algerian Departments, and appropriate regional and departmental executive organs and deliberative organs;

(b) Ensuring the cooperation of the communities as well as the guarantees appropriate to each of them;

(c) Instituting organs having jurisdiction relative to the domains of mutual concern to metropolitan France and Algeria and ensuring, within these organs, the cooperation of representatives of metropolitan France and representatives of Algeria.

Thus with a single ballot the voters were asked both to legitimize the long-standing Gaullist principle of self-determination and to legitimize newly defined details for the establishment of a new governmental structure. After having bided time for nearly fifteen months, de Gaulle now sought to clear three

[40] See pp. 168-170 below. *LM*, December 7-8, 1960.
[41] *LM*, December 10, 1960.
[42] *J.O., lois et decrets,* December 9, 1960.

hurdles in one month: legitimation of principle, definition of detail, and legitimation of detail. The second step, however, came first and the other two were telescoped into one. Although the government bill did not describe the future status with nearly the precision or comprehensiveness of the *loi cadre*, the fine points were to be elaborated by decree, and later legitimation was provided for only through the cabinet.

There was provision for three referenda in all: 1, the January one; 2, one in Algeria (which might possibly take place in two stages) on the nature of its ties with France; and 3, one in France accepting (or rejecting) the Algerian decision. Neither of the last two would necessarily permit popular judgment on the form of the internal governmental structure, although the questions could be framed to have that effect.

2. *The Campaign.* With his intentions now made public, de Gaulle set about at once to campaign for their acceptance. Leaving the Committee on Algerian Affairs to prepare for cabinet approval arrangements for conducting the referendum, he flew to Algeria on another of his royal tours, this time hitting both army and civilian audiences.[43]

In three major radio and television addresses after his return he appealed for support of his policy and, incidentally, elaborated on it slightly. By promising in the kick-off speech of the campaign on December 20 that each ethnic community would have "*organically* . . . appropriate guarantees,"[44] he made more explicit his apparent plan to provide communal representation in the political organs of government. By describing the future "regional and departmental organization" as "corresponding to the geographic and ethnic diversity of Algeria,"[45] he seemed to indicate that there would be regions and departments with European majorities.

Other statements in his speeches seemed designed to transform the referendum from being only a request for popular

[43] The decrees determining the arrangements for the conduct of the referendum were published in the *Journal officiel* of December 14.

[44] *French Affairs no. 108*, December 20, 1960, French Press and Information Service, New York (mimeo). Emphasis supplied. The other speeches were published as Nos. 110 and 111, December 31, 1960 and January 6, 1961 in the series.

[45] *Ibid.*

legitimation of the self-determination policy and of his plans
for organizing the Algerian governmental structure. By devoting
more than half of his first speech and two paragraphs of his
second to a review of the general accomplishments of his administration, de Gaulle made an appeal for endorsement of his
general policies. By saying in his first speech that "the affirmative
answer of our people in the referendum will also take on the
character of an appeal for . . . a peaceful confrontation," he
was calling for a mandate to negotiate with the rebels. His
statements in the second speech that "you well know what a
blow" a negative response would be to me, "preventing me from
carrying out my task" and in his third speech that "I am the
one to whom you are going to give your answer" were clearly
implied threats to resign if not satisfied with the results. They
gave the referendum more openly the plebiscitary character
that it inevitably would have had in any case.

The governmental administration took an active part in the
referendum campaign. Large amounts of public money were
spent on propaganda favoring a positive response and civilian
and military officials in Algeria were instructed by M. Joxe to
expend every effort to see that the results in their areas would
not contradict those on the mainland, that is, that they would
be favorable.[46] On the other hand, campaigning by the ministers
was limited to speeches at rallies organized by the U.N.R.,
except that Debré addressed military personnel in Algeria.
This conduct further underlined the extent to which de Gaulle
had become the only national "political" officer of the government.

To the surprise of few, de Gaulle won his referendum, 75
per cent of the voters and 55 per cent of the registered electorate
casting favorable votes.

3. *Significance.* On January 31, 1958 the *loi cadre* to provide
new political institutions for Algeria supplanting the 1947 statute
had been given final approval by the parliament of the Fourth
French Republic. On January 8, 1961 the government bill to
provide new political institutions for Algeria supplanting the
1947 statute was accepted by popular referendum in the Fifth
French Republic. In a sense, after thirty-one months of tortuous

[46] *LM,* December 29, 1960, January 1-2, 1961.

maneuvering de Gaulle had arrived at the point where Félix Gaillard had stood almost exactly three years earlier.

The new statute in each case established executive and legislative organs at departmental, regional, and all-Algerian levels; provided an agent of the Parisian government as the highest executive authority; maintained Algeria as an integral part of the French Republic but with its own "personality" and the possibility of later transformation toward greater autonomy; envisaged communal legislative and executive representation as one form of protection for the European minority; anticipated the joint conduct of certain "common affairs"; defined a federal relationship among the departmental, regional, and all-Algerian levels of government with ethnic contiguity as one criterion for determining boundaries; and assumed that suffrage would be universal and exercised within a single electoral college.

There were also important differences. For one thing, the de Gaulle statute left unanswered many questions to which the *loi cadre* had replied. By elaborating details, de Gaulle could easily transform the entire structure. On the other hand, the 1957 law contained a time clause that deferred implementation of some essential features of the plan until several years after the cessation of hostilities. The new bill was so drafted as to permit immediate implementation, a task to which the government promptly turned its attention. Because the referendum bill had been so sketchy, implementation also entailed elaboration of policy details.

IMPLEMENTATION

Even before the referendum, decrees to put into effect principles stated in the government bill were drafted. At the first meeting of the Council of Ministers after the referendum a communiqué was issued:

For the first application of the law adopted by the referendum, the Minister of State charged with Algerian Affairs obtained approval of measures leading toward the institution of *arrondissement* assemblies, toward an increase in the attributions of the General Councils in Algeria, toward administrative deconcentration, toward the institution of regional councils, and dealing with the attributions of regional prefects-inspectors-general. (*LM*, 1/13/61.)

Five decrees to implement those decisions were drafted by the Committee on Algerian Affairs and approved at the next weekly meeting of the Council of Ministers.[47] Further details on the government's intentions were provided by the Algerian Director of Information, M. Coup de Fréjac.

He stressed plans to develop strong regional organisms and insisted that no all-Algerian "executive apparatus" was to be created soon.

He added that these . . . "regional councils" . . . would be composed of the representatives of the General Councils, of the Chambers of Commerce and of Agriculture, and of labor, family, and cultural associations, and that they would contain about sixty members electing their president and meeting in two sessions annually. Endowed with extended consultative competence, they will be able to formulate proposals on all questions of economic and social character concerning the region. They will be obligatorily consulted on all regional plans and programs for equipment, construction, and development. As to the *arrondissement* assembly, it will be composed of all the general councilors in the *arrondissement* and will be presided over by the sub-prefect. It will meet twice a year, but it can be consulted in the interim by the sub-prefect. (*LM*, 1/14/61.)

Joxe flew to Algeria shortly after cabinet approval of his decrees to brief administrative officials there on procedures for their implementation. But growing indications that negotiations between the French government and the F.L.N. were impending soon cast the referendum law and its implementation under a shadow. Even before the referendum there had been speculation that the principal significance of a favorable vote would be its interpretation as a mandate for de Gaulle to negotiate. As the F.L.N. had strongly protested that the establishment of the system envisaged by the referendum law would "predetermine the self-determination," it apparently was feared that its vigorous implementation might endanger negotiations. In any case, it soon became abundantly clear that, provided fruitful negotiations became a realistic possibility, the referendum law would become simply another dead letter on the well-littered Algerian stage. Nothing more was heard publicly about its implementation.

Instead, as the negotiations began to take form, it became apparent that one of the bases of the French position was the in-

[47] *LM*, January 19, 1961.

corporation of as much as possible of de Gaulle's association formula, including the principles of the referendum bill, in any agreement reached with the rebels. As early as February 21 such reports circulated.[48]

Statements by M. Joxe at the time the Evian negotiations opened in May, confirmed those reports. Joxe listed among the principles advanced by his government:

1. That there be three alternatives (Frenchification, association, secession) presented to the Algerian voters in referendum.

2. That there be "cooperation" between the French and the Algerian Republics in certain areas of common interest such as economic, cultural, technical, and defense affairs.

3. That the restoration of "calm" be a prerequisite to the holding of the referendum.

4. That the possibility of partition or regroupment of the French in the event of secession was not excluded.

5. That the "peaceful coexistence" of the different ethnic communities be ensured through certain guarantees, including communal control of such things as education and the legal system.[49]

CONCLUSIONS

The Fifth Republic executive in seeking a "political" solution in Algeria has functioned very differently from the executive of the Fourth Republic. Most obvious, of course, is the shift of power from cabinet and premier to President of the Republic. The constitution gave the government authority to direct public policy and made the President of the Republic the custodian of the national conscience, who was to step in and reconcile conflicting views only when those with primary responsibility could not agree on policy to deal with grave national problems. As things have worked out, in those areas such as Algeria where de Gaulle has so chosen, he has assumed sole responsibility for the formulation of policy. He solicits counsel within the cabinet, but does not engage in discussion and reserves to himself the right to make the decisions. Apparently, the cabinet is sometimes not even made privy to the decisions until they are announced publicly. The formation of the Committee for Algerian Affairs downgraded the cabinet still further.

[48] *LM*, February 21, 1961.
[49] *LM*, May 28-29, 1961.

This has had the effect of insulating policy from politics. The 1957 *loi cadre* was worked out in a veritable maelstrom of politics. Not only was the Fourth Republic cabinet a highly political emanation of a highly political parliament, but the even more political device of the round-table conference was used. In contrast, the present deputies were elected less for their policy positions than for their attitudes toward de Gaulle. Thus, they have little political authority independent of de Gaulle. The cabinet has been rendered even less political by the granting of key portfolios to career civil servants. The premier holds his post entirely by the grace of de Gaulle. Yet, even the residue of politics in those organs has been bypassed increasingly as de Gaulle relies more and more on civil servants for counsel and aid.

The direct appeals to the people through provincial tours, radio-television addresses, the so-called press conferences, and referenda are not an effective substitute for the politics of the Fourth Republic. They do not permit the confrontation of authentic alternatives and without choice there is no politics. Under the Fourth Republic there were too many alternatives, too many avenues to use influence, and too much politics. De Gaulle's republic has reacted to the opposite extreme.

Another, less expected, difference has been the slow speed with which de Gaulle has acted to put his decisions into effect. Three months after he announced his intention of drafting a new statute for Algeria, M. Bourgès-Maunoury (who was hardly the most dynamic premier of the Fourth Republic) had his bill in the hopper of the National Assembly, despite the fiercest opposition. Yet, it was sixteen months after de Gaulle had declared he would permit the Algerians to decide their own destiny before he even requested popular sanction for his decision, much less attempted to implement it. This chapter and the previous one have dealt with the activities of the executives of the two French republics in formulating proposals for resolution of the "political" problem in Algeria. The next two will treat the handling accorded those proposals in parliament as a means of illustrating the roles played by parliament—or rather the dominant chamber of parliament—in the two republics.

FURTHER TRANSFORMATION

The policy-making dominance of the executive—and especially the President—increased during the year preceding the Evian Accords of March 1962. Negotiations with the F.L.N., by their nature an executive function, highlighted the search for a solution during that period. The French negotiators at the fruitless talks in May-July and at the successful talks from November through February worked directly under de Gaulle. Only when a draft accord had been framed was the cabinet consulted collectively. At that meeting, Louis Joxe, the chief negotiator, reported for one hour. Debre spoke for twenty minutes. Then de Gaulle polled each minister. There was no dissent. New talks modified the draft agreement to meet later objections of the F.L.N. National Council but the revised document was signed, announced by Joxe, and proclaimed by de Gaulle without further reference to the cabinet.

Military elements and European settlers opposed negotiations more violently as the likelihood of settlement increased. This led to further concentration of power in the Presidency. De Gaulle's broadcast appeal to the armed forces retained their loyalty during the April 1961 military pronunciamento and insured the collapse of the coup. From then until October he wielded *Article 16* of the Constitution, using it chiefly to try by summary tribunals the participants in the coup. All this was done in close consultation with the cabinet but de Gaulle's dominance was unquestioned. As the Europeans' O.A.S. intensified its campaign of bombing and random murder of Moslems, the emergency executive powers that had long been used against the F.L.N. were turned against it.

Finally, the executive—and especially de Gaulle—wielded full authority to work out and implement, in cooperation with the F.L.N., plans for the application of the Evian Accord through the provisional executive stipulated in the agreement.

These developments further accentuated the transformation of the executive from a collective, responsible cabinet supervised by an arbitral president, as the Constitution provided, to a monarchic president assisted by a council of advisers.

7

The Legislature:
The National Assembly
of the Fourth Republic

INTRODUCTION

THE FOURTH FRENCH REPUBLIC was called a strong-assembly regime. Parliament, and particularly the directly elected lower chamber, was constitutionally designated as the repository of national sovereignty. It was granted all legislative powers and virtually unlimited authority to install and remove cabinets at will.[1]

In practice much legislation originated in the cabinet, but, in most cases, it did not become law until formally approved by parliament. There were two principal exceptions. In the first place, there was legislation of the type that, in most political systems, is formulated by the executive in the regular performance of such traditional executive functions as armed forces command and diplomacy. Military policy in Indochina, for instance, and diplomatic policy was made and executed without the legislative endorsement required in other areas. In the second place, legislation was formulated to elaborate more general legislation enacted by parliament. In this latter category are the detailed regulations that inevitably must be worked out by the administration to apply any legislation. All legislation requires administrative articulation. The latter category also includes action taken in pursuance of special powers granted

[1] Because of the predominance of the National Assembly over the other chamber, these two chapters are primarily concerned with it.

by parliament. This practice was continuously followed from the early days of the Faure government.

The special powers bills were grants of legislative authority, not definitions of policy. They authorized the government to act in certain broad areas, but did not require nor even describe any particular action.[2] In fact, only in regard to the *loi cadre* did the parliament of the Fourth Republic play an active part in forming political policy to deal with the Algerian insurrection.

THE ORIGINAL BILL

Its Content

The *loi cadre* originally submitted to the National Assembly was designed to reorganize the governmental structure of Algeria to permit greater internal autonomy and to give the Moslems political equality with the Europeans.[3] "Autonomous territories" were to be established in Algeria by ministerial decrees that would become effective if not revoked by parliament within three months after submission. These territories would have the capacity to join together in creating "federative organs." The Paris government reserved authority over citizenship and nationality; foreign affairs, defense, and general security; the organization of the governmental structure and the electoral system; currency, taxation, tariffs, and the budget; most judicial matters; education; the public domain, mining, and energy resources; and publicly owned enterprises. All matters not expressly reserved to the central government came under the jurisdiction of the territories. After two years following the election of each territorial legislature it could delegate such powers as it wished to the federative organs. Parliament could transfer powers to either the territorial governments or the federative organs.

The federative organs would not constitute a complete government. They would include a federative assembly composed of members elected through universal, equal suffrage in the

[2] On the "special powers" see pp. 70-74 above.
[3] For the full text of the original proposal see *LM*, September 15-16, 1957. For the changes made by the time of its first consideration in committee see *LM*, September 19, 1957.

respective territories and a federative council composed of an equal number of members elected by each of the territorial legislative assemblies. The council would be responsible for executing the decisions of the assembly. It would elect annually one of its members in rotation to "direct . . . its work," but would be dependent on a proconsul, called "the depositary of the powers of the republic," for the means of execution. This depositary, who would be a minister and a member of the Paris government, would preside over the deliberations of the council, "direct the civil services of the State," and also perform roughly the same ceremonial functions in Algeria that the president of the Fourth Republic performed in France. He would promulgate the "decisions" of the federative assembly, though he could appeal them to the French Council of State or to a court of arbitration, appointed in its entirety by the president of the Republic, if he doubted their conformity with the *loi cadre* or the French constitution.

The Republic would be represented in the autonomous territories by agents appointed by the president of the Republic acting in full cabinet meeting. They would perform at the territorial level the functions performed by the "depositary" at the federative level. In addition they would designate the "person charged with forming the [territorial] government," which was invested by the territorial assembly.

With obvious regard for the European settlers, "minorities" were guaranteed equitable representation at all levels and discriminatory legislation or governmental action was forbidden.

The most controversial feature of the bill was its explicit substitution of the traditional "double college" electoral system by a single college regime. Under the existing electoral system Moslems in one college chose among Moslem candidates for public office and Europeans in the other chose among Europeans. The proposed bill threw all voters into the same bag, causing consternation among the settlers who feared that they would be swamped by the Moslem majority.

Committee Hearings

The *loi cadre* had an inauspicious introduction to the parliamentary mill. M. André Morice, the Defense Minister, whose

hostility to the bill was ill-concealed, failed to appear at the
Interior Committee hearings to join the Premier and the Minister
Residing in Algeria in its defense. Then the committee was unable to agree on a *rapporteur*.[4] Finally, a number of committee
members strongly opposed key features of the bill. The hostility
was so sharp that the government, already teetering on the verge
of dissolution, withdrew the bill and convoked the famous
"round-table" conference.[5] The bill returned from the round-
table conference accompanied by a "corrective letter" that
sweetened the pill for the right-wing of the committee and the
Assembly. In fact, most of the changes responded to objections
raised by conservative committee members at the abortive
hearing. The letter withdrew the designation "legislative" from
the territorial assemblies, limited the federative assembly to
coordinating functions, and deprived the federative council of
the right to choose one of its members to "direct" its works. The
clause permitting parliament to delegate additional powers had
been stricken and parliament was given primary authority over
alterations in the Algerian governmental structure with assent
required by the territorial and federative assemblies. A promise
that France would supply investment capital to Algeria was
added.

In the meantime, the committee had succeeded in electing a
rapporteur—M. Marcel Roclore, an Independent opposed to the
bill—but the success was illusory. M. Roclore submitted a pre-
report recommending suppression of all references to federal
relationships, to a single electoral college, to an executive council, and to any later evolution of the Algerian governmental
structure. The committee adopted the pre-report as a basis for
discussion, but rejected his recommendation that the *loi cadre*
omit provision for a single electoral college. Roclore resigned as
rapporteur because of this and was succeeded by M. Etienne
Gagnaire, a Socialist favorable to the government's bill.

The style and content of the deliberations on the bill are in-

[4] The *rapporteur* is the committee member charged by the committee with
preparing a report concerning a piece of proposed legislation for presentation to the Assembly on behalf of the committee. In most cases his viewpoint
on the bill is representative of the committee majority's.

[5] See pp. 85-87 above.

dicated by the following excerpts from an account of the committee meeting: [6]

The battle over amendments began with the opening of discussions by the Interior Committee.

M. Roclore and the moderates launched the first offensive by supporting . . . a new text eliminating any notion of federalism.

The first paragraph—"Algeria is an integral part of the French Republic"—was adopted without difficulty. . . . But in the second, M. Roclore proposed: "It is composed of autonomous territories which manage their own affairs freely and democratically."

M. Merigonde (Socialist) called on the committeemen to be content with the government's wording by returning to the expression "federal territories." The Committee agreed, by 16 votes . . . against 14 . . . and 12 abstentions. . . . But everything was called into question again by the vote on the complete article, for the "federalist" wording did not succeed in uniting a majority. . . .

This incident provoked a show of bad temper by the Socialists, who were amazed by the attitude of the Radicals and R.G.R., who, in the end, contributed only one affirmative vote. . . .

The meeting was recessed and during this intermission the Independent committeemen received from those who had negotiated in the name of the group at the "Round Table," the advice not to call into question the agreement arrived at.

With the resumption of the meeting, in the evening, a way was found to fix things up. As a pretext to obtain a second reading of this first article, M. Merigonde proposed a new wording: "Territories federated among themselves."

The Moderates still demanded that the Roclore text be passed, but they were beaten by 25 votes to 9.

The phrasing of M. Merigonde was then carried by 16 votes . . . against 15 . . . and 8 abstentions. And the complete article this time, was approved by 17 votes . . . against 15 . . . and 9 abstentions. . . .

For article 5 (single electoral college), M. Roclore proposed a completely different wording. "The Republic guarantees to all citizens the free exercise of their electoral right by universal, equal, and secret suffrage. It guarantees to each community, with the suppression of the double electoral college, equitable, obligatory, and authentic representation at all levels." The *rapporteur* argued that this would lead to a better understanding by the public of France's desire to suppress the double college.

A majority of 28 votes . . . against 15 preferred the positive affirmation of the single electoral college. . . .

[6] *LM*, September 25, 1957.

M. Soustelle then had added, by 20 votes against 11, and 11 abstentions, this detail, "in accordance with the means determined by laws."

This addition had the effect of modifying the distribution of the votes, and the complete article was rejected by 22 votes . . . against 21. . . .

The committee spent twenty hours debating proposed amendments to the bill and made a number of other changes, but, in the end, was unable to agree on recommendations and M. Gagnaire was instructed to report to the Assembly on the committee's deliberations without making recommendations. As a result, the government's original bill served as the basis of discussion in the Assembly.

The Assembly Debate

The following excerpts from the debate illustrate the atmosphere and manner in which the proceedings of the Assembly were conducted. For instance, in contrast with Assembly debate on the Algerian problem in the Gaullist regime, both the government and the opposition speakers attempt to change votes, to sway the opinions of their listeners.

1. Organizing the Debate. September 25, 1957—1st sitting.

PRESIDING OFFICER (M. ANDRÉ LE TROQUER (S.)): [7] The agenda calls for discussion of the government bill on the institutions of Algeria and the letter clarifying the bill. The conference on the organization of debates . . . has divided the time reserved for the debate as follows. . . .

Government, 3 hours;
Committee of the Interior, 3 hours;
Communists, 6 hours, 20 minutes;
Socialists, 4 hours, 25 minutes;
Independents and Peasants of Social Action, 3 hours 50 minutes;
Popular Republican Movement, 3 hours 20 minutes;
Radical Republican and Radical-Socialist group, 2 hours 5 minutes;
French Union and Fraternity (Poujadist), 1 hour 30 minutes;
Social Republicans, 1 hour;
Democratic and Socialist Union of the Resistance and the African
    Democratic Assembly, 1 hour;
Assembly of the Republican Left and the Republican Center, 40
    minutes;
Peasants, 40 minutes;

[7] For key to abbreviations, see the Appendix.

Overseas Independents, 20 minutes;

Progressive Republican group, 20 minutes;

Peasants of Social and Rural Action, 20 minutes;

African Socialist Movement, 20 minutes;

Unattached, 40 minutes;

Votes and Ballots, 1 hour;

M. Gagnaire, rapporteur for the Committee on the Interior has the floor. (*Applause on the left*)

2. *The Committees Report.* [M. Etienne Gagnaire reported on the work of his committee (described on pp. 137-140 above) and concluded with these comments:]

M. GAGNAIRE (S.): You will doubtless permit me, in my personal capacity, to go into a few details. I sincerely regret that the decisions reached at the round-table conference—

M. PIERRE MONTEL (I.P.A.S.): What round table? Does it appear in the Constitution? It's a wobbly table.

M. GAGNAIRE: —have not been respected by certain groups of the majority. (*Applause on the left and on several benches in the center. Interruptions on the right.*)

If they had been, the committee would have been able to report on the government bill and on the clarifying letter.

Let me hasten to add that the Algerian problem will only be settled by a political solution. The proposed *loi cadre* will permit us to arrive at this solution. (*Applause on the left.*)

Finally, the great majority of Algerians awaits the passage of the proposed *loi cadre*. To disappoint them, I am convinced, would bring us to the worst of all possible catastrophes. (*Applause on the left, and on several benches in the center. Lively interruptions on the extreme right.*)

THE PRESIDING OFFICER: M. Paul Coste-Floret, rapporteur for the advisory Committee on Universal Suffrage, Constitutional Laws, and Rules and Petitions, has the floor.

M. PAUL COSTE-FLORET (M.R.P.): Mesdames, messieurs, the discussion of the government's proposed *loi cadre* for Algerian institutions raises both political questions and technical problems. . . . It was the duty of your Committee on Universal Suffrage, Constitutional Laws, and Rules and Petitions, which decided unanimously to act in an advisory capacity concerning this proposed *loi cadre*, to examine the technical problems that it raises.

The committee first underlined the ambiguity of this proposed law which does not sufficiently distinguish between two fundamental matters, to wit, the problem of the bond linking Algeria to France, and that of the internal structure of Algeria.

It seems to me that it would be better to distinguish between these two matters clearly . . . and that is why we have proposed an amendment to that article . . . :

"Algeria is an integral part of the French Republic, one and indivisible; it is composed of territories federated to each other, which freely and democratically manage their own affairs."

This text was adopted unanimously by the members of the committee with the exception of the Communists. . . .

If, as is rumored, you are led to pose the question of confidence in this debate, perhaps it will be necessary to retain, if not all, at least some [of the amendments proposed by my committee and presented in the text which you have before you]. . . .

The serious work done by the Committee on Universal Suffrage is a reflection of its hope in the present debate. This debate is too important, M. Prime Minister, for you to disappoint this hope. (*Applause in the center, and on several benches on the right.*)

3. Dilatory Motions.

THE PRESIDING OFFICER: M. Ballanger poses the preliminary question by virtue of article 46 of the rules.[8] M. Ballanger has the floor.

M. ROBERT BALLANGER (C.): Mesdames, messieurs, the question which urgently requires discussion here is, to our minds, that of peace in Algeria. Peace in Algeria depends entirely on negotiations with the qualified representatives of the Algerian people, on a basis of recognition of Algeria's right to national independence. (*Lively interruptions on the right and on the extreme right.*)

M. JEAN-MARIE LE PEN (U.F.F.): Never! You have no right to say that! Shut-up! Leave this Assembly! (*Exclamations on the extreme left.*) Mr. Speaker, you have no right to let him say that!

M. BALLANGER (C.): The projected *loi cadre*, being conducive to the maintenance of the colonial regime and the aggravation of the war—

M. GUY PETIT (I.P.A.S.): That has nothing to do with it.

M. ROBERT BALLANGER (C.): —we feel that it is contrary to the interest of our country to discuss it. This is why the Communist group is posing the preliminary question, and asks a vote by open ballot on this point. (*Applause on the extreme left.*)

M. RAYMOND MONDON (I.P.A.S.): It's not receivable!

M. LE PEN (U.F.F.): I ask for the application of article 75 and 81 of the penal code. (*Exclamations on the extreme left.*)

(*On several benches on the extreme left*): Down with Fascism!

THE PRESIDING OFFICER: No one else wants recognition? . . .

I will consult the Assembly on the preliminary question posed by M. Ballanger. . . .

---

[8] A preliminary question asks, in effect, if the matter proposed for debate deserves the attention of the chamber. If the motion passes, the chamber is saying that it does not and passes to the next item on the agenda, thereby automatically defeating the proposal without debate. Only one supporter and one opponent of the motion may speak before the question is posed.

Here is the result of the ballot:

Number of Voters	560
Absolute Majority	281
For Adoption	150
Against	410

The motion is defeated. I have received the following prejudicial motion from M. Tixier-Vignancour, submitted in accordance with article 46 of the rules:

"The National Assembly.

"Recognizing that there can be no reform undertaken in Algeria before peace and order have been re-established there;

"Decides to suspend the examination of any *loi cadre* until the war, being waged on France by individuals, armed and aided by foreign powers, has been won."

M. Tixier-Vignancour has the floor.

M. JEAN-LOUIS TIXIER-VIGNANCOUR (N.-I.): Mesdames, messieurs, the discussion which opens today calls into question principles even more than individuals.

[M. Tixier-Vignancour launched into a speech in which he defended the French rule in Algeria, attacked the Communists, and displayed an intense chauvinism. The following passage shows something of the tone of his speech.]

M. TIXIER-VIGNANCOUR: Very well, Mr. Resident Minister [Lacoste, Resident Minister of Algeria], I'm going to speak to you with strong words, not only from myself, but from innumerable telegrams, letters, proposals, etc., which I have received as have many of my colleagues for the last two weeks: We have a sovereign and supreme contempt for being condemned by the slavers and the racists of the United Nations. (*Applause on the extreme right, and on several benches on the right.*)

Are you going to have us be judged by the people of Little Rock? (*Very good! very good! on the same benches.*)

Are you going to have us be judged by the slavers of Yemen?

Are you going to have us be judged by countries which still practice the slave trade?

Are you going to have us be judged by an Assembly within which we find the majority of our country's enemies, whether they are on the other side of the Iron Curtain, or whether they are those shop-keepers across the Atlantic who, one hand on the Bible and the other on their cash-drawer, want to teach lessons of morality and humanity to our country.

And, it's before this abominable jurisdiction—

(*Protests on the left and in the center. Applause on the extreme right.*)

THE PRESIDING OFFICER: M. Tixier-Vignancour, you have no right to employ such an expression.

M. TIXIER-VIGNANCOUR: Before these enemies— (*New protests on the left and in the center.*) Yes!

M. MARCEL DAROU (S.): You didn't know 1914-1918 and 1939-1945! Happily, you don't represent France! A little caution! What you just said is scandalous.

M. TIXIER-VIGNANCOUR: I am extremely surprised—

M. DAROU: We're not surprised at what you're saying! It's dishonorable!

M. TIXIER-VIGNANCOUR: I am extremely surprised to hear our Socialist colleagues, who, more than anyone have reason to complain—

M. DAROU: About you!

M. TIXIER-VIGNANCOUR: —about the United Nations, take its defense.

[M. Tixier-Vignancour continues despite several interruptions and concludes his address by saying that in voting on his prejudicial motion, the National Assembly will answer two questions: 1. How can anyone have the right to propose a *loi cadre* for Algeria in the absence of elected representatives from Algeria? 2. How can such a law be proposed when so many jurists have said that it is impossible to create a federated state within a centralized republic, and that there must first be constitutional revision?

He also does not want to see such a law adopted under foreign pressure and the armed menace in Algeria.

M. Bourgès-Maunoury, the Prime Minister, followed, speaking in favor of the *loi cadre*, underlining its importance, and, after many interruptions, asking the National Assembly to reject Tixier-Vignancour's prejudicial motion.

The motion was defeated, 343 to 77, and five other prejudicial motions proposed immediately afterward were also defeated or declared non-receivable.]

4. *The General Discussion.*

[Six speakers—an Independent, a Socialist, a Christian Democrat (M.R.P.), a Radical, a Communist, and the indefatigable M. Tixier-Vignancour—participated in the general discussion that ensued that day. Among them was M. Jacques Duclos, floor-leader of the Communist group. The following excerpts indicate something of the Algerian policy of his party at the time and the style with which it was presented as well as the attitude of the other deputies toward him and his party.]

M. JACQUES DUCLOS (C.): Mesdames, messieurs, the National Assembly is called on to make a decision on the proposed Algerian *loi cadre.* . . .

The government's policy has embarked on a path of nonrecognition of the Algerian right to independence, and the proposal which it presents leaves no other choice than war to the death.

The continuation of this war does not displease the American im-

perialists who cover their colonialism with a deceiving mask. . . .
We can be sure that the neocolonialists from across the Atlantic will
neglect nothing in order to take the place of their French accomplices
and rivals in Algeria.

M. PIERRE MONTEL (I.P.A.S.): With your support.

M. DUCLOS: For their part, the German imperialists to whom
Eurafrica offers prospects for the penetration of the African con-
tinent, are also ready, in concert with their American counterparts, to
play a game where the stakes are the domination of Africa. The old
fox, Adenauer, whom the French Europeans [9] have well served,
watches France bog down in Algeria. . . .

If it is like this, it is because the defense of colonial interests, fundamentally opposed to those of France, goes before everything for
those who govern us.

The colonialists get incontestably richer, but the people of France
must pay the deficit of the Algerian budget. . . .

The pretended Algerian prosperity . . . is that of a minority of
profiteers . . . they are trying to make us believe that the end of
colonial domination of Algeria will sink the French economy into
stagnation.

France spends nearly two billion francs a day on the war in Algeria. That is a burden which will lead us to ruin, but one which
matters little to the colonialist, provided that he can grow richer.
(*Applause on the extreme left.*)

By pursuing the war in Algeria, France has everything to lose. On
the other hand, if Algerian independence were acquired with the
permission of France, and not against her, conditions would be
created for the establishment of special Franco-Algerian relations,
economic as well as political and cultural. . . .

To tell the truth, those who govern us are in the act of selling out
the Sahara [to foreign oil interests], but the property rights that they
invoke are being contested.

M. MAX LEJEUNE (S.), MINISTER OF THE SAHARA:—Will you permit me to interrupt you M. Duclos?

M. DUCLOS: Certainly.

MINISTER OF THE SAHARA: M. Duclos, I do not have the right to
let you say that the government is getting ready to sell out the Sahara.

On the extreme left: It has already been done!

MINISTER OF THE SAHARA: We have no intention of selling out the
Sahara to any foreign power—

M. TIXIER-VIGNANCOUR: Nor Algeria!

MINISTER OF THE SAHARA:—and, in my own behalf, M. Duclos, I
declare to you—and you cannot make the same affirmation—that I have
never been in the service of a foreign power. (*Applause on the left,
in the center, and on the right. Interruptions on the far left.*)

[9] That is, the French who support European unification.

M. DUCLOS: That's a vulgarity from a minister who is trying to hide his anti-French labors under insults. (*Applause on the extreme left. Protests from the center, on the right and on the far right.*)

M. ROBERT BECHEL (M.R.P.): Oh, come now, M. Duclos, everyone knows that you are sold out to Russia.

M. DUCLOS: *M. le président,* will you please call that individual to order. (*Lively interruptions from the center, on the right, and on the extreme right. Applause on the extreme left.*)

PRESIDING OFFICER: M. Duclos, before calling one of your colleagues to order, I will begin by calling you, yourself, to order for calling the words of a minister a vulgarity. (*Applause in the center, on the right and on the extreme right.*)

Let me attend to my business and you attend to yours. Please continue your speech.

M. DUCLOS: American firms are participating in the prospecting of the Sahara, just as English firms and French capitalists are also embarked on the same path, and this enables us to foresee ferocious fights between petroleum trusts. . . .

The proposed *loi cadre* says . . . : Algeria is an integral part of the French republic.

M. MARCEL BOUYER (U.F.F.): All the members of the national parties have approved it.

M. DUCLOS: But this formula closes the door to any prospect of independence for the Algerian people, and does not take into account the principle of self-determination, inscribed in the charter of the United Nations.

M. MARCEL ROCLORE (I.P.A.S.): Tell us about Hungary!

M. DUCLOS: Nevertheless, some people would like to match the maintenance of colonial dominion with a few apparently progressive formulas in order to try to influence the Algerian people, and at the same time, to deceive world opinion. Others do not want these formulas, even if they are without practical significance, for they fear their subsequent repercussions, and of course, the ultras of Algiers, who are close relatives of the racists of Little Rock, insist that their colonial status be in no way changed.

All that explains the difficulties that the government ran up against in its elaboration of the *loi cadre,* and the reappearance in the Committee of the Interior of questions which had been supposedly solved at [the round-table conference at] Matignon. . . .

This project . . . divides . . . Algeria into several territories of which the division would not only be geographic, but will take into account ethnic realities. . . .

We are in the presence of provisions paralleling the official thesis of the South African racists. . . . There is also the question of the sincerity of elections, but we know what to expect from long experience with prefabricated elections in Algeria. (*Applause on the extreme left.*)

M. Antoine Guitlon (I.P.A.S.): No doubt you're talking about elections in the Soviet Union!

M. Jean Damasio (U.F.F.): It's a question that you're well placed to answer!

M. Duclos: The electoral provisions that the technicians are preparing for Algeria would not be fair and would trample underfoot the rights of the Algerian people to the profit of the colonialist minority whose demands become progressively greater as more concessions are made to them.

M. Jean Demarquet (U.F.F.): You know very well that's false!

M. Duclos: . . . Certain people . . . pretend . . . to assure Algeria a great managerial autonomy. . . . In fact . . . the territorial legislative assemblies and the federative institutions will have no competence on [so many important] questions [that] one wonders of what this "great managerial autonomy" . . . could consist.

All that aims at the continuation of a war that is "imbecile and a dead end" and which menaces the liberties of France where a concentration camp has already been set up at Mourmelon.

M. Tixier-Vignancour (N.-I.): There is no one at Mourmelon.

M. Duclos: All that facilitates the development of the Fascist danger, ruins our country, and gravely hurts its international prestige, as the commentaries of the international press on the violences and the tortures occurring in Algeria bear witness.

M. Demarquet (U.F.F.): At Melouza,[10] for example. Fascist!

M. Duclos: . . . Addressing himself to the public prosecutor, M. Henri Alleg explained how he was subjected to abominable tortures. . . .

"You're going to talk, you scum!" said his torturers to M. Henri Alleg. "You're cooked, you are in a state of suspended death! You wrote articles on extortions and tortures. Okay! now it's on you that the 10th Paratroop Division is committing them. And what we do here is going to be done in France." (*Interruptions on the far right.*)

"No one knows that you've been arrested, you're going to die, and we're going to blow your damned Republic to hell." (*Exclamations on the right and on the extreme right. Noise, applause on the extreme left.*)

M. Raymond Triboulet (R.S.): Proof!

M. Damasio (U.F.F.): He's the mouthpiece of the F.L.N.

The Presiding Officer: M. Damasio, don't interrupt.

M. Damasio (U.F.F.): It's the truth, Mr. Speaker.

[M. Duclos' discussion of alleged tortures in Algeria, culminated in this scene.]

M. Duclos: Thus, I am taking the liberty of asking several precise questions of the Minister for Algeria.

What has become of Maclouche M'hmed arrested on February 25,

[10] An Algerian village at which a massacre occurred that the French blame on the F.L.N.

1957 by the 2nd R.C.P. and the 2nd brigade of the police? He under-
went torture by water and by electricity. He stayed for fifteen days
in a cell one meter square. Sent at last to Beni-Messous, in a staging
camp guarded by paratroopers, he left it twenty days later and under-
went an "interrogation" lasting ten days, and was beaten with a bull
whip.

M. DEMARQUET (U.F.F.): Bravo for the 2nd R.C.P.! Impeccable!
That's good work! (*Lively interruptions on the extreme left.*)

THE PRESIDING OFFICER: No! M. Demarquet, you have no right
to say that.

M. DEMARQUET (U.F.F.): Twenty days later he wasn't dead!

On the extreme left: Scum, assassin, torturer!

M. RÉMY BOUTAVANT (C.): (*Indicating the right*) There they are!
The torturers!

M. DUCLOS: The war in Algeria with its attendant violences and
tortures, places many young Frenchmen in a crucial situation which
justly worries their parents. (*Interruptions on the right.*)

Here I refer to a moving document, written by a former soldier in
Algeria, Jacques Pucheu:

"In the month of January, a small convoy of thirty men was given
a rude blow about six kilometers south of Menaa. Two days later we
descended on two villages situated in a place about one kilometer
from the ambush, near the center of Chir. In reprisal a dozen civilians
were executed on the spot. The others were taken to a C.P. at Chir,
where some were executed after interrogation. The women were
raped and the two villages were blown up with dynamite." (*Interruptions on the extreme right and on the right. Applause on the extreme
left.*)

M. ANDRÉ MORICE (MINISTER OF NATIONAL DEFENSE AND OF THE
ARMED FORCES) (Rad.): Will you permit me to interrupt you, M.
Duclos?

M. DUCLOS: Certainly, *M. le ministre.*

M. MORICE: I will not permit, in this assembly, the declarations
made by M. Duclos—

M. DUCLOS: No, I quoted a soldier's letter.

M. MORICE: —which could stain the honor of our soldiers.

And I declare to you again, M. Duclos, that if we want to serve the
cause of our young . . . we must . . . help them in their fight, on
the moral plane as well as on the material plane, that is to say, exactly
the opposite of what you are doing here. (*Applause on the right and
on the extreme right. Exclamations on the extreme left.*)

On the extreme left: On their return, you will have an account
to settle with them.

M. DUCLOS: *M. le ministre,* I wish to answer you by asking you a
question. A little while ago, I demonstrated that while the French
people are paying for the Algerian war, French soldiers are getting
killed, and Algerians are falling—

On the right: It's your fault.

M. DUCLOS: —there are people who are getting rich from the Algerian war. I know that the initiative for the famous Algerian Tunisian frontier fortification comes from you. (*Applause on the extreme left.*)

M. MORICE: Will you permit me to interrupt you?

M. DUCLOS: Wait, I'm not finished. And as you are a specialist on fortified walls,[11] I ask you to publish the list of all those who have had any part in furnishing the supplies necessary for building that line of fortifications. Yes! This list must be published! (*Applause on the extreme left.*) And now, I give you the floor willingly.

M. MORICE: In answer to M. Duclos, I am not a specialist on fortifications.

M. DUCLOS: You know what I mean. We understand each other perfectly!

M. MORICE: Yes, we understand each other. . . . You and your friends have, at a certain time in the past—and I did justice to it in this chamber—spoken of an affair concerning the construction of the Atlantic wall—

M. DUCLOS: And concerning the demolition—

M. MORICE: —which occurred while I was in captivity.

M. DUCLOS: One could have an interest, even while a prisoner.

On the right: Scum!

M. AIMÉ PACQUET (P.): You are disgusting, M. Duclos.

M. DUCLOS: You're the one who's disgusting.

M. JEAN LEGENDRE (I.P.A.S.): M. Duclos was caught red-handed as a spy in 1923! A spy dares to give us lessons! (*Protests on the extreme left.*)

PRESIDING OFFICER: M. Legendre, please!

M. LEGENDRE: That man is a spy!

M. HENRI POURTALET (C.): Listen to Legendre, the blackmailer.

PRESIDING OFFICER: My dear colleagues, please. This time the subject is even more serious than before. A member of the Government has just been accused by the speaker who has asked him a serious question concerning his honor.

M. DUCLOS: Those who fight for peace in Algeria are the true defenders of the national interest. Faithful to glorious national traditions, they will take the flag of the fraternity of peoples into their hands.

M. DEMARQUET (U.F.F.): Via Melouza. That's perfect.

M. DUCLOS: Those who govern us . . . do not want . . . anyone to talk about the sons of men shot during the war, refusing to serve under the war-criminal Speidel.[12] (*Applause on the extreme left.*) We

[11] M. Duclos is alluding to allegations that a construction firm with which M. Morice had been associated had profited from work it had performed for the Germans in building fortifications in occupied France during World War II.

[12] A German general who held an office in the NATO command.

are going to vote against the *loi cadre,* both for reasons of principle and for national reasons. . . .

As the central committee of the French Communist party has recently emphasized, a French Algerian policy should be defined in the following manner:

"Repudiate the colonial relations between France and Algeria; recognize the Algerian people's right to independence; negotiate between equal peoples in order to create new relations and ties between France and Algeria based on free consent and conforming to mutual interest."

In order to make such a policy triumph, we call on the working class and the French people to unite, and to act with the goals of ending the war and of imposing a policy of friendship between the peoples of France and Algeria.

We hold the firm conviction that the central committee's appeal will be heard, and that everywhere, in the cities, and in the countryside, demonstrations, petitions and delegations to those whom we have elected, while in business, work stoppages, strikes, manifestations—

M. ROGER LEGER (U.F.F.): Subscriptions for the murderers!

M. DUCLOS: —will make next Thursday . . . a great national day for the fight for peace in Algeria. (*Applause on the extreme left.*). . . .

By union and action, we will impose an end to the Algerian war. We will prevent the colonialists from using France in order to preserve their privileges, we will make a triumphant French policy (*Exclamations on the extreme right, on the right, and on diverse benches*), a policy of peace, a policy of friendship and understanding between peoples. (*Prolonged applause on the extreme left. Exclamations on the extreme right.*)

[On the following day, September 26, the first speakers were two Socialists, two Communists, the Prime Minister, a right-wing extremist, and M. Jacques Soustelle—the leading orator of the Gaullist group.]

M. JACQUES SOUSTELLE (R.S.): There are many in the National Assembly who have declared and who continue to think that French Algeria should be a new Algeria. I am one of them. Still, the new Algeria must remain a French Algeria.

To disregard this exigency, or even while affirming it to move away from it slowly and to prepare to abandon it, would be to betray both the living and the dead. (*Applause on the right, on the extreme right, on certain benches in the center, and on some benches on the left.*)

Let us not forget that, since the beginning, the F.L.N. has always played the double game . . . of noisily protesting against the pretended absence of reforms, yet sabotaging them ferociously when we try to implement them. . . . (*Applause on several benches on the left, in the center, and on the right.*)

Without doubt . . . for our habitual critics . . . in the U.N. . . . we are colonialists and we would remain colonialists even after we have offered the presidency of the Algerian Republic to Ben Bella.[13] (*Very good! very good! on the right.*) The *loi cadre*, that is, the exposition of the decisions and the intentions of the French Republic relative to Algeria should not have to be made for the U.N. nor for M. Khrushchev nor for M. Dulles. (*Applause on several benches on the left, in the center, on the right and on the extreme right.*)

To go and wave it about in Manhattan as an element of the case for the defense, when we should only appear as prosecutors at the U.N., is, to my mind, a fundamentally erroneous tactic. . . . (*Applause on the same benches.*)

Finally, to finish with the chapter of illusions and chimeras, let us recognize, without circumlocution, that there is no text which can relieve France of carrying out its present war effort against the rebellion, and its future economic and social effort in Algeria. There is no text which can exempt us from fighting against defeatism and treason at home. (*Applause on the right.*)

You will say, then, what good is a *loi cadre*?

To my mind, this would be an attitude no less regrettable . . . than the myth of the miraculous drug. . . . We must have a law, since in our political system . . . governmental instability is the rule, and consequently, only the parliament can, through laws, bring a certain element of continuity, therefore of confidence, to the situation. . . .

But, though we are partisans of a *loi cadre*, we cannot accept anything other than a text which not only declares what is done, but which embodies in the mechanisms themselves that neither today nor tomorrow nor in the future will France envisage the separation of Algeria and, consequently, the independence of Algeria. (*Applause on several benches on the left, in the center, on the right, and on the extreme right.*)

It is only just and honest to recognize that [some] points [in the text] have been either improved or suppressed by means of a clarifying letter. This clarifying letter issued from a Council of Ministers, which had taken into consideration the exchanges of views which took place in a meeting now well-known under the name of the round-table conference.

I tried at the beginning of this speech and without much success, it seems, to specify that a meeting of representatives of political groups was not and could not be a new constitutional mechanism. There is a government which is responsible for the preparation and introduction of texts, there is a parliament which is responsible for their rejection or their adoption. There is no round-table conference unless it comes from the pens of the journalists who love striking formulas so much.

When we read the dithyrambs which greeted this conference and its results in the press, one would have truly believed—to quote the poet—that Saturday was:

[13] A leader of the F.L.N.

"... *La fameuse journée*
"*Où sur le mont Sinaï la loi nous fut donnée.*"

But, mesdames, messieurs, the *Hôtel Matignon* is not Mount Sinai, and the results of the round-table conference do not constitute a decalogue. (*Applause and laughter on numerous benches in the center, on the left, on the right and on the extreme right.*)

Thus, as much as it was legitimate, and even very well advised to bring men of good will around one table, to ask them for advice which the government can then take into account or not within the framework of its responsibilities, it would be excessive . . . to make this conference pass for a sovereign organ of the State, and the conclusions to which it came, for a sort of intangible treaty. . . .

I believe that everyone here knows what has for a long time been [my] position . . . on the problem of the single electoral college. First of all, I feel that this institution is to a large degree tied to the complete integration of Algeria within the parent state, for the more Algeria becomes a French territory as the others, the more it becomes inadmissible that any discrimination be established among the French citizens who people it.

Then . . . I have wanted to establish a difference between the national elections of the parliament of a French territory, essentially political elections for which the installation of a single electoral body was necessary, and territorial or local elections to administrative assemblies in which a representation, adjusted to local interests, is much more understandable and necessary. . . . To my mind, every electoral law ought to fulfill the minimum conditions in the framework of the single electoral college in Algeria. The first of these conditions would be, that in each electoral division, the minorities would be represented in the elected bodies, by a number of members not less than the numerical proportion of these minorities in the electorate.

The second condition is that the election of these representatives should result from the suffrage of a majority of the electors belonging to the interested minority. . . .

M. PIERRE COT (R.P.): That is no longer a single electoral college.

M. SOUSTELLE (R.S.): At this moment, I am expressing the minimum conditions, and I don't see what a democrat like you can find to reproach in these exigencies, which arise from the purest democratic spirit. We do not want the organized crushing of any minority under any formula. (*Applause on the right and on certain benches on the left and in the center.*)

M. COT (R.P.): Then don't talk about a single electoral college. Say that you're against such a college. It would be more moral.

M. SOUSTELLE (R.S.): M. Pierre Cot, I am not letting myself be deceived by a dilemma, which, like all dilemmas has a third solution.

M. COT (R.P.): Show it to us. Tell us how the electors can vote separately in a single electoral college. You would be squaring the circle!

M. ROBERT CHAMBÉIRON (R.P.): You're contradicting your demonstration.

M. SOUSTELLE (R.S.): . . . Let no one ever be able to say of us: they have, certainly, without wanting it, provoked the loss of Algeria. Neither our country nor history would ever pardon us for that, and still less would our conscience. (*Applause on the right, on the extreme right, and on several benches in the center and on the left.*)

M. CHERIF SID CARA, SECRETARY OF STATE FOR ALGERIA: Will you permit me to interrupt you, my dear colleague?

M. SOUSTELLE: Certainly.

M. CHERIF SID CARA: I should like to ask for some brief explanations from you. While watching the deliberations, either of the National Assembly, or of the Assembly of the French Union, I noticed something quite paradoxical. I saw the right wing, and the left wing of these Assemblies agree in order to reject the government's *loi cadre* project.

The left wing rejects it while declaring for the nationalists, the separationists, and the F.L.N. . . . The right wing rejects it because they want to defend the position of France in Algeria, that of the Algerian French. That is entirely normal and I agree with their decision to defend France, and the Algerian French at the same time.

But if I defend the Algerian French, it is not because I wish to defend their privileges, it's simply because I am convinced that Frenchmen who have lived in Algeria for several generations have the right to consider Algeria as their fatherland. . . .

The Moslems loyal to France count on the promises that have been made to them for over a year. They had the hope, until now, that France walked a liberal road. Take care! If, by the rejection of this *loi cadre*, or if this law is passed by a feeble minority, they will have the grave and discouraging feeling that each time the Algerian problem is put before public opinion, the French parliament refuses to discuss it, and procrastinates in order to escape an examination of the question and to put it off indefinitely. (*Applause on the left and in the center.*) . . .

M. SOUSTELLE: . . . I remain attached to every formula which comes as close as possible to the pure and simple integration of Algeria into France with perfect equality for all citizens.

M. PAUL COSTE FLORET (M.R.P.): Very good!

M. SOUSTELLE: In my mind, without doubt excessively simple, that is the republican solution, *par excellence*, the progressive solution.

M. CHAMBÉIRON (R.P.): With 140 Algerian deputies here!

M. SOUSTELLE: I have already heard that argument 140 times, and it is no better the hundred and fortieth time, than it was the hundred and thirty-ninth.

That said, integration is in no way incompatible with the setting-up of local decentralized institutions. . . . One can therefore conceive perfectly of an integrationist system in which local decentralization exists in a state as advanced as possible, such that these citizens, equal in rights and in duties, have, in addition, local responsibilities, and such that local elites can freely emerge.

That is all that I have to say. (*Applause on certain benches in the center, on the left, on the right, and on the extreme right.*)

[Two members of the government followed Soustelle to the podium. The principal defense of the proposed law was made by M. Robert Lacoste, Minister for Algeria.]

M. ROBERT LACOSTE (S.): Mesdames, messieurs, certain people among you, who, however, are less numerous than I thought, have come to this podium to contest the advisability and the effectiveness of the *loi cadre*.

On the contrary, I believe, and I express the profound conviction that the *loi cadre* comes at a propitious moment, that its adoption is imperative, that its effectiveness will be certain if the conditions of its passage make it a positive act, clearly translating the will of France.

At the same time that we are carrying on the struggle into which we have been forced . . . we have tried to do constructive work. Our double concern has been, first to lead the Moslems to the point where they can manage their own affairs. Then, we have wanted to create institutions of administrative autonomy, and concrete conditions which will permit the representatives of all the Algerian populations to fix, in agreement with the French parliament, the status of a new Algeria within the framework of the French republic. . . .

But isn't it too early for this vote, certain people will say? Order has not yet been entirely re-established; what good will it do to construct texts that you won't be able to apply for a long time?

I understand the objection, but all the same I should like to say that for several months, after a long period of getting started, the Algerian situation has been improving every day, in spite of the foreign effort. . . .

The moment has come, mesdames, messieurs, to consecrate this work with the *loi cadre* and to develop all that it contains in germ on the legal level for the Algerian future. . . .

The Army has the right to know for what sort of Algerian future it is fighting. The French Algerians have the right to demand that the capital's irresolution end. The French Moslems have the right to be confirmed in the confidence that they have given us, with daily risk to their lives.

This is true (*applause from the left*), and it is the objective of the *loi cadre*.

In any case, I am afraid, if the *loi cadre* is not passed, that Moslem opinion as well as international opinion will see the mark of a selfish and negative attitude on the part of France. . . . We must therefore pass the *loi cadre*. But what are its principles? . . .

First, we wish to maintain indissoluble bonds between France and Algeria. That means that Algeria is an integral part of the French Republic, that all Algerians are French citizens, that the Algerian populations participate in the exercise of national sovereignty through the intermediary of their elected representatives in the constitutional assemblies of the Republic.

It means that the attributes of sovereignty in Algeria are possessed by the Republic and that a group of functions, supposedly of sovereignty, are in the exclusive jurisdiction of the Republic. . . .

The second principle to which we must answer: that of equality of rights. To say that all Algerians are French citizens means that they are equal in rights, and especially in political rights. That assumes that we have accepted the suppression of the privilege of representation that has existed until now: . . . that assumes therefore . . . the institution of a single college. . . .

We understand that the Europeans in Algeria . . . are afraid of being submerged beneath the wave [of Moslems] and of losing their homeland. But . . . democracy is not the crushing of minorities, and the present project guarantees an equitable and obligatory representation of the diverse communities at every level.

Mesdames, messieurs, then we must organize recognition of the Algerian personality. Too many people have confused, and still confuse the Algerian personality with Algerian unity, an organic and monolithic unity. In fact, Algeria's dominant characteristic is diversity. It is a country which presents the aspect of a true patchwork of political, geographical and ethnic entities. . . .

We are, therefore, driven to organize Algeria as a union of distinct territories to which it will be convenient to give the maximum administrative autonomy to permit them to affirm their own personality and to cooperate to the best of their abilities in the common task. It has been provided in the law that the assemblies of these territories will have the possibility . . . of forming a federative assembly, . . . which . . . will give, in fact, a representation to minorities more important than they could have had under any other system. . . .

Another principle is that of arbitration. In order to assure the coexistence, the free development of these distinct communities, we thought that it would be good to install a new device, an arbitration court which would hand down decisions . . . on every appeal against arbitrary discriminatory measures sent to it.

Finally, mesdames, messieurs, the last principle which must be satisfied is the following: the *loi cadre* that we are about to vote on must not be a unilateral act, in spite of the sovereignty of the French parliament; it should not constitute an imposed statute, and it is for that reason that it guarantees the possible evolution of Algerian institutions.

M. Tixier-Vignancour (N.-I.): Toward independence.

M. Lacoste: The French parliament will decide, M. Tixier-Vignancour. . . .

M. Tixier-Vignancour (N.-I.): It's a mechanism for independence.

M. Lacoste: The mechanism that I have described, M. Tixier-Vignancour, is very precise. It carries in itself all the desirable guarantees and at the same time it gives the Algerians the certainty that the *loi cadre* that we are going to pass is not an imposed statute. . . .

My dear colleagues, . . . if this *loi cadre* receives your massive approval, it will become a powerful trump in our hand. It will permit us to say that France knows what she wants, that she has just committed a deed of national will. We can tell our people that we know where we're going and just how far we're committing ourselves. We can tell the Algerians in complete good faith that we are taking on obligations for the Republic and for them. We can tell international opinion that all the reproaches that were made to us were baseless, and that we need no one's advice to decide for ourselves what Algeria, that is to say, France, will be tomorrow. (*Applause on the left and on numerous benches in the center.*)

[Nine more orators spoke in the general discussion before the session was adjourned at 11:25 P.M. after a decision to begin discussion the following day on individual articles. The morning session of September 27 was consumed in parliamentary maneuvers by opponents of the bill endeavoring to amend it or to defer action on it. At the outset of the afternoon session the following exchange took place.]

M. Jacques Isorni (I.P.A.S.): I rise to a point of order.

The Presiding Officer: M. Isorni is recognized to make a point of order.

M. Isorni (I.P.A.S.): My dear colleagues, during the sitting this morning, the Assembly decided to defer action on the articles which had been read, as well as on the amendments which relate to them.

In the name of my group, I ask that the Assembly vote by ballot, now, on the amendments which have been submitted. Indeed, we fear that the Prime Minister is going to put the question of confidence immediately, which would end the debate.

If it is true that the general discussion took place, it is equally true that the true prerogative of the parliamentarian is his right of amendment, which permits him to discuss the law.

M. Cot (R.P.): Very good!

M. Marcel Bouger (U.F.F.): Exactly!

M. Isorni (I.P.A.S.): Furthermore, if the question of confidence is put immediately, there will be no debate before Monday, and thus we shall not know the government's opinion on the grave news that the United States and Italy have decided to deliver arms to Tunisia. . . . Now, it is not admissible that the Assembly adjourn without knowing . . . if Italy is going to deliver to Tunisia, weapons which will be turned against us, and if supported by the United States, she is not again on the point of knifing us in the back, but this time with the knife in the hands of Christian democracy. (*Applause on the right and on the extreme right.*)

5. *Question of Confidence.*

M. MAURICE BOURGÈS-MAUNOURY, PRIME MINISTER: I ask for the floor.

THE PRESIDING OFFICER: The Prime Minister has the floor.

THE PRIME MINISTER: Mesdames, messieurs, in answer to M. Isorni, I maintain the terms of the so-called denial that I made yesterday. Besides, as far as I know, I am only responsible for the French Government.

The debate this morning, showed that the government bill under discussion was a single entity, a whole, that it was difficult to defer action on an article or an amendment without deferring action on them all and that it was awkward to alter this equilibrium without detracting from the entire project. . . .

I am sure that the Assembly has understood the great national argument that can be drawn from the vote of a substantial majority.

I do not think, and I assume all responsibility, that more ample discussion can enlarge the majority that so many of us want.

I shall have to answer many criticisms which have already been expressed in this hall, but right now, I think I must pose the question of confidence.

Therefore, I pose the question of confidence for the adoption of articles 1 to 27 of the initial bill, completed by the clarifying letter, modified by M. Paul Coste-Floret's amendment No. 1, second rectification to article 1, M. Guy Petit's amendment No. 13, rectified to articles 7, 9, 10, 11, 12, 18, 22, and 23 by M. Brocas' amendments No. 34 and 35 to articles 5 and 25, and by M. Cayeux's amendment No. 32 rectified and completed by M. Paul Coste-Floret's sub-amendment No. 36 rectified to article 24, and against all motions, all other amendments and all additional articles, as well as on the entire government bill. (*Lively protests on the extreme right and on numerous benches on the right.*)

On the extreme right: Dictatorship!

M. JEAN BERTHOMMIER (U.F.F.): You're not permitting discussion in parliament. That's Fascism! . . .

PRESIDING OFFICER: I take note that in the terms of article 46 of the Constitution, the vote on the question of confidence can be taken not less than twenty-four hours after it has been posed to the Assembly.[14] On what day does the Assembly wish to proceed with this vote?

[14] Actually, the constitution stipulated that "one clear day" had to elapse between the day on which the question of confidence was posed and the day on which the vote was taken.

On several benches: Monday!
On the extreme left: Saturday! . . .
[The National Assembly voted 300 to 245 to schedule the vote of
confidence for Monday, September 30, 1957. There were two sittings
on Monday, during which, several groups explained their votes.]

6. *Explanations and Voting. Third Sitting, Monday,*
September 30, 1957.

M. Guy Petit (I.P.A.S.): I only ask you for several minutes of
patience, and for the opportunity of expressing my thought to its
end. My intervention will be much shorter—I assure you—if you will,
please not demonstrate.

If, hostile to the *loi cadre* in its present form, because the question
of confidence was put prematurely, and because the discussion on
amendments was not brought to its natural conclusion, we were to
drop hostile ballots in the urn—for I speak here, not only in my name,
but in the name of a certain number of my friends—we know that we
would open a power vacuum and there are many of us here who do
not know how it will end. . . .

If we decide to finish it off this evening, we do not know what
could happen tomorrow but there is a danger that it will be particularly
grave.

M. Prime Minister, even though we are hostile to the law as you
presented it—

M. Duclos (C.): You're going to vote for it even so. That's what
you're going to say. (*Laughs on the extreme left.*)

M. Petit (I.P.A.S.): —we think that this law should be examined
by the Council of the Republic with all care and wisdom.

The Council of the Republic, which is not held to a calendar, could
attach amendments to it which we are certain would be maturely
studied, since that Assembly has the advantage of Algerian representation, while here we have none.

The day when the text would come back to us, M. Prime Minister,
amended by the Council of the Republic in the way that we want,
if then you decide to pose the question of confidence to remove the
amendments that the Council of the Republic has judged useful to
introduce, then, whether you pose the question of confidence or not
we will vote resolutely against. (*Laughs on the extreme left. Exclamations on the extreme right.*)

Mesdames, messieurs, I terminate, declaring that it is unfortunate
that such a grave affair cannot be discussed seriously here. . . .

Mme Jeanette Prin (C.): You're the one who's not serious.

M. Duclos (C.): You're putting on a music-hall number.

The Presiding Officer: No one else wants the floor? . . .

I am going to put the question of confidence to the vote, by ballot
at the tribune. . . .

I invite our colleagues to hand a single blue or white ballot to the secretary tending the urn.

I indicate also, that in the terms of article 10 of general instructions to the bureau, every deputy is permitted to hand a written note, legibly signed to the same secretary, indicating his voluntary abstention.

I am going to draw the letter by which the roll call will begin.

(*The letter "R" is drawn.*)

The ballot is open. . . .

(*The roll-call takes place. The vote is opened at 9:20* P.M.)

The roll-call is over. . . .

No one else wants to vote?

The ballot is closed.

(*The vote is closed at 10:20* P.M.)

The votes will be counted. . . .

Here, after verification, is the result of the vote on the question of confidence.

> Number of voters 532
> Constitutional majority required to
> refuse confidence 298
> For adoption 253
> Against 279

In conformity with the third paragraph of article 89 of the constitution, confidence has not been refused to the cabinet, but in terms of the 3rd paragraph of article 89 of the rules, the entirety of the projected law on the institution of Algeria is not adopted.

Though the government was not constitutionally required to resign, it conformed to the well-established practice in the Fourth Republic of refusing to remain in office after defeat on a major policy vote. It resigned at once.

THE GAILLARD BILL

Investiture and Redrafting

That resignation opened a government crisis of more than a month that ended with the investiture of M. Félix Gaillard, youthful Radical Finance Minister in the Bourgès government. The investiture debate on the Gaillard government lasted about five hours and forty-five minutes. Approximately thirty-four minutes (that is, less than 10 per cent of the time) was spent discussing the *loi cadre*, or French policy in Algeria, in a more general way. Gaillard promised to prepare a new *loi cadre* incorporating most of the principles of the previous version, but defining the electoral provisions in a separate bill.[15]

The Gaillard government was invested by a vote of 337 to 173. Less than three weeks later it submitted a new *loi cadre*. The new bill was a clear retreat from the previous one.[16]

The influence of the Assembly on the bill is obvious. To win the support of right-wing deputies who had opposed the Bourgès-Maunoury project, Gaillard increased the "guarantees" to the European community and, consequently, trimmed the political wings of the Moslems. Furthermore, his amendments dealt with the provisions that had been most criticized by the right during the first debate. Finally, again in response to right-wing pressure, the law was not to go into effect until after the restoration of "calm" in Algeria.

Passage of the Bill

The Interior Committee made amendments that were self-contradictory. On the one hand, they liberalized it by striking out the phrase that limited the federative organs to "coordinating" functions and by providing that the federative council and the territorial assemblies would have executives. On the other hand, they rendered the creation of the federative organs more difficult by requiring that all the territories, rather than a simple majority of them, adhere before the federative organs could be established. Some of the territories were expected to have European majorities. This gave the Europeans, in effect, a veto over establishment of the federative organs.

The debate in the National Assembly was largely a repetition of the one of September. Most of the speakers repeated their earlier arguments. By invoking questions of confidence, Gaillard obtained passage of both bills without further amendment. On November 29 the *loi cadre* was passed, 269 to 200, and the electoral law was passed, 267 to 200. The opposition was composed of 132 Communists, 26 Poujadists, and 42 rightwing Radicals and Conservatives. The Council of the Republic concurred

---

[15] For the text of this part of the address, see p. 88 above.

[16] For a detailed description of the new bill see pp. 88-89 above. See also *LM*, November 19 and 20, 1957.

and, with the publication of the law in the *Journal officiel* on February 5, 1958, France for the first time since 1947 had significant new legislation for Algeria. Three months later the Fourth Republic collapsed.

THE LEGISLATIVE ROLE OF THE NATIONAL ASSEMBLY

During the more than three and a half years that the Fourth Republic was faced by the Algerian insurrection, the National Assembly initiated no significant legislation to solve it and delegated most of its legislative competence over Algerian security, economic, social, and administrative matters to the cabinet. Only in the realm of constitutional matters (the organization of the political branches of government and the electoral system) did the Assembly deal with substantive legislation.

In that area the influence of the National Assembly was determining. Not only was the initial bill undoubtedly drafted with regard for the views of the majority of the members of the Assembly, but also it was transformed to bring it more in line with prevailing opinion in the Assembly before it was finally enacted. This transformation was effected by the Bourgès cabinet after its initial bout with the Assembly's Interior Committee and the round-table conference, by the Assembly in plenary session acting on the Bourgès bill, by the Gaillard cabinet acting in the light of the Bourgès-Maunoury experience, and by the Interior Committee during its consideration of the Gaillard bill. The hand of the Assembly was heavy and served as a conservative restraint on the cabinet. Its direct legislative influence was negative, tending to the preservation of the Algerian status quo.

The role of the Fourth Republic's National Assembly in the formation of Algerian policy was not, however, limited to direct legislative action. Its power to make and unmake governments gave it even more influence over Algerian policy than did its legislative power. Despite the efforts of the framers of the 1946 constitution to ensure eighteen months' tenure to most governments through an effective power of dissolution, the Assembly was, in practice, able to overthrow a government at almost any time and did so. Governments knew this and acted accordingly.

If more deputies opposed its personnel, promises, policies, or performance than favored them, the government fell. This danger kept governments in line. As the gravity of the Algerian situation deepened, it assumed a greater place in the preoccupations of the deputies. Their reaction to Algerian policy became increasingly decisive in determining their attitude toward the government. This attitude found clearest expression in the sixteen debates directly and exclusively concerned with general North African or purely Algerian questions between November 1, 1954 and de Gaulle's return to power. But during that period the deputies also manifested their Algerian views fully in nine investiture debates and in two debates on general governmental policy that were dominated by the Algerian question. Furthermore, their opinions and votes on other questions were probably influenced by their feelings toward the government's handling of the Algerian question.

Life is no less complicated in a so-called strong parliament regime than in the world at large. The factors influencing the statements and voting of a deputy cannot be identified or measured with accuracy and precision. But, in any case, in the forty-three months that Fourth Republic governments were wrestling with the Algerian insurrection, premiers or premiers-designate were compelled to defend themselves before the National Assembly in no fewer than twenty-seven debates devoted exclusively or primarily to Algeria.[17] In each of them the life of the government was at stake, for they were all followed by votes of confidence. As a result of the Assembly voting after those debates three governments fell and three others were refused investiture.

Obviously, then, the Assembly was not shy about calling governments to account if it found their Algerian policies unsatisfactory, and the governments, accepting its authority, adjusted their policies to its desires. They attempted to conduct their policies so as to offend as few of the members of their majorities as possible and to avoid giving oratorical ammunition to their enemies.

In initiating legislation, then, the Assembly was ineffective. On the other hand, indirectly through its power to defeat gov-

[17] Fifteen during the last fourteen months of the regime.

ernmental legislative proposals and to remove governments from office it was able to control Algerian policy closely.

The National Assembly of the Fourth Republic was divisive and irresponsible, but it was also a reasonably accurate reflection of the political views of the nation. The struggles over policy that wracked the Assembly represented the disagreements in the nation. Through elections that gave the voters authentic opportunities to express political preferences, the French people produced an Assembly in whose work was involved their own responsibility. The Assembly, in turn, exercised such close and effective control over the executive that it was clearly responsible for governmental policy. The faults of the Fourth Republic Assembly arose from its being too responsive, too representative of a divided nation, involved too continuously in the formation of governmental policy. It had power that could not be exercised decisively by any large assembly, much less an assembly that was both large and badly fragmented, still less an assembly faced by a problem of the proportions of the Algerian dilemma. Paralyzed, it made policy that was not policy, that had form but not content, that sought to attain contradictory objectives by making promises that might be fulfilled it knew not when. Furious battles were waged over trifling semantics in statutes that were stillborn or expired quickly from neglect. In short, the weaknesses of the National Assembly were the weaknesses of the nation it represented too well.

8

The Legislature:
The National Assembly
of the Fifth Republic

CONSTITUTIONAL LIMITATIONS

THOUGH THE National Assembly of the Fifth Republic bears the same name as the legislature of the Fourth Republic, it is quite a different animal. Its predecessor roamed the political wilds devouring hapless governments with greedy abandon, but the present beast has been confined in a narrow constitutional cage where it cowers, growling and snarling in frustration under the whip of a stern master. It still goes through the motions it acquired by habit and instinct, but knows full well that its sound and fury signify nothing. Only time can tell how long the beast will remain caged.

The 1946 constitution conferred all legislative power on parliament. Its successor enumerates a limited, though important, list of subjects which may be regulated, except during emergencies, only by laws enacted by parliament or by decrees issued by the government under authorization of a specific grant of power from parliament. All powers not enumerated are reserved to the government, which has meant, in effect, the president of the Republic. Among the subjects within the jurisdiction of parliament are "the electoral systems for the houses of parliament and the local councils" and "the fundamental principles . . . of the free administration of local communities, of their power, and of their resources." Therefore, it seems reasonable to assume that the 1957 *loi cadre*—the only significant Algerian legislation enacted by the Fourth Republic's National

Assembly after 1954—would have required parliamentary action under the 1958 constitution.

Besides limiting the scope of jurisdiction of parliament, the 1958 constitution prescribes legislative procedures in a way that gives cabinets certain advantages that they did not have under the old regime. For instance, the government's text of a bill rather than the committee version serves as the basis of discussion on the floor of the chamber. Thus, the Gaillard government would have been defending its bills rather than the revised committee bills with its questions of confidence in November 1957. The clause permitting the cabinet to require consideration by large, nonspecialized parliamentary committees also tends to strengthen the government at the expense of the Assembly, for small, specialized, standing committees are the most effective instrument of a parliament in legislating.

The new text permits the cabinet to compel the Assembly to pass judgment on its proposal without Assembly amendments, but the same result was obtained by Gaillard through invoking a confidence vote.

Of greater import is the new mechanism by which the Assembly may dismiss a government. Formerly if a government feared that an important bill faced defeat, it posed a question of confidence, saying, in effect, that it would resign if the bill were defeated. Though a government was not constitutionally compelled to resign unless hostile votes were cast by a majority of the sitting members, almost invariably they quit even when, because of abstentions, there was only a hostile majority of voting members. Now, if the government declares a bill urgent it is considered adopted without vote unless a motion of censure, introduced within twenty-four hours, attracts the votes of a majority of the sitting members. Votes opposing the motion and abstentions are not recorded so there is no relative majority. The Bourgès-Maunoury government would have survived under this arrangement though the Mendès-France and Gaillard governments would not have.

The constitution also seeks to render less likely the irresponsible dismissal of cabinets by making it possible for the president of the Republic to punish parliament by dissolving it. This power may be exercised only once in any twelve-month period, however, which makes it less attractive. A president who does not get a completely amenable Assembly on the first try might find twelve months a long time to struggle against recalcitrant deputies.

ALGERIAN POLICY BEFORE THE ASSEMBLY

During the first three years after de Gaulle's return to power as last premier of the Fourth Republic, the Assembly debated Algerian policy on seven occasions.[1] The first two debates (on de Gaulle's investiture and on the renewal of the special powers originally granted to Mollet) occurred under the old constitution. In both cases, the question of Algerian policy was eclipsed by the controversy over the *coup* of May 13 and the emerging new regime, though it was closely related to both these questions. In the first twenty-nine months after the new institutions were set into operation in January 1959, there were only five Assembly debates treating Algeria to any substantial extent.

The new constitution does not require that prime ministers obtain the investiture of parliament, though they may be removed by the National Assembly. Nevertheless, in an obvious move to demonstrate the parliamentary character of the Gaullist system, M. Debré made a declaration of policy, followed by a debate and a division of the house, when he was appointed premier in January 1959. In June the debate on the government's currency reforms and budget for Algeria was broadened by the speakers to deal with Algerian policy in general. The Premier's general policy declaration of October 13 also became the occasion for a debate concentrating on Algerian policy, though no division followed.

After the settlers' revolt of January 1960, the government convoked parliament in a special session at 5 P.M. February 3, and requested authorization to "take by ordinances, in the conditions stipulated by article 38 of the constitution,[2] certain measures relative to the maintenance of order, to the security of the

---

[1] Not included is a very insipid discussion of social policies in the Sahara departments in May 1961.

[2] "Art. 38. The government may for the implementation of its program, request of Parliament authorization to take by ordinance, during a limited period of time, measures which are normally in the domain of law.

"Ordinances shall be enacted in the Council of Ministers with the advice

State, to the pacification and to the administration of Algeria"
until April 1, 1961.[3] After the Prime Minister's declaration, the
Assembly recessed from 6 P.M. until 9 P.M., while the Committee on Constitutional Laws questioned the Prime Minister
and discussed the request. The committee recommended five
amendments to define the powers more closely, but the Prime
Minister rejected three. He accepted one that required the
signature of the president of the Republic to all ordinances
issued by virtue of the law and one that would terminate the
powers with the end of the Debré ministry. The bill was passed
in that form by a massive majority.

DEBATE ON SELF-DETERMINATION

The only debate expressly devoted to general Algerian policy
during the three years in question took place in December 1960.
It followed a declaration by the Premier, but was not terminated
by a division. Therefore, the government's life was not at stake.
Coming some three months after de Gaulle's promise of self-
determination for Algeria, it afforded the colonialist wing of the
Assembly its first opportunity to vent its anger at de Gaulle's
"betrayal" of May 13.

Excerpts from the Premier's declaration and the debate follow:

Organizing the Debate

THE PRESIDING OFFICER M. JACQUES CHABAN-DELMAS (U.N.R.):
The agenda calls for a declaration by M. the Prime Minister on
Algeria and a debate on this declaration.

[The President of the Assembly then announced a time distribution
similar to that of the 1957 debate. See pp. 140-141 above.]

M. the Prime Minister has the floor. (*Applause on the left and in
the center.*)

Declaration by the Premier

M. MICHEL DEBRÉ, PRIME MINISTER: The debate which is opening
today in the National Assembly has, mesdames, messieurs, and

---

of the Council of State. They shall take effect upon publication but shall become null and void if the Government bill for ratification is not submitted to
Parliament before the date set by the enabling act. . . ."

[3] The text was published in *LM*, February 3, 1960.

deputies, a special character. In conformity with article 11 of the constitution, a government bill will soon be submitted to referendum.

The purpose of this bill . . . is double. It is, on the one hand, to obtain solemn approval for the principle of self-determination when security has returned to the Algerian departments; it is, on the other hand. . . . to provide for a decentralized organization of the political branches of government in Algeria.

The government bill has not yet been drafted. The government, in fact, has arranged to have a debate in the National Assembly precede its deliberation on the bill in order that it may take into account observations or suggestions which are presented to it in the course of the discussion. (*Exclamations on the right. Applause on the left and in the center.*)

M. JEAN LEGENDRE: That's making fun of everyone!

[M. Debré then reviews the evolution of the Algerian situation under the de Gaulle regime and the achievements of the government. It is now time, he says, to prepare for the Algerian self-determination announced by de Gaulle on September 16, 1959.]

It has seemed necessary to the President of the Republic and to the government to call on all French citizens, in the motherland as in Algeria, to confirm in the most solemn manner that such is the commitment by France and the objective of French policy.

When security has been re-established, the Algerians . . . will be called upon to decide their destiny. I can no more today than in October 1959 specify the means of a solemn consultation of which the date can be set, of which the organization can be defined, only after the time necessary, not only for security to be re-established, but in order that the appeasement of troubled spirits may be well under way. As was said in October 1959 the determination of these means will, moreover, be preceded by a discussion among all the Algerian factions that will participate and by a debate in parliament. But the main lines have been set. As General de Gaulle said in September 1959: ". . . three solutions will be the object of the consultation." They are secession, frenchification, and the governing of Algeria by Algerians supported by the aid of France and in close union with her. (*Murmurs on various benches on the right and the center right.*) . . .

This consultation will take place freely. French authority with all its means will assure public order and oversee the conduct of the balloting. No pressure on the voters will be tolerated, no impediment to the presence of observers from the entire world will be raised.

In any case—that is, whichever option is generally accepted—the rights and the interests of those who wish to remain French citizens will be safeguarded. (*Applause on the left and in the center.*)

(*Numerous voices in the center right and on the right*): How?

M. JEAN LEGENDRE: That was already said to the French of Tunisia and Morocco. We know what has happened to them!

M. HENRY DUVILLARD: You come here, M. Legendre, only to cause trouble. Otherwise, we never see you!

THE PRESIDING OFFICER: Please, my dear colleagues do not interrupt M. the Prime Minister.

THE PRIME MINISTER: . . . The necessary measures—

(*Numerous voices in the center right and on the right*): Which ones?

THE PRIME MINISTER: —will, if necessary, be taken toward this end as will also be taken . . . the measures indispensable for the respect of the interests of France. Regrouping—that is, partition—would be a rending from which everyone would suffer. (*Interruptions on the center and on the right.*)

M. EDOUARD BOICOURT: At least have the courtesy to listen!

THE PRIME MINISTER: . . . The problem which is now presented is that of knowing if . . . it is better to wait without moving toward the hour of self-determination. We do not think so. It is better, on the contrary, to give to the Algerian people, and in particular to the population of Moslem origin, the possibility of an Algeria run by Algerians—

M. JEAN-MARIE LE PEN: You do not have the right to do it! (*Protest on the left and in the center.*)

THE PRIME MINISTER: —and at the same time united to France. That is why the government bill— (*Interruptions on the right.*)

M. PIERRE PORTOLANO: M. The Prime Minister, I ask your permission to interrupt. (*Protests on the left and in the center.*)

M. MICHEL HABIB-DELONCLE: Sign up for the debate.

M. LE PEN: Those are falsehoods, intolerable to hear.

THE PRIME MINISTER: I said that thus the bill submitted to the referendum will contain a second article by which the government will ask for the powers necessary to [reorganize] . . . the political organs of government in Algeria, a reorganization that will naturally be provisional since any permanent organization depends on the results of the self-determination consultation.

M. LE PEN: You don't have the right. (*Interruptions on the left and in the center.*)

THE PRESIDING OFFICER: M. Le Pen, you are to take part in the debate. For the moment, I ask you to be still. (*Applause on the left and in the center.*)

M. DUVILLARD: If the Prime Minister cannot speak, no one will speak after him.

THE PRIME MINISTER: This provisional organization rests on three principles, which it seems suitable to indicate in the bill.

The first principle is the management of the Algerians' own affairs by Algerian organs of deliberation and execution responsible, some for the entire Algerian territory, others for determinate regions. This organization does not impair the sovereignty of the Republic, whose representative has charge of the national interests. But, on new bases, according to new structures, the citizens of Algeria will have charge of the direction of the affairs of their regions and of the territory.

The second principle is the necessity of assuring not only . . . the coexistence of the communities, that is, guarantees for each of them, but also the institutional participation of the communities in the common management of the Algerian affairs in the regions as in the territory.

The third principle is the organization of the collaboration between mainlanders and Algerians by common organisms for the areas of activity in which the motherland aids Algeria.

On the basis of the law, if it is adopted by the nation, the implementation of these three principles will be determined by decrees in the Council of Ministers. . . .

Mesdames, messieurs, we are ready for peace. We are ready for self-determination. But we will not surrender and we will not wait. We will not surrender to movements which threaten to plunge Algeria into irreparable misfortune. We will not wait to pursue the political, economic, and social development of Algeria, work to which only France can contribute fraternally, but which requires two conditions: the accord of the Algerians, of all the Algerians, and the accord of the mainlanders.

The referendum, of which this debate is the preface, has as its objective to obtain this accord. (*Applause on the left, in the center, and on several benches on the right.*) . . .

M. Arrighi, ex-Gaullist

THE PRESIDING OFFICER: M. Arrighi has the floor. (*Applause in the center right and on several benches on the right.*)

M. PASCAL ARRIGHI: M. the President, mesdames, messieurs, by endeavoring to proceed to a serious and closely reasoned analysis of the Algerian events, the declarations which concern it, the choices that are proposed to us, I would like to indicate first of all my desire to take part without passion, with the sole concern of seeking where the truth lies in the facts, attitudes, and decisions which, all of us feel, cannot leave us without real disquiet. Knowing your divergences, your various leanings, my aim is to be less polemical than analytical, more perhaps to induce reflection than to try to convince.

It is already fourteen months since the Assembly . . . discussed the Algerian problem. By the will of its majority and the tacit consent of a great part of the opposition, the governmental authorities have had a free hand. The authority, the means for which they asked in order to settle the Algerian problem, was neither measured nor bargained over. The chairmen's conference even refused to inscribe on the Assembly's agenda an oral question that the chairman of our group had posed last June 22 to the government and in which it asked what difference existed between Algerian Algeria and secession. No attempt to give an answer, even partial, was made.

During more than a year, we have debated the problems of agriculture, of the Community, of the budget. But we have never stopped thinking that one problem dominates and crushes all the others, that of Algeria. Yet, Algeria has remained outside our discussion. . . . Algerian policy has been formulated outside parliament and even outside the cabinet; on the other hand, this policy has undergone an evolution which has now led in a direction that many of us believe is dangerous and perhaps mortal.

That this policy has been formulated outside parliament and the government is most obvious. . . . The President of our Assembly has indicated . . . that this Algerian policy appertained to the domain reserved [to the government]. Constitutionally speaking, parliament and especially the National Assembly know only the government. We know that it is not alone in question and we cannot avoid—no matter how reserved we are now, how carefully we do it—citing the declarations of the highest authority of the State [President de Gaulle.]

Parliament and the groups that compose it have had no part in these declarations; indeed, it has often happened that the government itself has been kept ignorant of the decisions that these declarations implied . . .

[For] example: the last declaration was recorded and had arrived in Algeria—it was therefore definitive—even before the government met on Friday, November 4 at 4 P.M., even before knowledge of it had been given to the ministers. Article 20 of the Constitution declares, however: "The Government determines and conducts the policy of the nation." This constitutional principle has not been respected. . . .

[Another] example: a minister of state charged with Algerian affairs was designated on November 22 . . . and since his nomination, unofficial reports and the press, all in agreement, have informed us that in the future Algerian policy appertains only to the President of the Republic and the Minister of State and last Sunday a decree countersigned by M. Michel Debré confirmed that this policy has escaped the jurisdiction of the Prime Minister. (*Diverse movements.*)

Thus, since Algerian policy is determined at the highest level and since the Assembly must not vote after this debate, it is clear the government no longer plays a part in the elaboration of Algerian policy and that parliament no longer has a part in approving it. . . .

Two propositions . . . will form two parts of my speech. . . . First proposition: the declaration of September 16, 1959 has been modified; it leads to an Algerian republic. Second proposition: the Algerian republic means the republic of the F.L.N. oriented toward the East.

But then, a question comes to mind: Could this be avoided? I will try to reply to that question in the third part of my remarks. . . .

[M. Arrighi elaborated his propositions and answered his question affirmatively, though he advanced no positive suggestions on how

Algeria could be kept French except that it required a firm will by the government. On the whole, the speech was quite dispassionate, was interrupted by applause only occasionally and even more rarely by hostile comments.

M. René Moatti, another right-wing opposition deputy and former Gaullist, followed M. Arrighi and made similar allegations that de Gaulle had usurped the constitutional prerogatives of parliament and the government. To this he added the observation that the device of the referendum was also being used in an unconstitutional way to erode the authority of parliament. M. Moatti announced at the conclusion of his speech that he had promised during the election campaign to resign if he found that he could not support de Gaulle on an important policy question, that he now disagreed with him on Algeria, would resign, and run for re-election in the by-election to fill his vacancy.[4]]

A Lively Moment

[For the most part, debate proceeds with greater calm, or perhaps one should say lassitude, than it did under the Fourth Republic and the Algerian debate of December 1960 was not an exception, especially in view of the importance of the subject and the length of time since the deputies had last been able to express their views on it in the chamber. Nevertheless, there were occasional bursts of passion such as this incident:]

M. Henri Tremolet de Villers: . . . We are committed not only because we do not wish to deceive our voters, but also, beyond that, because we bear a responsibility for the destiny of France.

This entire destiny is at stake in Algeria and the plebiscite is a proof of it. I do not know if we will run risks and it matters little. I do not believe, however, that they are so great, for France is not decadent and only her leaders may be [*peuvent être*] old, tired, and sad. But your proposal endangers France and, with her, peace and liberty. (*Lively interruptions on the left and in the center.*)

I said, "*peuvent être*"! (*New, prolonged interruptions on the same benches. Banging of desk tops.*)

The Presiding Officer: M. Tremolet de Villers, I ask you—

M. Cerf Lurie: It is inadmissible to speak thus!

M. Tremolet de Villers: M. the President—

M. Georges Bourriquet: You are a dreadful person. And you supported a certain marshal [5] don't forget!

[4] M. Moatti was badly defeated in the by-election, June 4, 1961, running fourth and polling 13.5 per cent of the votes in the first round and withdrawing before the second round. His Gaullist opponent, M. Kasperit, won the seat with 39 per cent of the vote on the first ballot. *LM*, June 6, 13, 1961.

[5] A reference to Marshal Petain, who was 84 when he became head of the wartime French State, the "Vichy" regime.

M. Tremolet de Villers: You are not even listening! (*Desk tops bang on the left and in the center.*)

M. André Fanton: He should get out!

M. Bourriquet: He should leave the tribune! It's scandalous!

The Presiding Officer: Will the Assembly permit me to speak. M. Tremolet de Villers, I really think that the Assembly, as I, has shown a very great mildness toward you. (*Applause on the left and in the center.*)

The Presiding Officer: For the second time, as far as I am concerned, I asked you to measure your words.

M. Henri Caillemer: That's what he did.

The Presiding Officer: I think I did it with enough courtesy to hope that my observations would be heard. I regret noting that, despite these repeated appeals, nothing has been changed in certain of your expressions, I do not say in your comportment or in your attitude. I am therefore, obliged to ask you, on the one hand, to withdraw the last two expressions that you used when you described those who have charge of conducting French policy at present, on the other hand, after you have withdrawn those expressions, to conclude immediately, your speaking time, after all, having been used up. (*Applause on the left, in the center and on various benches.*)

I do not seek applause. I wish that what I have just asked for be done.

M. Tremolet de Villers: Permit me to point out to you, M. the President, that if my speaking time is used up, it really is not my fault.

The Presiding Officer: I have taken that into account. I know what I'm saying.

M. Tremolet de Villers: I will repeat, if you wish, what I said. (*Lively, prolonged interruptions on the left and in the center. Banging of desk tops.*)

Well, then, I express the wish that France, which I said is not decadent, may have young, dynamic leaders who will lead her to victory. (*Lively prolonged interruptions on the left and in the center. Applause in right center.*)

The Presiding Officer: It is not through an evasion that this incident can be settled—

M. Tremolet de Villers: That's not an evasion, M. the President. I find it extraordinary—

The Presiding Officer: Let me speak, please!

I do not intend to brandish the whip of a certain article in the rules, although I could very well do it. It is not through an evasion— I repeat the expression—that this incident can be settled, I expressly asked you to declare that you withdraw the expression that you used a moment ago.

M. Tremolet de Villers: But M. the President—

The Presiding Officer: After which, I asked you to conclude immediately.

M. Tremolet de Villers: I will conclude.

The Presiding Officer: No! I asked for two things that I invite you to do! if you don't do them I shall feel obliged to tell you that your words will not appear in the *Journal officiel* and to suspend the sitting.

M. Tremont de Villers: M. the President, we obviously understand each other very poorly and probably— (*Interruptions on the left and in the center.*)

The Presiding Officer: I understand what I say, believe me.

M. Tremolet de Villers: Let me explain myself; if everyone talks, I cannot.

I did not at all say that France had old, tired, and sad leaders. (*Lively and prolonged interruptions on the left and in the center. The members of the government leave the chamber.*)

Mesdames, messieurs, if you don't listen to me, don't judge me!

I said that France is not decadent and that only her leaders could be [*pourraient être*] old. (*No! No! on the left and in the center. Desk lids bang.*)

The Presiding Officer: I did not hear the conditional.

M. Bourriquet: M. Tremolet de Villers, you should be ashamed of those words. We have not fought for years in order to hear that today.

The Presiding Officer: Twice I invited the speaker, on the one hand, to withdraw certain expressions, spoken by him, on the other hand, to conclude. He has not deferred to the request of the President!

M. Tremolet de Villers: I cannot admit that I said an insult that I did not make!

The Presiding Officer: Under those conditions, I am going to suspend the sitting. (*Applause on the left and in the center. Diverse movements.*) The rest of the debate is deferred until the next sitting . . .

[M. Waldeck-Rochet, Communist group spokesman, succeeded M. Tremolet de Villers to the tribune. The attitude of the Assembly was in sharp contrast to the previous incident as well as to the usual reception given Communist speakers in the Fourth Republic. He was heard in complete silence without a single interruption, neither applause from his nine party colleagues nor heckling from his other listeners.]

The Minister for Algeria and the Premier

[The debate was terminated shortly before 8:00 the next morning with statements by M. Louis Joxe and by the Prime Minister.]

M. Louis Joxe, Minister of State Charged with Algerian Affairs: M. the President, mesdames, messieurs, at this uncertain hour of the night, or of the day—

M. Jean-Baptiste Biaggi: It is the image of your policy!

M. Joxe: —I will not speak long, but I must give some explanations to those who have preceded me, at the end of a debate which has lasted nearly twenty hours. You will excuse me if I do not answer each of the speakers individually, since, indeed, they have, for the most part, disappeared. (*Light laughter.*) I will content myself, therefore, with bringing together a certain amount of information, of arguments, of details about the theme of this debate.

Well, after all, what does it concern? It concerns two questions which will be posed soon to the nation, one concerning self-determination, the other concerning the organization—while awaiting self-determination—of the political branches of government in Algeria. . . .

M. Jean-Baptiste Biaggi: It is not a question of the organization of the political branches of government.

M. Joxe: Self-determination is the first question. It was said that there was a certain lack of continuity in this affirmation and in this policy. I would like to remind you, very simply, that the idea was expressed by the Chief of State, that it was adopted by the government, then by parliament, in principle, by 441 votes against 23 the 23rd of October 1959 at the end of a debate on general policy.

M. Biaggi: Of what use was it?

M. Joxe: It served to fix the question. It was understood that later a popular consultation would take place on the issue of self-determination and we have not merged the consultations. Tomorrow we are going to ask the nation in the form of a proposed law solemnly to confirm the approval that parliament has already given. It is a matter of the questions that we are going to pose on Algeria and only on Algeria.

M. François Valentin: That is not proper.

M. Joxe: That's perfectly proper.

M. Valentin: No, M. the Minister, for there is an option to take. And it is to be taken in advance. You do not have to have the nation confirm a decision taken in a regular manner by parliament. It is one or the other.

M. Joxe: We have a perfect right to consult the nation on this point. . . . The principle of self-determination was approved in its principle by the National Assembly in a debate on general policy. We ask that this intention be confirmed. It's perfectly regular.

M. Valentin: No!

M. Joxe: I am terribly sorry, but I have the right to present the point of view of the government.

M. Valentin: We have the right not to agree.

M. Joxe: It is the right of everyone here and this right will be respected. . . .

In his relatively brief speech, M. Joxe said very little in reply to points raised in debate, largely repeating the main lines of the government's policy. M. Debré in concluding remarks of equal brevity, interrupted only by occasional applause from the majority benches, showed even less concern with replying to issues raised in the debate. No voting followed the debate.

During the last six months of the three-year period, the Assembly had no opportunity to debate Algerian policy, despite the fact that it met in concurrent special and regular sessions during six weeks of that time and despite the fact that there was a great deal of political activity in regard to Algeria (referendum, attempted generals' coup, peace feelers, etc.). There is a touch of irony in this because of de Gaulle's invocation of article 16 of the constitution [6] as an aftermath of the coup. The article requires that the Assembly meet in special session by right, but it does not give it the right to discuss the use of the power and no such discussion was held on this occasion.

THE LEGISLATIVE ROLE OF THE NEW NATIONAL ASSEMBLY

The National Assembly of the Fourth Republic was not able to formulate Algerian policy directly, but had great indirect influence. Its successor has had no direct influence of any significance. Furthermore, as long as the great prestige of General de Gaulle shelters the premier, it cannot influence policy indirectly by making and unmaking governments nor even by refusing to pass legislation proposed to it by the government. In fact, as the Algerian referendum shows, its approval of legislation may not even be accepted as adequate legitimation. The

[6] "Art. 16. When the institutions of the Republic, the independence of the Nation, the integrity of its territory, or the execution of its international commitments are endangered in a grave and immediate manner and the regular functioning of the constitutional organs of government is interrupted, the President of the Republic shall take the measures required by these circumstances, after official consultation with the Prime Minister, the Presidents of the Assemblies, and the Constitutional Council.

"He shall inform the nation of this by a message.

"These measures must be inspired by a desire to assure to the constitutional organs of government, in the least possible time, the means to accomplish their mission. The Constitutional Council shall be consulted about them.

"Parliament shall meet by right.

"The National Assembly may not be dissolved while the emergency powers are being exercised."

constitutional provisions designed to restrict the powers of the Assembly could no doubt be circumvented by it. French parliaments have never lacked the boldness and ingenuity necessary to mutilate the letter and spirit of constitutional texts. If there were the will, parliament would find the way; but with de Gaulle in the saddle it has lacked the will.

Another means of parliamentary influence over policy has disappeared with the application of the principle of separation of powers. The constitution makes the holding of a cabinet office incompatible with membership in parliament.[7] To join the government, a deputy must resign his seat. This contrasts with the Fourth Republic. All but two of the Fourth Republic's ministers [8] were members of parliament and became private members again when they left the government. As a result, relations between government and parliament were close on a purely personal basis. The cabinet was run by the Assembly's "own boys." Not only has this situation come to an end, but successive reshuffling of the Debré government has reduced the role in it of former parliamentarians. Two senators and seven deputies were among the fifteen ministers in de Gaulle's original cabinet. The Debré ministry originally included four senators and eight deputies among its twenty-one ministers. By the time of the settlers' revolt of 1960 there were only three senators and six deputies among twenty-one ministers and nonparliamentarians held the key posts of Foreign Affairs, Finance, Algerian Affairs, and the Interior.

The new constitution introduced the device of reserved periods of parliamentary time for questions—oral or written, with or without debate—directed to members of the government by members of the assembly. This provision has had little effect on Algerian affairs as it has elicited no significant statements on Algerian policy.

On the other hand, in the manner of American presidents, de Gaulle has consulted leading parliamentarians and especially the presidents of the political groups, i.e., parties, in the Assembly and the members of the directorates of the chambers on important Algerian questions, such as the referendum of January 1961.

---

[7] Article 23.

[8] Léon Blum presided over a caretaker government for one month and General Catroux was Minister Resident in Algeria for one week.

Also, he has appointed parliamentarians to *ad hoc* commissions, including the *commissions d'élus*.

These acts of grace do not, of course, outweigh the much more substantial loss of Assembly power through the restrictions imposed by the new constitution and by the force of de Gaulle's personality. As long as the constitution operates in its present manner and as long as de Gaulle's popularity carries its present weight, the French parliament will remain a clearly subordinate organ of government unable to exercise any substantial and continuous influence over policy, at least in an area of policy as complex and important as Algeria.

The National Assembly of the Fourth Republic had been too responsive, too representative, too involved in policy formation and fell into a paralytic fit as a result. Its successor has been too insensitive, too little representative, too isolated from the seats of power. The artificiality of Fifth Republic elections has deprived the National Assembly of political legitimacy. The disdain of the executive renders impotent such spasms of political life as remain. It floats between the parties and the people, on the one hand, and the government, on the other, without making solid contact at either pole. Policy is doubly insulated from politics; policy is severed from parliament and the parliament is severed from the people.

TWILIGHT OR DAWN?

During the final year of the Algerian war the French parliament went still further into eclipse. Prime Minister Debré's statement of Algerian policy was debated at the end of the regular spring session of parliament in June 1961, but, although the policy was attacked fiercely by most elements in the Assembly, no vote was taken. The special emergency session convened until Article 16 resumed in September before the regular autumn session, but it was ruled incompetent to discuss the Algerian question so long as the government objected.

Perhaps the most striking evidence of the low state into which parliament had fallen appeared during the final settlement of the Algerian problem. Parliament was not even informed of the negotiations in progress at Les Rousses and Evian until after agreement with the F.L.N. had been reached, had been accepted by the French cabinet and the Algerian National Council, had been signed, had been made public, and had begun to go into effect. Then, the two houses of parliament were summoned into special session, confronted with a *fait accompli,* presented with reports by members of the government, and given an opportunity to blow off steam harmlessly. This they did. Most of the speakers in the debates and probably most of the members of the two chambers were hostile either to de Gaulle's Algerian independence policy or to his request for new special powers. Yet, so few were prepared to oppose the President at that crucial juncture with no-one-knew-what consequences that a censure motion was not even proposed and the debates ended without votes being taken.

Two later acts by the government before the summer recess further humiliated parliament. Between the brief special session on Algeria and the regular spring session the government refused to permit a delegation of the National Assembly's National Defense Committee to visit Algeria to investigate "the use of the army in the maintenance of order" there. This precipitated the protest resignation of five of the seven members of the committee's steering committee and three of the seven members of the steering committee of the Assembly's Committee on Constitutional Law and Legislation. Then, immediately upon announcement of the results of the July referendum, the mandates of the 102 parliamentarians from Algeria were terminated by ordinance of the Council of Ministers, virtually without discussion, with no prior indication, and without parliament even being informed.

At this writing it is too early to say, but that moment of supreme indignity when parliament did not know from one day to the next who were its members may also have marked its nadir. With the Algerian war over there is no longer the pressing need for executive domination. Conditions may again permit parliament to recover much, if not all, of its former power and influence. This possibility was not put to a test before the summer recess, but there was much speculation that in the autumn there might be a "return to normalcy" in the French parliament and generally on the French political scene.

9

Conclusion

THE MEMBERS of a democratic political society tend to have a common interest regarding an external problem and diverse interests regarding an internal issue. The external interest, being one, is best defended through a single voice. The executive branch of government is the organ best equipped to speak with such a voice because it generally has unity of command and direction. It has unity because its distinctive function is administrative and efficient administration requires the clear-cut lines of authority and focus of responsibility that only such unity can provide.

The particular interests within a community, being diverse, are most easily reconciled within an organ in which a variety of points of view are expressed. Those interests can be reconciled only when they have been identified, and they can be identified only when they have been articulated. The adjustments are most likely to be accepted by the interested members of the community if they are confident that their points of view have been presented by valid spokesmen and if there has been serious public deliberation of the issue. The branch of government best suited to perform this function is a representative, deliberative assembly. This, of course, does not exclude initiation of internal policy by the executive. It does mean that internal policy, from whatever source, is most likely to reconcile most satisfactorily conflicting interests when framed with a view toward its acceptability by a genuinely representative and deliberative legislature and when subject to amendment by such a body.

In a country such as twentieth century Britain, which has a

basic ethnic and economic homogeneity and broad political consensus, the chief political problems tend to be external. This favors the dominance of the executive and, especially, the prime minister. In less blessed lands—France, the United States, or eighteenth and nineteenth century Britain—internal issues tend to be more important and legislatures tend to play bigger roles.

In this era of the legitimacy of popular sovereignty, effective political authority derives, at least nominally, from the people. In order for a governmental organ to speak with authority, it must claim a mandate from the people. In Britain the transfer of power from parliament to prime minister was accomplished by transforming the House of Commons from a deliberative body composed of representatives to an essentially electoral body whose members are elected almost solely on the basis of their endorsement of one or the other of the prime ministerial candidates. In the United States the president acquired his popular authority through the transformation of the electoral college into a nondeliberative, nondiscretionary recording structure. The separation of the electoral process from the legislature enabled both Congress and the President to claim mandates from the people. In Fourth Republic France, the executive derived its authority from parliament in a manner superficially similar to the contemporary British system. However, in contrast to Britain, the French Assembly remained representative and deliberative. It retained this status because the French people felt the need of an organ within which the voices of their diverse elements could be heard and brought into a rough, if dynamic and unstable, harmony. Though such an arrangement was untidy and inelegant, it usually contained French social tensions within the manageable dimensions of a single baroque chamber. Only occasionally, as in 1934, did they spill over into its front yard, the *Place du parlement* or the misnamed *Place de la concorde*. The system was also eminently democratic, for it permitted presentation to the electorate of candidates representing a wide range of political viewpoints and gave to the successful candidates genuine influence over policy. Directly, they influenced policy through their power to install and remove governments. Governments ignored or defied the Assembly at their peril. M. Bourgès-Maunoury, painfully aware of this, carried cabinet servility to its logical, if absurd, extremity with his famous "round-table" conference.

Every link in the chain of authority from people to policy was solid. It is difficult to conceive of a more democratic and representative system if by that is meant popular control of governmental policy. The underlying French social disunity was reflected in governmental weakness and instability, but even this was a virtue—indeed a necessity—in a country where the various social elements distrusted one another and feared that strong State authority might be used by one group against the others.

On the other hand, the system was not democratic in the sense that it did not permit the French voter to express a clear preference among alternative governments. Coalitions were always necessary because of the absence of a majority party so that the most the voter could do was influence the relative weight of the members of the coalition. Even so, though the voters did not control directly the selection of the government, the resultant coalition was usually composed of those parties that were the least disliked by the most Frenchmen.

The system operated fairly well when domestic issues predominated. At least it maintained the modicum of social cohesion that might have evaporated before a strong central authority. When external problems came to the fore, however, it was less satisfactory. In 1914 the nation was still convalescent from the recurrent crises over the form of regime, and the Assembly bowed submissively to the whiplash of the Old Tiger. In the years immediately prior to World War II the situation was different. The internal threat to the regime was still virulent but no longer mortal. The Assembly, because of its deliberative, representational character was incompetent to deal with the external threat and conferred virtual dictatorial powers on a series of governments that lacked popular mandates and the authority that only they confer. In the end, both government and parliament abdicated to the Vichy regime whose only claim to legitimacy and authority was the personal prestige of its leader.

Despite the determined efforts of the constitution-makers of the Fourth Republic, the postwar French regime soon evolved into a close replica of the Third Republic. The dominance of domestic issues ensured the dominance of the Assembly. After 1954, as the Algerian insurrection pushed all other problems into the wings, however, the old dilemma was posed anew. Algeria was primarily an external problem. Its key elements lay in the Aurès Mountains, Tunis, Moscow, Washington, New Delhi, the U.N., and in the impact on Algerian minds of influences emanating from those places. All of these were beyond the control of the Palais Bourbon. The cloak of legislative anonymity had provided the least unsatisfactory means for negotiating solutions of internal problems, but only a Cincinnatus from his lonely spire could scout the foreign foe and sound the nation's clarion call. Because the Algerian insurrection was primarily external, an authoritative executive was needed. On the other hand, the Algerian problem also had roots deep within the French body politic. For more than 130 years sinews had grown to bind the territory to France. All possible solutions had domestic implications of momentous importance. To resolve the internal ramifications of the issue, to adjust the diverse domestic French interests, the involvement of a representative, deliberative assembly was necessary.

The constitutional problem, then, that was brought into focus by the Algerian insurrection was that of building an authoritative executive to deal with its external aspects while maintaining a viable assembly to facilitate solution of the related domestic issues. This constitutional problem was not new, as French history for nearly a century clearly shows, but it was made dramatically acute by the Algerian crisis.

De Gaulle, as he approached the problem of reconstructing French institutions, seems to have developed a similar analysis. He believed that authoritative executive power was essential. But he also recognized that French social disunity is endemic and accepted the need for a representative, deliberative, and influential assembly.

These principles were incorporated in the constitution of the Fifth Republic. The executive function was vested in a cabinet deriving its authority from both the Assembly and the president. The Assembly was based on direct, universal suffrage, expressed through an electoral system that, in the abstract, was at least as sensitive to popular will as the former system. The authority of the political executive was to be enhanced by partially insulating it from the disunity of the representative assembly and by giving it a second, independent base of support in the president of the Republic. M. Debré, in his speech to the Council of State in August, 1958, proclaimed that the new regime was parliamentary, not presidential, because it maintained, however restricted, the principle of ministerial responsibility.

The intentions of Debré and de Gaulle have not been fulfilled. The regime, with a modified parliamentary constitution, has become a modified presidential system. Parliament is neither representative nor influential, so its deliberations are doubly sterile. The premier and the cabinet are neither ministerially responsible nor the formulators of public policy as the constitution directs. The president of the Republic was supposed to be an arbiter, resolving disagreements between the houses of parliament and between the parliament and the cabinet. Instead, he has become the prime formulator of public policy. Yet, his action in the face of difficult problems has been timid and uncertain.

Why has the system departed so far from the intentions of its founders? In my view, de Gaulle's analysis of the constitutional problem was correct, but the remedy was defective for two reasons. First, it failed to give the president of the Republic (and hence also the government) an authentic basis for popular support. The bizarre electoral college from which he emanates permits no expression of popular will. Not being placed in office by popular will, he derives no legitimate authority through the electoral process. This lack of a constitutional popular mandate seems to have been a cause of de Gaulle's reluctance to act decisively in Algeria and of his search for popular endorsement through referenda and royal tours.

Yet, de Gaulle had an implicit popular mandate through the 1958 referendum and elections. In effect, those consultations were transformed into virtual personal plebiscites. A successor, elected without the concurrence of parliamentary elections, would speak with a still weaker voice. De Gaulle's mandate is also questionable, and therefore weakened, by the fact that he had no serious rival for office. Consequently the French were denied an opportunity to express an authentic choice even through the 1958 consultations.

The other defect in the Gaullist remedy was its failure to take into account adequately the traditional French constitutional assumption that parliament and the executive will operate in a relationship of reciprocal political confidence. This is the assumption, essential to parliamentary government, that no government will hold office unless it has the political confidence of parliament. It was this assumption, cultivated by the Gaullists, that transformed the 1958 elections into a plebiscite, because it was understood that de Gaulle would resign if a hostile Assembly were elected. It is this assumption that deprives parliament of its influence on policy, that renders it impotent for the expression and resolution of the diversity of French political opinion, because it is understood that de Gaulle will resign if the Assembly acts contrary to his will.

By isolating the political executive and the Assembly from the disunity of French political opinion, de Gaulle also isolated them from popular will, thereby depriving the executive of the democratic authority necessary to act decisively and the Assembly of the representativeness necessary to effect needed internal political adjustments.

The basic constitutional problem now facing de Gaulle is how to endow the presidency with institutional authority (as opposed to his personal prestige) while restoring the representativeness and part of the influence of the Assembly. Considering the situation abstractly without taking into account French political traditions and prejudices, it would seem that the problem might be resolved by the introduction of a more orthodox presidential regime. The presidential electoral process might be reformed to permit the constitutional expression of clear popular preference and the president's electoral dependence on parliament might be eliminated by letting it be known that de Gaulle would not resign if faced by a hostile parliament. He could act as do American presidents, using the powers of the office to influence the Assembly but not expecting to win all the battles.

In a parliamentary regime one or the other of the political branches of government dominates. It subordinates the political executive of an essentially divided nation during periods when internal problems predominate. It casts parliament into limbo during periods of external crisis. The tendency of the French to construct rigid constitutional frameworks makes it difficult for the balance of power to shift constitutionally within a given system, so a new system must be established each time a shift in the balance of power is desired.

The presidential regime permits an evener distribution of power between the two organs and also permits the focus of power to shift in accommodation to the political situation. The branches are independent of each other in the sense that each has constitutionally defined powers, a separate source of popular authority, and is not expected always to be in policy agreement with the other. Thus, each branch has constitutionally independent status and, when the situation is favorable because of the nature of the predominant problem, it can assert its preeminence. During periods of external crisis, the executive is dominant; during periods when domestic issues predominate, the legislature is dominant, or at least has an authentic "last say."

The development of a presidential system in France is open to the obvious criticism that it would require the transplanting of foreign governmental institutions. The response is threefold. In the first place, the French have a long tradition of attempts to import foreign governmental institutions. With one exception these have been brought from Great Britain. The French, quite justifiably, have admired the efficient operation of the British system. This advantage has been so dazzling that they failed to realize that France lacks the foundation of social homogeneity and political consensus that makes the British system work. American society with its great diversity is more like the French. Therefore, the American presidential system might find French soil more congenial than has the British system.[1] If it is then remarked that the French tried the presidential system in 1848 with disastrous results, it should also be noted that they had the incredible folly to place in the presidency the pretender to the imperial throne. Their giddiness in the aftermath of the

---

[1] It should be noted in passing that such eminent French political scientists as Professors Maurice Duverger and Georges Vedel have advocated the establishment of presidential-type regimes.

1848 revolution and the precipitate introduction of universal suffrage, and not defects in the system, proved their undoing.

A second reply is that the biggest step has already been taken. The executive has, in fact, for nearly four years operated without effective responsibility to parliament. This relationship needs merely to be regularized, rationalized, and institutionalized so that de Gaulle's departure will not alter it radically.

The third reply is that a French presidential regime would undoubtedly and should, of course, take a peculiar Gallic form. To suit the French political clime it would have to be pruned and bent. For instance, the ideological orientation of French politics or the multiparty system might survive. The cabinet might remain responsible to parliament as an expendable buffer between parliament and the political executive. It would be foolish to suggest that a French presidential regime should take any particular form in detail. It need only combine an independent political executive representing the unity of French popular will with an influential assembly representing its diversity. Then it would be structurally suited to deal with the varying national problems in as efficient and effective a manner as the nature of French society and political problems permits.

In any case, if the French regime is metamorphosed into presidential form, it is more likely to occur through the accretion of precedent than through deliberate reform. It is altogether possible that the natural process of institutional evolution will produce a presidential-type regime or one that has the same general qualities. Changes in that direction, especially insistence on the part of de Gaulle that he will hold office even if the Assembly gainsays him, should be encouraged, but it is unlikely that much solid progress will be made except by prescriptive accommodation to fortuitous and gradually changing circumstances. The regime has already moved in the direction of a presidential system, not only without design by the Gaullists but apparently even contrary to their intentions. This suggests that French soil has now become more hospitable to the exotic plant. If there has been such a change it may be because of the recent, dramatic evolution of France into a progressive, prosperous, more completely modern and industrial nation. Whatever the exact form of the regime, however it is developed, it is

unlikely that France will find the political peace of mind she
has so long sought in vain until her institutions permit her to
deal flexibly and efficiently with her varied and changing problems through the effective expression of the diversity of her
popular will in one way and the effective expression of its unity
in another.

Epilogue

THE ROAD TO EVIAN

ON MARCH 18, 1962 France and the F.L.N. signed a ceasefire agreement at Evian-Les-Bains, ending seven and a half years of fighting. The longest, bloodiest, and most ravishing war for independence was over. Estimates of the number of persons killed ranged from 250,000 to two million. Its monetary cost has been set at $20,000,000,000. More than 20,000 native villages had been destroyed. One million Moslems had been incarcerated in regroupment camps, about 250,000 others were refugees in Tunisia and Morocco, and half a million were expatriates in France. All this happened to a country with a total Moslem population of only nine million.

From its tiny beginning in 1954 the rebel army grew to a peak of about 120,000 men in 1957-1959 and numbered about 40,000 at the ceasefire. Although strenuous military efforts under de Gaulle limited the activities and power of the rebels, he was no more able than his predecessors to wipe them out. "We know that we cannot defeat the French Army in battle," Mr. Abdel Kader Chanderli, Algerian representative in New York, told me in 1959, "but we can fight a guerilla war for ten years, if necessary, and the French will some day weary of the struggle."

If there had been doubt before, the 1961 referendum made it clear that the French were weary and wanted only a graceful exit. It was this exit which de Gaulle sought during the year preceding the agreement at Evian. His search aroused increasingly violent resistance to "capitulation" by certain French military elements and European settlers.

The F.L.N. had always insisted that France could find such an exit only through negotiations granting Algerian independence. De Gaulle took a first step toward acceptance of that alternative in September 1959 with his "peace of the brave" proposal for a ceasefire. The F.L.N. charged that the proposal was, in effect, an invitation to surrender. By June 1960, de Gaulle accepted a broader frame of reference and preliminary talks were held at Melun near Paris. The F.L.N. withdrew, expressing dissatisfaction with the conference arrangements, especially the French refusal to permit F.L.N. negotiators access to the press. The Algerians again feared to be appearing to negotiate a capitulation.

The 1961 referendum ostensibly approved the self-determination policy and authorized the establishment of an interim, semi-autonomous regime in Algeria. In fact, it was regarded by de Gaulle mainly as a mandate to begin serious negotiations. Immediately after the referendum the cabinet authorized certain measures tending toward the establishment of the new regime, but it was clear to all that no such regime could succeed without the participation of authentic Moslem spokesmen and equally clear that no such spokesmen would serve without the concurrence of the F.L.N. The F.L.N. refused to accept any Algerian regime that was not worked out in negotiations with it. Furthermore, the F.L.N. refused to negotiate if steps were taken to establish the interim regime, reasoning that such a regime would "predetermine the self-determination." This situation made the referendum article on the interim regime meaningless and negotiations with the F.L.N. essential. Therefore, no serious effort was made to implement the interim regime and contacts were made at once with the F.L.N. with a view toward early negotiations. Several disagreements over prior conditions and procedure had to be resolved. De Gaulle sought to treat the F.L.N. as only one of several Algerian political "tendencies" to be included in any talks. The F.L.N. balked and de Gaulle retreated. Then de Gaulle's reluctance to begin political negotiations before a ceasefire had to be overcome. By the third week in April and after several delays, it appeared that serious talks would begin within two weeks.

The imminence of such talks ignited the April 1961 "Generals' Coup," the third insurrectionary effort by European opponents of French policy in Algeria. The first had been May 13, 1958 and the second was in January 1960. After the 1961 referendum plastic bombs began being exploded in metropolitan France. They were planted to cause property damage rather than bodily harm and to demonstrate the depth and intensity of opposition to a liberal Algerian policy. The campaign was given central direction when the Secret Army Organization (O.A.S.) was formed in a two-day meeting in Madrid in March. General Raoul Salan, former commander of French armed forces in Algeria, was designated O.A.S. head. Retired Air Force General Edmond Jouhaud; retired Air Force General Maurice Challe, Salan's successor as Algerian commander; and retired Army General André Zeller were among the other leaders.

The O.A.S. organized the April coup. It had been planned for April 24 but was set off prematurely on April 21 when the plans were uncovered. The First Foreign Legion Parachute Regiment moved into Algiers, occupied key strategic spots, and kidnapped General Fernand Gambiez, commander in chief of armed forces in Algeria. Jean Morin, Delegate General, and Robert Buron, Minister of Public Works, who happened to be in Algiers, were also captured. The coup leaders broadcast appeals for popular support to help them maintain the French hold on Algeria. With the exception of a few individuals in the officer corps, the revolt was joined only by two other paratroop regiments. De Gaulle's broadcast appeal to the army to remain loyal was successful and the revolt collapsed. Challe and Zeller surrendered. Salan and Jouhaud went into hiding.

The effect of the Generals' Coup was opposite to that intended; it facilitated rather than prevented negotiations. It convinced the F.L.N. of de Gaulle's firmness and determination and showed that—at least for the time being—the army was under his control. On the other hand, de Gaulle now knew that he was stronger than ever and could move with the assurance that he had the massive support of the French people. Both sides were also aware that protracted delays might enable internal French opposition to rally again and perhaps succeed where the generals had failed.

In any case, formal negotiations were underway less than a month later at the Lake Geneva resort of Evian-les-Bains. After three weeks they were suspended by the French, with manifest regret on both sides, on the grounds that insufficient progress was being made. On four main points the F.L.N. refused to accept the French position and no compromise formulas were found:

1. The French wanted a ceasefire to precede agreement on political questions.

2. The French declined to recognize Algerian sovereignty over the Sahara and insisted that its future status had to be negotiated with all the "bordering" countries.

3. The French refused to release the five F.L.N. leaders whom they had captured in 1956.

4. The French maintained that organic guarantees to the European community as a community should be incorporated in any agreement.

Reconvened talks at Lugrin in July were suspended by the F.L.N. over alleged French refusal to acknowledge Algerian sovereignty over the Sahara. This failure led de Gaulle to rumble a bit about establishing the interim regime authorized by the January referendum and about partitioning the territory between Moslem and European states if the F.L.N. did not show signs of getting down to business on negotiations. Also, he lifted the unilateral truce he had declared at the beginning of the Evian talks. That truce had covered French offensive operations in the interior but not along the Tunisian and Moroccan borders. Nor had it excluded French troop movements, though F.L.N. movements were forbidden. It was never recognized by the F.L.N. as anything but a propaganda play. Originally, the truce had been declared for thirty days, but it was tacitly extended for another month and a half. Another of de Gaulle's tactical moves in conjunction with the summer negotiations was his announcement that a combat army division would be withdrawn from the territory, ostensibly as a prelude to partition. He did not explain why the withdrawal of troops to France would be a step toward partition. Later he asserted that the troops were being withdrawn because of a decline in the fighting. A second division was pulled out later in the year.

The Algerians, too, were involved in diplomatic maneuvering away from the conference table. A cabinet shakeup late in August replaced Premier Ferhat Abbas by Ben Youssef Ben Khedda, who was reported to be a leftwing extremist, hostile to the West. At the same time, the F.L.N. expressed gratitude and made new overtures to "the Socialist countries of Africa, Asia, and Latin America." A week later the Belgrade conference of neutral nations promised "diplomatic and practical" aid to the Algerians.

Through all this sideline action, however, both sides were careful to make it clear that they continued to hope for a resumption of the suspended talks and avoided any words or action that might have precipitated a definitive break. This caution bore fruit in the late fall when negotiations were secretly resumed. Rumors of the talks were rife throughout the winter, but were not officially confirmed until a draft agreement was reached at the Swiss-French border village, Les Rousses, on February 18.

The accord was submitted to the French cabinet and the G.P.R.A. The French cabinet approved it without dissent in a meeting on February 21 and authorized the French negotiators to sign a formal agreement. Parliament was not even consulted. The G.P.R.A. approved the accords on February 20, but could not authorize formal conclusion of the treaty without the concurrence of its "parliament," the National Council. The 54-member National Council met in closed session in Tripoli for six days. After debate that apparently was somewhat more than perfunctory, the Council voted by a large majority to authorize the F.L.N. delegation to return to Evian and conclude an agreement, provided certain conditions were met. It was reported that the Council required assurances that the French would deal forcefully with the rising anti-Moslem terror of the O.A.S. and also insisted that the final agreement treat in detail the transitional phase between the ceasefire and what everyone assumed would be ultimate independence. In particular, it expected detailed stipulations concerning the size, composition, and authority of the transitional Provisional Government and of the forces at its disposal to maintain order. Also, it insisted on precise schedules for the withdrawal of French troops, the release of prisoners, and the repatriation of refugees.

A final two-week negotiating session at Evian resolved the remaining disagreements. The most difficult issues seem to have been the designation of the four "neutral" members of the Provisional Executive and the procedure for disbanding the F.L.N. Army. On March 18 the accord was signed. The ceasefire began the next day. The agreement provided for a transitional regime to carry out its terms, an Algerian self-determination referendum, and a special relationship to be established between France and Algeria if the Algerian voters ratified independence.[1]

Actually, the outcome of the referendum was virtually dictated by the agreement. The French bowed to realities and accepted what the F.L.N. had been fighting for in this emphatically tautological masterpiece of eloquent double talk:

The formation, after self-determination, of an independent and sovereign state appearing to conform to the realities of the Algerian situation, and in these conditions, cooperation between France and Algeria corresponding to the interests of the two countries, the French government considers, together with the F.L.N., that the solution of the independence of Algeria in cooperation with France is the one which corresponds to this situation.

In accordance with that assumption, the agreement stipulated that the Algerian voters would be asked by the two governments to make known through a referendum to be held within six months whether they "want Algeria to be independent and in that case whether they want France and Algeria to cooperate in the conditions defined by the present declarations."

The French also admitted that their 126 years of efforts to bind the Sahara to Algeria had been more successful than their efforts since 1956 to separate it again. "The Algerian territory" was defined, as the Algerians had insisted, to include the Saharan departments of Oases and Saoura.

On the other hand, the F.L.N. agreed to do what they had earlier charged would breach their sovereignty. They agreed to give Algerians of French civil status certain special civic privileges. For three years they were permitted to remain French nationals while exercising Algerian civic rights. They could then become either Algerian citizens or resident aliens under a special convention. Proportionate representation in popular assemblies, free access to the civil service, fair compensation for expropriated property, and retention of a special court system to adjudicate personal status cases were guaranteed to the Europeans as a community. A "Court of Guarantees" was to enforce those provisions. The F.L.N. also agreed that France should have certain rights in exploiting the Saharan oil resources in return for economic and

[1] *French Affairs*, No. 130, March 18, 1962.

technical assistance and that she might lease the Mers-el-Kebir military and naval base for 15 years.

The agreement provided that a Provisional Executive should be created immediately after the ceasefire to 1) operate the public administration, 2) maintain law and order with police and security forces, and 3) prepare and implement the referendum. Prisoners, refugees, and displaced persons were to be liberated and permitted to return to their homes. France was to begin withdrawing her troops at once. Within a year after the referendum her Algerian forces were to be cut to 80,000 and in another year completely withdrawn.

Though the agreement went into effect upon signature, the French cabinet scheduled a three-day parliamentary debate on Algerian policy which, however, closed without a vote. No less a formality was the French referendum of April 8 in which 90 per cent of the voters endorsed the agreement. By that time the accord was rapidly being implemented. Fighting had stopped. Ben Bella and the other four imprisoned members of the G.P.R.A. had been released. The release of other prisoners and transfer of refugees had begun. Christian Fouchet, who had been Minister of Tunisian and Moroccan Affairs when the first steps to withdraw from those two countries were taken in 1954, had been designated French High Commissioner in Algeria. Abderrahmane Fares, a longtime friend of the French and former speaker of the Algerian Assembly who had come late to the F.L.N., had been appointed president of the twelve-man Provisional Executive and the liberal French mayor of Philippeville, Roger Roth, had been named vice president. Two other Frenchmen, four Algerians sympathetic to the national cause but not members of F.L.N., and four other F.L.N. representatives completed the executive. The members gathered at the Algerian administrative capital of Rocher Noir by the end of March and began, in cooperation with the French authorities and the F.L.N., to prepare for the referendum, which they scheduled for July 1.

The most serious problem confronting the Provisional Executive was the O.A.S. terrorist campaign which was rising in intensity and brutality. During the formation of its own security forces, the Provisional Executive was entirely dependent on the French Army and police for counter-terrorist action. Even later, after it had its own forces, it expected to rely partly on the French. After the failure of the "Generals' Coup" in April 1961, the O.A.S. had conducted a bombing campaign to maintain French sovereignty over Algeria by 1) dissuading de Gaulle from his liberal policy, 2) overthrowing his regime, or 3) disrupting the peace negotiations. Initially, the campaign was concentrated in metropolitan France and was designed mainly to create a noisy demonstration of the *Algérie française* sentiment. As late as May 1962 only six persons (three of them terrorists) had died—probably accidentally—in O.A.S. attacks in France. As the likelihood of successful ceasefire negotiations increased, the O.A.S. altered its operations. First, it launched a systematic campaign of "executions" of Europeans and Moslems suspected of disloyalty to *Algérie française* and of members of the French police and military counter-terror forces. These were deliberate assassinations, planned individually, and carried out almost entirely in Algeria. By the time the Les Rousses talks were concluded in February 1962, the O.A.S. had been blamed by French authorities for the deaths of 158 Europeans and 183 Moslems in Algiers alone. At that time the O.A.S. was believed to have a full-time force of 3,000 to 4,000 members organized in a military manner.

The announcement of the accord at Les Rousses signalled the failure of the O.A.S. in its original aim of deterring the French government from reaching agreement. The Secret Army changed its tactics again. Now it began random killing of Moslems in the streets. Gangs armed with machine guns and automatic pistols raced through the streets in automobiles, shooting such Moslems as had the misfortune to come within range. Mortar shells were lobbed into Moslem residential districts. Booby-trapped autos, timed to explode when they would be most lethal, were parked in busy locations. Hardly a day passed without at least a dozen murders. Ninety-one were killed on one bloody day. By early May the total casualties since the ceasefire numbered more than 2,500, of which over 1,000 were deaths.

Two objectives of this campaign were suggested. One was that the O.A.S. hoped to incite the Moslems to mob violence against the Europeans, expecting that the French Army would then be compelled to intervene against the Moslems. They believed that this would force the F.L.N. to retaliate against the French Army and the war would be on again. The Moslems refused to be panicked into mob action, although there were some incidents of organized, individual retaliation. The formation of a militarized police force composed of Moslems drawn from the Moslem "Harkis" formations of the French Army and placed under the jurisdiction of the Provisional Executive removed the danger of the infernal circle desired by the O.A.S. Another objective of the O.A.S. was said to be the imposition of *de facto* segregation. Only Moslems who ventured into the European sections of the cities were attacked individually. It was difficult to see, however, how segregation so imposed could be expected to continue after violent coercion ceased and it was equally unlikely that the O.A.S. wished to, or believed it could, continue such attacks in perpetuity. Also, the mortar shellings were incompatible with that strategy.

In any case, by early June the O.A.S. campaign collapsed amidst bitter dissension and the evaporation of settler support. The July 1 referendum approved independence overwhelmingly.[2]

CONSTITUTIONAL REGIMES AND POLITICS

The massive approval by the French electorate of the Evian Accords registered in the referendum of April 8, 1962 closed an important chapter in French postwar history. By that act the French people accepted a final solution for the Algerian question as an internal French problem. No one doubted that the Algerian referendum provided for in the Accords would take the last portion of French North Africa out of the French Republic. After the Algerian consultation, questions regarding the form of Algerian governmental institutions would no longer fall within the area of competence of the French Republic and thus would no longer be an issue of direct concern to French politics. The chapter opened by the All Souls Day Insurrection was closing. The closing of that chapter ended the process that has been the subject of this study. The search for a constitutional settlement in Algeria is over as far as French politics are concerned.

---

[2] 91.23 per cent of the registered voters and 99.72 per cent of the ballots were favorable. Registered voters increased from 4,703,482 in 1961 to 6,562,478 in 1962, revealing how narrow had been de Gaulle's Algerian support in 1961. Although 66 per cent of the 1961 voters cast *"oui"* ballots, this was only 29.2 per cent of the number of registered voters in 1962, 31.4 per cent of those actually voting in 1962, and 27.1 per cent of the population.

That search was conducted over a period of some ninety-one months within the framework of two successive constitutional regimes. The strong-assembly system of the Fourth Republic collapsed during the forty-fifth month of the rebellion and was replaced after a seven-month transitional emergency constitutional dictatorship by the strong-executive system of the Fifth Republic. During the Fourth Republic, six Premiers succeeded one another in assuming primary responsibility for directing the search. During the Fifth Republic, President de Gaulle continuously held that responsibility with Michel Debré as his chief aide.

A summary review of the operation of the two regimes governing the same country in search of a solution to the same overriding problem for virtually the same length of time offers an unusual opportunity to make comparisons between the character and effectiveness of two distinctly different types of governmental structures. It also permits some conclusions to be drawn concerning the impact of the problem on the institutions.

THE FOURTH REPUBLIC

During most of the Fourth Republic there was broad agreement among responsible political groups on the general end of governmental policy in Algeria. All but the Communists agreed that the nationalist rebellion should be suppressed with all available force, that Algeria should remain an integral part of the French Republic, and that political, constitutional, social, and economic reforms should be introduced. Disagreement arose primarily on three questions: 1) What should be the relative emphasis and timing of suppression and reform? 2) What should be the extent of the reform? 3) Who should be in charge of formulating and implementing the policies?

These disagreements were brought to the surface and into focus in parliament; they were conveyed to the people through the political parties, public statements and speeches, and the press; they were projected into the executive because of its dependence on the confidence of a parliament in which no politically homogeneous majority existed. The reconciliation of disagreements that was prerequisite to the elaboration of policy was effected in a series of political organs. Investiture of a government may be regarded as the first step in that process. Acceptance by an Assembly majority of an investiture declaration implied a commitment to support the Algerian policy enunciated in it. To assemble a parliamentary majority a Premier-designate had to present a program that would win more support than opposition. Widely divergent views on Algeria had substantial representation in any possible Assembly majority. Algerian policy was usually among the chief determinants of parliamentary attitudes toward governments. Thus, it was usually necessary for a Premier-designate to propose an Algerian policy capable of winning the support of deputies holding irreconcilable views. Consequently, the professed Algerian policies of the Premier-designate tended to be broad and vague, trying to be all things to all men or, more exactly, different things to different men. The investiture, then, placed a framework around Algerian policy, marking its outer limits but doing little to define its substance.

Those details were referred to the cabinet. However, because the disagreements of the parliamentary majority were represented with fair accuracy in the cabinet, the problem of reconciling irreconcilables recurred. During the Faure and Mollet cabinets the basic issue was evaded by deferring Algerian reform until after that conveniently indefinite date when the fighting would have stopped. By mid-1957, however, the advocates of authentic reforms had become convinced that if there were no reforms there would be no ceasefire, and they pressed the issue insistently. With great reluctance the cabinet opponents of reform acquiesced in a modest reform program.

The process was not yet complete. The sovereign Assembly could reopen questions that had been settled by its executive committee, the cabinet. In committee and then in plenary session the stand-patters could fight again and often win the battles they had lost in the cabinet. By using dilatory motions, repeated amendment motions, protracted debates, private members' bills, and committee versions, the government's adversaries could wear it down, extracting concessions to render bills more and more vacuous. As if this were not complicated enough, Premier Bourgès-Maunoury devised the so-called "Round Table." This was supposed to provide another means which the Premier could use to rally support. Instead, it only gave his opponents another chance to hack away at his projects.

This struggle between the parliament and its agent may seem rather incongruous, but there was, after all, a difference in outlook between them. However accurately the divergent views of the deputies were represented in the cabinet, the ministers acquired with their governmental functions a different perspective. Having the responsibility for government they were impelled to try to enact policy that would realistically serve the national interest. The backbenchers, on the other hand, remained primarily representatives of various political points of view. Their conduct was motivated chiefly by a desire to protect the particular interests which they represented and to oppose any policy that seemed to jeopardize those interests. By giving to the Assembly the final say, the regime insured that the reconciliation of conflicting interests would gain priority over the consistent application of a dynamic policy, however sterile might be the reconciliation and however lethal to the national interest.

The damage this wrought to the effectiveness of government was particularly serious and especially evident in the case of Algeria. The Algerian insurrection was essentially an external problem requiring the forceful and united action of the nation and its government to effect the most advantageous solution. Yet, it so deeply involved conflicting internal interests that the full force of the Assembly was aroused. As a result, the gap between the demands of the situation and the tolerance of the Assembly yawned ever wider as the crisis deepened.

The government and parliament that dealt with the Algerian problem were the same government and parliament that dealt with other problems. The gap that had been widened so enormously, the paralysis with which those organs were struck because of Algeria, could not but affect their functioning in dealing with other problems. Governmental prestige and authority cannot be compartmentalized; losses sustained in one area affect all areas. Thus, the incapacity of the regime to cope with the Algerian problem had a general debilitating effect on the Fourth Republic and led directly to its collapse.

THE FIFTH REPUBLIC

Late in the Fourth Republic the conviction began to develop among many who had most strongly advocated Algerian reforms that the continued strength of the Algerian nationalist movement meant that no reforms could succeed unless they were acceptable to the F.L.N. This development undermined the general agreement that Algeria should remain an integral part of the French Republic. At the same time, there was a decline in the ranks of those who believed that all reforms should be deferred until after a ceasefire. Finally, with the wave of Gaullism after May 13, general agreement emerged on the desirability of having de Gaulle in charge of policy.

As a result of these shifts, the Algerian issues under the Fifth Republic were different from those of the Fourth Republic. Now there was general agreement on the need for extensive reforms at once and on de Gaulle's leadership, but disagreement on the future international status of Algeria and on whether the insurrection should be reduced by force or by negotiation.

Thus, de Gaulle's return to power did not end political controversy regarding Algeria. In fact, the differences between the points of view on the new policy issues were even greater than had been the case before. Under the Fourth Republic all responsible discussion of reform concerned the amount of political participation to be permitted the Moslems within the republic. To this question was now added the question of whether Algeria should be allowed to secede partially or completely. Politicians under the previous regime had not even dared raise that question.

Though the range of disagreement was not narrowed under the Fifth Republic, it was no longer projected into the policy-making organs of government. De Gaulle's popularity so dominated the minds of candidates and voters in November 1958 that it obscured all policy questions in the parliamentary elections. Thus, though the deputies in the new National Assembly held widely differing views on Algeria, they had not been sent there to represent those views but to support de Gaulle. His continued popularity restrained open violation of that mandate. Those few, like M. René Moatti, who returned to the hustings for a new and anti-Gaullist mandate were repudiated by the voters. Because the disagreements were only imperfectly articulated in the Assembly they could not be reconciled. The Assembly was denied its natural function.

The same phenomena that undercut the authority of the Assembly enhanced that of the President. The 1958 elections were a blank check to de Gaulle. The executive was given the authority to act in the general interest without first effecting the reconciliation of particular interests that had been necessary under the Fourth Republic.

There was no parliamentary investiture of the political executive when the Fifth Republic was put into operation. De Gaulle had been invested by the people in September and November 1958. That was enough. Furthermore, there was no representation of particular interests in the cabinet. The ministers held office with the confidence of de Gaulle. The attitude of parliament was largely immaterial. The general interest that had so often been obscured during the Fourth Republic by the competition among representatives of particular interests now predominated.

It is more accurate to say that de Gaulle articulates the national will than that he represents the national will. His claim to formal delegation of authority from the French people rests on four popular consultations in none of which was there an authentic opportunity for choice because in none of them was there a visible and realistic alternative to de Gaulle.

All of de Gaulle's action (ambiguity in early policy statements; delay and vacillation in implementing the liberal policy that, apparently, he always preferred; constant direct popular contact to elicit support; successive referenda not proposed by the September 1959 self-determination declaration) indicates a profound feeling of uncertainty concerning the strength of his claim to popular legitimacy. Yet, every objective indication is that he had continuous and massive French popular support for whatever Algerian policy he chose to pursue. This phenomenon was not new. The governments of the Fourth Republic always had popular support for their Algerian policy even when they lacked parliamentary support. Popular support for de Gaulle was greater because of his personal *mystique* and because the French public was, in its war-weariness, more willing to follow. Furthermore, it was not offset by a strong parliament. The deputies were specialists in the representation of particular interests. Their divisions reflected their awareness that their social, ideological, or geographic constituents had conflicting particular interests. But this specialization blinded them to what the majority of the French public seemed to realize at an early point: that the national interest required strong leadership to solve the essentially external Algerian problem and that the national interest took precedence over particular interests in such a situation. During the Fourth Republic, the National Assembly, expressing those particular interests, had a stronger and more direct impact on the executive than had raw public opinion expressing the national interest. During the Fifth Republic, de Gaulle's prestige, the Constitution, and the electoral and referendal system combined to make the impact of popular will more direct.

The great tragedy of de Gaulle's Algerian policy was that he failed to exploit this support to obtain a rapid solution. Not only would such a solution have spared many lives in the struggle between the French Army and the F.L.N., but also it would have prevented effective, organized, violent resistance of the sort mounted by the O.A.S. Repeatedly, de Gaulle sought and received massive manifestations of support for whatever Algerian policy he might pursue. There is every indication that he wanted from the outset to negotiate a settlement with the F.L.N. that would define a relationship very similar to the one finally agreed upon at Evian. Yet, he cast about for more than three years before undertaking serious negotiations in an atmosphere acceptable to the F.L.N. The Algerian regime that was ratified in the 1961 referendum was as surely stillborn as the *loi cadre* of 1957 because neither had been negotiated with the F.L.N. One prominent French statesman privately suggested to de Gaulle soon after his return to power and again after the self-determination declaration of September 1959 that he should move rapidly to reach agreement with the F.L.N. before opposition to his policies could solidify and become better organized. "No," the general replied. His preoccupation with national unity dictated that every effort be made to help France's blinded children to see the light and to come to his support, before irrevocable steps be taken that could cause still another rip in French social fabric.

Had he moved with less caution the breaks might have come sooner but, also, they might not have been so deep or complete and they might have been more quickly mended.

THE IMPACT OF ALGERIA ON THE FRENCH REGIMES

Initially, the gravity of the Algerian problem was not grasped by the politically conscious public in France. During that early stage, issues with essentially domestic roots continued to dominate French politics and the National Assembly retained an ascendancy that more or less conformed to the necessity of the situation. It provided the necessary forum for compromise. As the French became increasingly preoccupied with Algeria, the belief grew that strong executive leadership was required. The Algerian problem became one of those national crises of catastrophic magnitude with its principal causes lying outside the French body politic that has an especial need for such leadership. The tension between the capacities of the system as it was operating and the requirements of the situation exploded on May 13 and brought to power the one Frenchman who could command the requisite authority. De Gaulle probably could have exercised that authority through the structure of the Fourth Republic, but his past commitments and certain traditions of French constitutionalism led him to insist upon a new regime. The Fifth Republic was designed as an essentially parliamentary regime on which an independent non-political chief of state could impose his arbitration. The new regime was no more able than the old to resist the pressures generated by the Algerian problem. From the outset, it was clear that the balance which had been sought by the framers of the new Constitution was not being struck and that the executive, in practice, held all power. Whether de Gaulle and his Republic will be able to adjust to a situation in which Algeria no longer imposes a restraint on the Assembly is, at this writing, the great unknown of French politics. Upon the extent and character of that adjustment depends the future of French democracy.

Chronology

1954

Nov. 1	Algerian nationalist insurrection begins.
Nov. 5	M.T.L.D. dissolved by decree.
Nov. 12	French aerial bombardments in the Aurès mountains.
Nov. 12	Nat. Assembly Debate on Algeria, Tunisia.
Nov. 24	Council of the Republic debate on Algeria.
Dec. 10	Nat. Assembly debate on No. Africa.

1955

Jan. 5	Min. of Interior presents Algeria reform plan.
Jan. 18	Special session of Algerian Assembly.
Jan. 20	46 delegates in Algerian Assembly demand equality.
Jan. 25	Soustelle named Algerian Governor-General.
Feb. 3-5	Mendès-France govt. falls on No. African policy.
Feb. 18	Nat. Assembly refuses to invest Pineau.
Feb. 25	Nat. Assembly invests Faure govt.
Mar. 31	Nat. Assembly votes Algerian state of emergency.
Apr. 17, 24	Canton elections in Algeria.
Apr. 21	Bandung Conference backs F.L.N.
July 30	State of Emergency in Algeria extended 6 mos.
Sept. 13	Algerian Communist Party dissolved by decree.
Sept. 26	61 Moslems in Algerian Assembly reject integration.
Sept. 27	Soustelle adjourns Algerian Assembly session.
Sept. 30	Algerian affair placed on the U.N. agenda.
Nov. 30	Council of Ministers dissolves Nat. Assembly.
Dec. 12	Legislative elections in Algeria postponed.

1956

Jan. 2	Nat. Assembly elections.
Jan. 4	61 in Algerian Assembly back "Algerian nationality."
Jan. 9	Gen. Catroux named Algerian Resident Minister.
Jan. 31	Nat. Assembly invests Mollet govt.

Jan. 31	Mollet advocates free elections after cease-fire.
Feb. 6	Europeans in Algeria demonstrate against Mollet.
Feb. 6	Catroux resigns as Resident Minister.
Feb. 9	Robert Lacoste named Resident Minister.
Mar. 12	Nat. Assembly votes special Algerian powers.
Apr. 11	Algerian Assembly dissolved by decree.
May 22	Mendès-France quits cabinet over Algeria.
May 29	Algerian debate in the Council of the Republic.
June 5	Govt. wins confidence vote on No. African policy.
July 3	Territorial reorganization in Algeria.
Aug. 20	F.L.N. Congress.
Sept. 25	Algerian question placed on U.N. agenda.
Oct. 17, 18	Algerian debate in Nat. Assembly.
Oct. 29	Mollet, Lacoste call for cease-fire.
Dec. 5	Algerian General, Municipal Councils dissolved.

1957

Jan. 9	Mollet "declaration of intentions" on Algeria.
Feb. 15	Conciliatory Algeria motion passed by U.N.
May 21	Mollet cabinet falls.
June 12	Nat. Assembly invests Bourgès-Maunoury govt.
July 19	Special powers renewed, extended to France.
Sept. 13	Council of Ministers approves the *loi cadre*.
Sept. 20	"Round-table" on the *loi cadre*.
Sept. 30	*Loi cadre* rejected, govt. falls.
Oct. 18	Pinay govt. refused investiture.
Oct. 28	Mollet govt. refused investiture.
Nov. 5	Nat. Assembly invests Gaillard govt.
Nov. 12	Special powers renewed.
Nov. 29	*Loi cadre*, electoral laws adopted.

1958

Jan. 31	Final vote on *loi cadre*.
Feb. 8	French bomb Sakhiet-Sidi-Youssef.
Apr. 15	Gaillard govt. falls on No. Africa issue.
Apr. 22	Bidault govt. refused investiture.
May 8	Pleven's attempt to form govt. fails.
May 13	Pflimlin govt. invested.
May 13	Insurrection in Algiers.
May 15	Declaration by de Gaulle, prepared to take power.
May 16	Nat. Assembly votes state of emergency.
May 23	Committees of Public Safety formed in Algeria.
May 25	Committees of Public Safety formed in Corsica.
June 1	De Gaulle govt. invested.
June 3	De Gaulle obtains special powers.

June 4	De Gaulle speaks at Algiers.
June 9	Gen. Salan named Delegate-General in Algeria.
June 16	Gen. Massu named Prefect of Algiers.
Sept. 18	G.P.R.A. proclaimed.
Sept. 28	Referendum on constitution.
Oct. 3	De Gaulle announces Constantine plan.
Oct. 23	De Gaulle calls for Algerian cease-fire.
Oct. 25	G.P.R.A. rejects negotiations.
Nov. 23, 30	Nat. Assembly elections.
Dec. 11	M. Delouvrier named Delegate-General in Algeria.
Dec. 21	De Gaulle elected Pres. of the Republic.

1959

Apr. 19, 20	Municipal elections in Algeria.
May 31	Senatorial election in Algeria.
June 4	Govt. declaration on Algeria.
June 9, 10	Algeria debate in Nat. Assembly.
June 23-25	Algeria debate in Senate.
Sept. 16	De Gaulle proposes self-determination.
Oct. 27	Algeria debate in Senate.
Oct. 28	De Gaulle message to army in Algeria.
Nov. 11	Algiers' demonstration against de Gaulle policy.
Dec. 12	Failure of Arab-Asian U.N. motion on Algeria.

1960

Jan. 19	Gen. Massu summoned to Paris.
Jan. 24	Settlers' revolt breaks out.
Jan. 25	Radio-TV message by de Gaulle.
Jan. 29	Speech by de Gaulle.
Feb. 1	End of the revolt.
Feb. 14	Creation of cabinet Committee on Algerian Affairs.
Mar. 3-5	De Gaulle travels to Algeria.
June 14	Speech by de Gaulle proposing negotiations.
June 20	F.L.N. accepts de Gaulle offer.
June 25	G.P.R.A. emissaries arrive in Paris.
July 19	*"Commissions d'élus"* established.
Aug. 22	G.P.R.A. calls for U.N. referendum.
Sept. 5	De Gaulle press conference.
Nov. 22	M. Joxe named Minister of Algerian Affairs.
Nov. 23	M. Morin named Delegate-General.
Dec. 7-8	Algeria debate in Nat. Assembly.
Dec. 9-13	De Gaulle travels to Algeria.
Dec. 11-13	Moslem demonstrations in Algeria.
Dec. 15	U.N. Political Commission vote.
Dec. 19	Opening of referendum campaign.

1961

Jan. 3	Ferhat Abbas urges "no" vote.
Jan. 9	De Gaulle wins referendum.
Jan. 17	Rebels ready to begin talks with France.
Feb. 28	De Gaulle-Bourguiba conference.
Mar. 16	French agree to talks before cease-fire.
Apr. 22	Army revolt in Algiers.
Apr. 23	Cabinet declares national emergency.
Apr. 26	Revolt collapses.
May 21	Evian peace talks open.
May 21	De Gaulle declares unilateral ceasefire.
May 31	Challe, Zeller get 15 years for role in April coup.
June 13	Evian talks suspended.
June 27	De Gaulle withdraws army unit.
July 20	Lugrin talks begin.
July 28	Lugrin talks suspended.
Aug. 11	De Gaulle ends unilateral ceasefire.
Aug. 27	Ben Khedda becomes G.P.R.A. Premier.
Sept. 5	Belgrade neutralists back F.L.N.
Sept. 9	De Gaulle assassination attempt fails.
Sept. 30	De Gaulle ends use of emergency powers.
Nov. 1	86 die, 150 hurt in Algerian riots.
Nov. 1-19	Hunger strike by F.L.N. prisoners in Paris.
Dec. 29	De Gaulle makes conciliatory speech.

1962

Feb. 8	French leftists demonstrate against O.A.S.
Feb. 19	Les Rousses talks end with accord.
Feb. 20	G.P.R.A. approves accord.
Feb. 21	French cabinet approves accord.
Feb. 28	F.L.N. National Council approves accord conditionally.
Mar. 7	Second Evian talks begin.
Mar. 18	Ceasefire agreement signed.
Mar. 19	Ceasefire begins.
Mar. 29	Provisional Executive installed.
Apr. 8	Referendum approves Evian accord.
Apr. 13	Jouhaud sentenced to death.
Apr. 14	Debré resigns; Pompidou named French Premier.
June 1	O.A.S. truce begins.
July 1	Algerian referendum approves independence.

Glossary and Abbreviations

A.P.—L'Année politique, Presses universitaires de France, Paris, an annual volume. Volumes 1944-1945 through 1950 were published by Editions du Grand Siècle. The 1951 volume was published jointly by P.U.F. and Grand Siècle. P.U.F. has been sole publisher since 1951.

Algérie française—French Algeria, the slogan of those who have opposed any relaxation of French control in Algeria.

C.—See Comm.

C.F.T.C.—Confédération française des travailleurs chrétiens, organization of trade unions affiliated with M.R.P.

C.G.T.—Confédération Générale du Travail, General Confederation of Labor, largest French trade union organization. Affiliated with Communist Party.

C.G.T.-F.O.—Confédération Générale du Travail-Force Ouvrière, General Confederation of Labor—Workers Force, the smallest of the major labor union organizations, affiliated with the Socialist party (S.F.I.O.).

C.N.I.—Centre National des Indépendants et Paysans, National Center for Independents and Peasants, conservative political party.

Cabinet Council—All the members of the government and, especially, a meeting of the full cabinet, including subministerial political officials such as secretaries of state.

Comm.—Communist, especially, a member of the Communist group in the National Assembly.

Commune—The territorial subdivision at the lowest level in the structure of French political-governmental institutions.

Community, The—The organization incorporating France and her former colonial possessions in tropical Africa and Madagascar (except Guinea, which severed all organic links with France in 1958, and Mali, which seceded in 1960).

Council of Ministers—That portion of the French cabinet composed of the members who head ministries and, especially, a meeting of the ministers.

Council of State—A body of high civil servants which performs a variety of important governmental functions, including the rendering of advisory opinions on the constitutionality of laws and decrees.

Département—Department, the principal territorial subdivision in France, roughly the size of a large American county.

diss.Rad.—Dissident Radical, member of the party formed by the right-wing faction after the 1956 Radical-Socialist scission.

double (electoral) college—The represententational system used in Algeria during the Fourth Republic, under which the members of the electorate subject to the jurisdiction of the French legal code filled half of the seats in an assembly or council and the electorate under the jurisdiction of Islamic law filled an equal number.

Elysée Palace—The French presidential residence.

F.L.N.—*Front de Libération Nationale,* National Liberation Front, the Algerian nationalist insurrectionary organization. In 1958, it was redesignated the Provisional Government of the Algerian Republic (G.P.R.A.). For reasons of simplicity it has been referred to in this study as the F.L.N. even after 1958.

G.P.R.A.—See F.L.N.

Hôtel Matignon—The residence of the French premier.

Ind., Indep.—Independent, especially a member of the I.P.A.S. See also C.N.I.

I.P.A.S.—*Indépendants et paysans de l'action sociale,* Independents and Peasants of Social Action, parliamentary group of the C.N.I.

J.O.—*Journal officiel,* the French government gazette. If no series designation is cited, the reference is to the *Débats parlementaires, Assemblé nationale.*

LM—*Le Monde,* leading French daily newspaper.

loi cadre—Framework law, legislation defining general principles and leaving the details to be elaborated by later laws or, usually, decrees.

loi Defferre—A 1957 framework law reforming and decentralizing the governmental structure of the French possessions in tropical Africa and Madagascar.

M.N.A.—*Mouvement national algérien,* National Algerian Movement, Messali Hadj's nationalist group as reconstituted after dissolution of the M.T.L.D. in 1954; a nationalist rival of the F.L.N.

M.R.P.—*Mouvement républicain populaire,* Popular Republican Movement, the major French Christian democratic party.

M.T.L.D.—*Mouvement pour la triomphe des libertés démocratiques,* Movement for the Triumph of Democratic Liberties, see M.N.A.

Métropole—The territory of the French Republic located in Europe. The terms "mainland France" and "the mainland" have often been used in this study instead of the infrequently used English cognates.

N.-I.—*Non-inscrit,* unaffiliated, a deputy who belongs to no parliamentary group.

Overseas Departments—Certain small French colonial possessions with populations composed predominantly of inhabitants of French stock, i. e., Réunion, Guyane, Martinique, Guadaloupe.

Overseas Territories—The French possessions of tropical Africa and Madagascar during the Fourth Republic.

P.—*Groupe paysan,* Peasant Group.

P.C.F.—*Parti communiste français,* French Communist Party.

P.S.A.—*Parti socialiste autonome,* Autonomous Socialist Party, left-wing dissident S.F.I.O. party, merged in the P.S.U.

P.S.U.—*Parti socialiste unifié*, Unified Socialist Party, left-of-center party.

Pays.—*Paysan*, member of the Peasant parliamentary group.

prefect—The chief governmental and administrative official of a *département*, a career civil servant.

R.D.A.—*Rassemblement démocratique africain*, African Democratic Rally, moderate West African nationalist party.

R.G.R.—*Rassemblement de la gauche républicaine*, Rally of the Republican Left, centrist Radical party.

R.P.—*Républicain progressiste*, Progressive Republican, member of a parliamentary group, allied with the Communist group.

R.P.F.—*Rassemblement du peuple français*, Rally of the French People, Gaullist political party, 1947-1955.

R.S.—See *Rep. Soc.*

Rad., Rad.-Soc.—Radical-Socialist.

Rep. Soc.—*Républicain social*, Social Republican, Gaullist political party, 1955-1958.

S. or S.F.I.O.—*Section française de l'internationale ouvrière*, French Section of the Workers' International, the principal French socialist party.

single (electoral) college—The Algerian representational system adopted for the 1958 elections whereby all voters are on a common roll and vote to fill only one set of seats.

Soc. Rep.—See *Rep. soc.*

triptyque—The official French Algerian policy during the Mollet government, 1956-1957: an end of the fighting to precede free elections and the future political status of Algeria to be negotiated with the representatives elected (cease-fire, elections, negotiations).

U.D.C.A.—*Union de défense des commerçants et artisans*, Defense Union of Merchants and Artisans, interest group of small shopkeepers. See U.F.F.

U.D.S.R.—*Union démocratique et socialiste de la résistance*, Democratic and Socialist Union of the Resistance, a centrist, Radical-type party.

U.D.T.—*Union démocratique du travail*, Democratic Union of Labor, small left-wing Gaullist party of the Fifth Republic.

U.F.D.—*Union des forces démocratiques*, Union of Democratic Forces, left-wing Radical group; merged in P.S.U.

U.F.F.—*Union et fraternité française*, Union and French Fraternity, electoral and parliamentary arm of the U.D.C.A.

U.G.S.—*Union de la gauche socialiste*, Union of the Socialist Left, a left-wing Marxist political party; merged in P.S.U.

U.N.E.F.—*Union nationale des étudiants français*, National Union of French Students, the largest French university student association.

U.N.R.—*Union de la nouvelle république*, Union of the New Republic, centrist Gaullist party of the Fifth Republic.

Index

213